THE CHARLTON STANDARD CATALOGUE OF

WADE WHIMSICAL COLLECTABLES

FIFTH EDITION

BY
PAT MURRAY

PUBLISHER
W. K. CROSS

The Charlton Press

TORONTO, ONTARIO • PALM HARBOR, FLORIDA

Canadian Cataloguing in Publication Data

The National Library of Canada has catalogued this publication as follows:
Main entry under title:
The Charlton standard catalogue of Wade whimsical collectables

Biennial.
3rd ed.-
ISSN 1205-8025
ISBN 0-88968-223-2 (5th ed.)

1. George Wade and Son—Catalogs. 2. Miniature pottery—England—Catalogs.
3. Figurines—England—Catalogs.

NK8473.5.G46A4   738.8'2   C98-390075-2

PRODUCTION

Editorial Assistant	Cindy Raycroft
Graphic Technician	Davina Rowan

ACKNOWLEDGEMENTS

The Charlton Press wishes to thank those who have assisted with the fifth edition of the *Charlton Standard Catalogue of Wade Whimsical Collectables*.

Special Thanks

Many thanks to the George Wade Pottery and staff for providing information on the manufacture of Wade porcelain and the sales staff in the Wade shop, particularly Cynthia, for providing new information on Wade products and sending their sales leaflets. Many thanks to The Official International Wade Collectors Club. And special thanks to Gordon for his time, patience and photography.

Contributors to the Fifth Edition

The Publisher and the Author would like to thank the following collectors and dealers for their assistance in supplying photographs, measurements, and backstamp details:

BJ Promotions (Bob Dawson); Catherine Barlow; John and Lisa Bonsey; John Borza; Peter Brooks; Jennifer Brown; C&S Collectables Direct (David Chown and Russell Schooley); Camtrak; Peter and Lesley Chisholm; Elizabeth and John Clark; Ellen and Martin Clayton; The Collector; Susan Cook; Cotswold Collectables; Father David Cox; Debbie Crouch; Darren Edwards; David Elvin; Janet and Mike Evans; G&G Collectables; Mrs. P. Gamble; Mary Lee Graham; Nancy Graham; Vince and Fatima Harvey; Jean and Rachel Higham; Beth Horka; Pat and Connie Hoyle; Marion and Gareth Hunt; Peg and Fred Johnson; Patty Keenan; Key Kollectables; Peter Lavendar; Dave Lee; Tina Lister; Jeanie Lucas; Carl Martin; Crystal Morton; Geoff Nash; Molly and Pete Newman; Cathy Norton; O.I.W.C.C. (Adele Hall, Jenny Wright and Kim Rowley); P&R Collectables; Adam Parker; Alison Pease; Phillips Auctioneers, U.K.; Potteries Specialist Auctions; Richleigh Promotions; Janet and Brian Robinson (New Zealand); Liz Ross (Victoria's Mall); Lorraine Sargeant; Claire Sims; Glenda Skeat; Carla Skinner (New Zealand); William Skirving; Jane Smith; Marcia Stoof; David Trower; U.K. International Ceramics; Derek, Kim and Del Watson; Sue Williams; Anthony Wixen; Julie Wright; Mary and Steve Yager; Yesterday's Collectables

And many thanks to all those who have helped with information and photographs for this book and preferred to remain anonymous.

A SPECIAL NOTE TO COLLECTORS

We welcome and appreciate any comments or suggestions in regard to the *Charlton Standard Catalogue of Wade Whimsical Collectables*.

If you would like to participate in pricing, please contact Jean Dale at the Charlton Press.

To provide new information or corrections, please write to Pat Murray, Box 746, RR #2, Stroud, Ontario L0L 2M0, Canada.

**Printed in Canada
in the Province of Ontario**

The Charlton Press

**Editorial Office
2040 Yonge Street, Suite 208, Toronto, Ontario M4S 1Z9
Telephone: (416) 488-1418   Fax: (416) 488-4656
Telephone: (800) 442-6042   Fax: (800) 442-1542
www.charltonpress.com   e-mail: chpress@charltonpress.com**

BURSLEM
1994-1995

CONTENTS

NOVELTY ANIMALS AND BIRDS

STORYBOOK FIGURES

WALT DISNEY FIGURES

MISCELLANEOUS SETS

WADE FAIR AND EVENTS

EVENT FIGURES

THE OFFICIAL INTERNATIONAL WADE COLLECTORS CLUB MODELS
COMPLIMENTARY FIGURES

THE OFFICIAL INTERNATIONAL WADE COLLECTORS CLUB
MEMBERSHIP EXCLUSIVES

COMMISSIONED MODELS

CHRISTMAS PUPPY
1995-1996

HOW TO USE THIS CATALOGUE

THE PURPOSE

This publication has been designed to serve two specific purposes. Its first purpose is to furnish the collector with accurate and detailed listings that provide the essential information needed to build a rewarding collection. Its second function is to provide collectors and dealers with current market prices for the complete line of Wade whimsical collectables.

This guide is divided into three main sections. The first section includes models produced for and by the Wade product line (for example, *English Whimsies*), which are listed alphabetically. The second section focuses on models produced for fairs, events, and membership exclusives, and is listed chronologically. The third section includes models produced by Wade under commission for other corporations. These are listed alphabetically according to the issuing company.

STYLES AND VERSIONS

STYLES: A change in style occurs when a major element of the design is altered or modified as a result of a deliberate mould change. An example of this is *Snow White and the Seven Dwarfs*, 1938, (style one) and *Snow White and the Seven Dwarfs*, 1982-1984 (style two).

VERSIONS: Versions are modifications in a minor style element of the figures, such as the open- and closed-eared rabbits in the Red Rose Tea series. A version could also indicate a change in colourways; for example, the variety of hat colours of the *Lucky Leprechauns*.

THE LISTINGS

A Word On Pricing

The purpose of this catalogue is to give readers the most accurate, up-to-date retail prices for whimsical Wades in the markets of the United States, Canada and the United Kingdom. However, one must remember that these prices are indications only and that the actual selling price may be higher or lower by the time the final transaction agreement is reached.

To accomplish this, The Charlton Press continues to access an international pricing panel of experts who submit prices based on both dealer and collector retail-price activity, as well as on current auction results in the U.S., Canada and the U. K. These market prices are carefully averaged to reflect accurate valuations for models in each of these markets.

This catalogue lists prices for figures in the currency of a particular market (e.g. U.S. dollars for the American market and sterling for the U.K. market). The bulk of the prices given are not determined by currency-exchange calculations, but by actual activity in the market concerned.

Additionally, collectors must remember that all relevant information must be known to make a proper valuation. When comparing auction prices to catalogue prices, collectors and dealers must remember two important points. First, compare "apples and apples." Be sure that auction prices realized for figures include a buyer's premium if one is due. Buyer's premiums can range from 10 to 15 percent, and on an expensive piece, this amount can be substantial. Secondly, know whether a figure is restored, repaired or in mint condition. This fact may not be noted or explained in the listings, and as a result, its price will not match that of the same piece in mint condition. Please be aware of repairs and restorations and the effect they have on values.

A last word of caution. No pricing catalogue can, or should, be a fixed price list. This book must be considered as a price guide only, showing the most current retail prices based on market demand within a particular region for the various models.

The Internet and Pricing

The Internet is changing the way business is being done in the collectables marketplace. Linking millions of collectors around the world through chat rooms, antique and collector malls, Internet auctions and producer web sites, e-commerce has become big business.

Some of the effects caused by the Internet and e-commerce on the collectable business are as follows:

1. Collectors deal directly with other collectors, changing the dynamics of the traditional customer/dealer relationship.

2. Information concerning new issues, finds and varieties is readily available, twenty-four hours a day. Collectors' wants are made known instantly to a wide spectrum of dealers and collectors.

3. Prices:

(a) Price differentials will disappear between global market areas as collectors and delivery services team up to stretch the purchasing power of the collectable dollar/pound.

(b) Prices of common to scarce items will adjust downward to compensate for the temporary expansion of merchandise supply. Conversely, prices of rare and extremely rare items will increase, a result of additional exposure to demand.

(c) After a time even prices of common items will rise due to the growing worldwide demand for collectables.

4. Internet auction sites listing millions of items for sale on a daily basis continue to grow as more and more collectors discover the viability of using this method to buy and sell merchandise.

5. Traditional marketing strategies (retail stores, direct mail retailers, collectable shows and fairs, and collectable magazines and papers) face increased pressure in a more competitive environment.

The Internet is user-friendly: no travelling required, twenty-four hour accessibility, no face-to-face contact or other pressure to buy or sell. Without a doubt, the arrival of e-commerce will change the way a collector collects.

A Word on Condition

The prices published herein are for models in **mint condition**. Figures with minor imperfections resulting from processing at the pottery will be discounted in the range of 10 to 20 percent from these prices. The early models with a cellulose glaze are almost impossible to obtain in mint condition, so their prices are for figures in reasonable condition, meaning that a minimum number of flakes of glaze are missing. The early figures in "strictly" mint condition will command a price much higher than the listed price. Models with minor chips, due to packaging by the commissioning company, are just "fillers" in collections and will command only a fraction of the mint price, in the area of 10 percent. Cracked or chipped figures are not really collectable.

Models that are broken, repaired or have major chips are worthless and should not be collected.

Technical Information

The whimsical Wades in this book were produced in the George Wade Pottery, the Wade Heath Pottery and in the Wade Ireland Pottery between the 1930s and 2000. For each model, the name of its series, the year of production, the model's name, its size (the height first, then the width in millimetres), the colours and its present value are presented. All known backstamps of the models are listed above the tables. If the figures can be found with a variety of backstamps, then each backstamp is followed, in parenthesis, by the model numbers applicable to it. For a few listings, only approximate dates of issue are given, as they could not be confirmed by Wade. When known, the year the model was discontinued and its original issue price are also given.

FURTHER READING

Pre-War and More Wades, 1st Edition, 1991, by Pat Murray

The Charlton Standard Catalogue of Wade Volume Four Liquor Containers, 3rd Edition, 1999, by Pat Murray

The Charlton Standard Catalogue of Wade Volume One General Issues, 3rd Edition, 1999, by Pat Murray

The Charlton Standard Catalogue of Wade Volume Three Tableware, 1998, by Pat Murray

The Charlton Standard Catalogue of Wade Volume Two Decorative Wares, 2nd Edition, 1996, by Pat Murray

The Wade Collector's Handbook, 1997, by Robert Prescott-Walker

The Wade Dynasty, 1996, by Dave Lee

The World of Wade, 1988, by Ian Warner with Mike Posgay

The World of Wade Book 2, 1994, by Ian Warner and Mike Posgay

The World of Wade Price Trends, 1996, by Ian Warner and Mike Posgay

Whimsical Wades, 1st Edition, 1996, by Pat Murray

CLUBS AND NEWSLETTERS

The Official International Wade Collectors Club, run by Wade Ceramics, was founded in 1994. Members receive an annual Wade membership model upon joining and the opportunity to purchase club limited edition models. The full-colour quarterly *Wade's World* magazine has information on new and old Wade models, dates and locations of Wade shows and exhibitions, and much more. To join the club, write to: The Official Wade Collectors Club, Royal Works, Westport Road, Burslem, Stoke-on-Trent, ST6 4AP, Staffordshire, England.

The Wade Watch, a quarterly six-page newsletter, is published by Wade Watch, Ltd. For more information, please contact: Wade Watch, Ltd., 8199 Pierson Court, Arvada, CO, 80005, USA or www.wadewatch.com.

INTRODUCTION

WHIMSICAL WADES

By the early 1950s, the Wade Potteries had filled the demand to replace industrial ceramics damaged in the war, and there was not sufficient work to keep the employees busy. This was when Sir George Wade decided to produce his now world-famous miniature animals—the *First Whimsies* — which he referred to as his "pocket money toys." They first appeared in spring 1954 at the British Industries Fair. The miniatures were intended for school children, but they soon attracted the attention of adults and became very collectable.

George Wade's policy was to limit the number of whimsical models produced, so they would not flood the market and lose their appeal. Models of the early 1950s were produced in sets, usually of five, and most sets were in production for only a year or two, some for as little as a few months. Whenever a large industrial order was received, the whole pottery would revert to the production of industrial wares, leaving some sets or series unfinished. Perhaps the pottery intended to go back to unfinished series, but because of slow sales, high production costs, copyright laws, or a new interest by the public, they were never completed.

In some of these cases there were only a few thousand models made, usually as a test run, and therefore they were not issued for nation-wide sale. To recoup production costs, some models may have been sold only in one area of the United Kingdom.

In 1958 the three English Wade Potteries were restructured under the name Wade Potteries Ltd., later renamed Wade PLC. Wade (Ulster) Ltd. was renamed Wade Ireland Ltd. in 1966.

Sir George Wade died in 1986 at age 95, to be followed a year later by the untimely death of his son Tony. With their passing, 120 years of Wade family involvement in ceramics came to an end.

In 1989 Wade PLC was taken over by Beauford PLC and renamed Wade Ceramics Ltd., which is still in production today. Wade Ireland was renamed Seagoe Ceramics and continued to manufacture domestic tablewares until 1993, when it reverted back to the production of industrial ceramics.

THE PRODUCTION PROCESS

The Wade Pottery manufactures a particularly hard porcelain body which has been used in many different products. It consists of a mixture of ball clays, china clay, flint, feldspar, talc, etc., some ingredients imported from Sweden, Norway and Egypt. These materials are mixed in large vats of water, producing a thick sludge or "slip." The slip is passed into a filter to extract most of the water, leaving large flat "bats" of porcelain clay, approximately two feet square and three inches thick. The clay bats are dried and then ground into dust ready for the forming process. Paraffin is added to the dust to assist in bonding and as a lubricant to remove the formed pieces from the steel moulds.

Once pressed into the required shape, the clay articles are dried, then all the press marks are removed by sponging and "fettling," which is scraping off the surplus clay by hand, using a sharp blade. From the early 1960s, a new method of fettling was used, whereby the base of the model was rubbed back and forth on a material similar to emery paper. This resulted in a lined or ribbed base, which is the best method of identifying the majority of post-1960 Wade figures.

One or more ceramic colours is applied to the clay model, which is then sprayed with a clear glaze that, when fired, allows the colours underneath to show through. This process is known as underglaze decoration. On-glaze decoration is also used by Wade, which includes enamelling, gilding and transfer printing, and is done after the article has been glazed and fired.

Some whimsical Wades are hollow, usually because they were prototype models that were discarded or removed from the pottery by workers. Other models may be found in different colour glazes than the originals, due to one or more of the following reasons:

1. The first colour glaze was laid down for a test run, but when the models came out of the kiln at the end of the firing period (sometimes as long as three days), it was either too light or too dark. This occurred in the case of the black *English Whimsies* "Zebra," which was so dark when it emerged after its run through the kiln that the striped pattern could not be clearly seen. The colour glaze was then changed to beige.

2. When the model was shown to the client he did not like the initial colour, so another was chosen.

3. Some models were reissued in different colour glazes for use in promotions for Red Rose Tea and for Tom Smith Christmas crackers.

WADE MODELLERS, 1954-1994

Listed below are the modellers who helped to create whimsical Wade figures. The year that each modeller started working at Wade is given and, if known, the year he or she left.

After leaving Wade, many modellers went on to work for Royal Doulton, Szeiler, Sylvac, Dilsford Studio and other well-known British potteries. This accounts for the great number of other collectable models that bear a distinctive and characteristic likeness to Wade models.

Jessica Van Hallen, 1930
    Snow White set, 1938

Robert Barlow, Late 1930s
    Tinker, Tailor, Soldier, Sailor
    Comic Duck Family

Nancy Great-Rex, Late 1930s-Early 1940s
    Butcher, Baker and Candlestick Maker

William K. Harper, 1954-1963
    First Whimsies
    Bernie and Pooh
    Hat Box models
    Drum Box series
    Minikins series
    Noddy set
    Tortoise Family
    TV Pets
    Shamrock Cottage
    Irish Comical Pig
    Pink Elephant
    Flying Birds
    Disney Blow Ups

Leslie McKinnon, 1959-1961
    The British Character set
    Happy Families series

Paul Zalman, 1961
Mabel Lucie Attwell models

Ken Holmes, 1975 to the present
Dinosaur Collection
Burglar and Policeman series
Children and Pets

Alan Maslankowski, 1975
Snow White set, 1982

MODEL BOXES, 1954-1995

Most collectors have seen or purchased Wade models in their original boxes. In order to catch the eye of a collector, early Wade boxes were made to be just as colourful, appealing and decorative as their contents.

When Wade models were issued in the 1950s, their appeal to collectors was not as avid as it is today; as a result, few boxes from the 1950s were kept by the original purchasers. Models in their boxes can command a higher price than a model alone, and depending on the age and condition of the box, the price of the model may increase by 30 to 50 percent.

In the 1970s the rising cost of paper and the fact that Wade produced an established collectors' product caused the company to produce less appealing containers. But by the 1980s, the boxes again became colourful and eye-catching, although they had lost the old-world charm of the boxes of the 1950s.

Box designs and colours can vary depending on the year of issue and the length of the production run. Some popular models that were reissued two or more times can be found in two, and at times three, different box sizes and colours (as in the *Happy Families* series, which was issued and reissued in three different box designs).

WADE MARKS, 1930s-1998

Wade Heath Ltd. and George Wade and Son Ltd. not only shared their pottery moulds, they also shared the Wade trademark during the late 1940s and into the 1950s. This makes it difficult to distinguish which pottery a particular model came from. As a general guide for those models produced in both potteries, the Wade Heath postwar novelty models have a green or greenish brown "Wade England" mark on their bases, and the postwar George Wade figures have a black or blue "Wade England" transfer on their bases.

Later, with the addition of Wade Ireland, it became even more difficult to determine the origin of a model. The potteries had a habit of helping each other out in order to speed up production. These figures all had the mark of the originating pottery on their bases and were packed in boxes from that pottery, even though they may have been made in another location.

A good example of this practice is the 1977 *Bisto Kids* set. During one of our conversations, Tony Wade told me that, although they were marked "Wade Staffordshire" on their bases, these models were in fact produced in the Wade Ireland Pottery. The George Wade Pottery had had another large order to complete, so Wade Ireland took over.

Similarly, some of the 1950s *First Whimsies* are believed to have been produced by Wade Ireland, although none of the models have a Wade Ireland mark, and the entire series of ten sets was packed in Wade England boxes.

Many small open-caste models (models with no bases and standing on thin legs) do have enough space on them for a Wade label or an ink stamp. They were originally issued in boxes with "Wade England" clearly marked on the box or packet front. Once removed from their container, however, these models are hard to identify without the aid of Wade collector books (the *First Whimsies* is a good example of this).

Larger, more solid-based models were marked with a Wade ink stamp or with a black and gold label on their bases. But over the years the label or the ink stamp can wear off or be washed off by previous owners, leaving them unmarked.

Wade Heath

Ink Stamps

1. Black ink stamp "Flaxman Ware Hand Made Pottery by Wadeheath England," 1935-1937.
2. Black ink stamp "Flaxman Wade Heath England," 1937-1938.

3. Black ink stamp "Flaxman Wade Heath," 1937-1938.
4. Black ink stamp "Wadeheath Ware England," 1935-1937.
5. Green-brown ink stamp "Wade England," late 1940s-early 1950s.
6. Green ink stamp "Wade England [name of model]," late 1940s-early 1950s.

7. Black ink stamp "Wadeheath by permission Walt Disney England," 1937-1938.
8. Black ink stamp "Wade" and red ink stamp "Made in England," 1938.
9. Black ink stamp "Wade England," late 1940s-early 1950s.

Wade

Hand-painted Marks

1. Black hand painted "Wade Alice 2," with black ink stamp "Made in England," 1930s.
2. Black hand painted "Wade Alice 7" and red ink stamp of leaping deer, 1930s.
3. Black hand painted "Hiawatha Wade England," 1937.

Ink Stamps

4. Black ink stamp "Wade England," late 1940s.
5. Black ink stamp "Wade Made in England," 1955.
6. Brown ink stamp "Wade England," with brown cricket in large C. Only seen on some of the *Happy Families* models.

Transfer Prints

7. Small black transfer "Wade England [name of model]," 1950s.
8. Large black transfer "Wade England [name of model]," 1950s.
9a. Black transfer "Wade Snippet No. 1 Mayflower Carried 102 Pilgrims to North America 1620-Real Porcelain-Made In England," 1956.
9b. Black transfer "Wade Snippet No. 2 Santa Maria Flag ship of Columbus 1492-Real Porcelain-Made In England," 1956.
9c. Black transfer "Wade Snippet No. 3 Revenge Flag ship of Sir Richard Grenville 1591-Real Porcelain-Made In England," 1956.
9d. Black transfer "Wade Snippet No. 4 Hansel-Real Porcelain-Made in England," 1957.
9e. Black transfer "Wade Snippet No. 5 Gretel-Real Porcelain-Made in England," 1957
9f. Black transfer "Wade Snippet No. 6 Gingy-Real Porcelain-Made in England," 1957.

10. Blue transfer "Wade England," 1956-1957.
11. Black transfer "Wade Porcelain England," 1961.

12. Black transfer "Wade Porcelain Copyright Walt Disney Productions Made in England," 1961.
13. Brown transfer "Wade Made in England," 1962.
14. Brown transfer "Copyright RHM Foods Ltd. & Applied Creativity, Wade Staffordshire," 1977.
15. Black transfer "Wade Made in England," 1978-1987.

16. Black transfer "Walt Disney Productions" in an oval shape, with "Wade England" in centre, 1981-1987.
17. Black transfer "Wade Porcelain England S/F [1-6]," 1984-1986.
18. Red transfer "Wade Made in England," 1985, 1994.
19. Black transfer "Harrods Knightsbridge," 1991-1994.
20. Black transfer "Wade Limited Editions Modelled by Ken Holmes [includes model name, series number and limited edition number]," 1993-1994.

21. Black transfer "Arthur Hare [Holly Hedgehog] © C&S Collectables Wade England," 1993-1995.
22. Black transfer "Wade," enclosed in an outline of the Isle of Wight and numbered, 1994.
23. Black transfer "[Limited edition number] © H/B Inc, Scooby-Doo, Limited edition of 2,000, Wade England, G&G Collectables," 1994.

24. Black transfer "1994 [1995] Mirror Group Newspapers Ltd © C&S Collectables Wade England," 1994-1995.

Impressed Marks

25. Impressed "Wade Porcelain Made in England," 1958.

Embossed Marks

26. Small embossed "Wade," 1954-1983.

27. Embossed "'Whimtrays' Wade Porcelain Made in England," 1958-1965.

28. Embossed "Wade Porcelain Made in England," 1958-1984.
29. Embossed "Wade Porcelain - Mabel Lucie Attwell © Made in England," 1959-1961.
30. Embossed "Angel Dish Wade Porcelain Made in England," 1963.
31. Embossed "Robertson," 1963-1965.
32. Embossed "Wade England," 1965-1994.

33. Large embossed "Wade Made in England," 1975-1984.
34. Embossed "Mianco [year of issue] Wade England" on rim of base, 1989-1995.
35. Embossed "Wade England 1990 [1991]," 1990-1991.

36. Embossed "Wade England 1991" on rim of base and ink stamp "GSG," 1991.
37. Large embossed "Wade," 1993-1994.

Labels

38. Small black and gold label "Wade England," 1954-1959.
39. Black and gold label "Genuine Wade Porcelain Made in England," 1959-1965.
40. Large black and gold label "Wade England," early 1970s-1981.
41. Black and gold label "Walt Disney Productions Wade England," 1981-1985.

Wade Ireland

Ink Stamps

1. Black ink stamp "'Pogo' Copyright, Walt Kelly, Made in Ireland 1959," 1959.
2. Black ink stamp "Made in Ireland," 1974-1985.
3. Purple ink stamp "Made in Ireland," 1974-1985.

Transfer Prints

4. Green transfer "Shamrock Pottery Made in Ireland," 1953-1956.

Impressed Marks

5. Impressed "Shamrock Pottery Made in Ireland," 1953-1956.

6. Impressed "Irish Porcelain Made in Ireland by Wade Co. Armagh," with shamrock, early 1950s.
7. Impressed "Made in Ireland," early 1970s.

Embossed Marks

8. Embossed "Irish Porcelain, Made in Ireland," with a shamrock leaf, 1953-1956.
9. Embossed "Shamrock Pottery Made in Ireland," 1959.
10. Embossed "Wade Porcelain Made in Ireland," 1970s-1980s.
11. Embossed "Made in Ireland, Porcelain Wade, Eire Tir-Adheanta," 1980-1988.
12. Embossed "Wade Ireland," 1984-1987.

COMIC ANIMALS AND BIRDS

COMIC ANIMALS AND BIRDS

From the late 1940s to the 1950s, the Wade Heath Royal Victoria Pottery and the George Wade Pottery produced a large series of animal and bird models, some described as comic or novelty. Because the two Potteries produced the same models using the same moulds and both used the "Wade England" mark, it is hard to tell which models were made in which pottery. But it is believed that models stamped "Wade England" in green, brown or black were produced in the Royal Victoria Pottery before 1953, and those models transfer printed with a black or blue "Wade England" mark were produced in the George Wade Pottery in the early to mid-1950s. The *Comic Families* models have been found with creamy beige background glazes and dark coloured clothing and are also found in white with pastel blue and grey colours.

During this period whenever Sir George Wade would come across surplus models, he would say, "Stick'em on something." The figures would be sent to the Wade Heath Pottery, where they were joined onto surplus bramble-ware mustard pots (minus their lids) or basket-ware eggcups, then mounted on a moulded leaf-shaped base to make a novelty bowl. The finished product was then recoloured and called a "Posy Bowl."

For ease of reference, the models are listed in alphabetical order, not in order of issue.

DONKEYS

Circa 1948-1952

The *Comic Donkeys* set is a pair of comic figures, one happy and one sad, which were produced in the Wade Pottery between the late 1940s and the early 1950s. The original price was 2/6d each.

A model of Cheerful Charlie with the words "Cheerful Charlie" hand written on his body and "Montreal" hand written on his ears has been found and is possibly a souvenir model exported to Montreal, Quebec, Canada. For other models with similar hand written souvenir place names please see "Staffordshire House Gifts."

Cheerful Charlie and Doleful Dan

Cheerful Charlie "Montreal"

Backstamp: Black ink stamp "Wade England"

No.	Name	Description	Size	U.S. $	Can. $	U.K. £
1a	Cheerful Charlie	Beige; coffee mane, tail, hooves	110 x 55	290.00	395.00	190.00
1b	Cheerful Charlie	Pink; coffee mane, tail, hooves; black lettering Montreal	110 x 55	300.00	400.00	195.00
2	Doleful Dan	Beige; coffee mane, tail, hooves	110 x 55	300.00	400.00	195.00

Donkey Derivatives
Circa 1948

Cheerful Charlie Salt Pot

Backstamp: Green-brown ink stamp "Wade England"

No.	Name	Description	Size	U.S. $	Can. $	U.K. £
1	Cheerful Charlie	Pink; beige mane, tail, hooves	110 x 55	115.00	300.00	150.00

Cheerful Charlie Posy Bowl

Doleful Dan Posy Bowl

Backstamp: Green-brown ink stamp "Wade England"

No.	Name	Description	Size	U.S. $	Can. $	U.K. £
1a	Cheerful Charlie	Blue egg-cup posy bowl	105 x 105	110.00	150.00	75.00
1b	Cheerful Charlie	Cream egg-cup posy bowl	105 x 105	110.00	150.00	75.00
1c	Cheerful Charlie	Multi-coloured egg-cup posy bowl	105 x 105	125.00	170.00	85.00
2a	Doleful Dan	Blue egg-cup posy bowl	105 x 105	110.00	150.00	75.00
2b	Doleful Dan	Green egg-cup posy bowl	105 x 105	110.00	150.00	75.00
2c	Doleful Dan	Multi-coloured egg-cup posy bowl	105 x 105	125.00	170.00	85.00

DUCK FAMILY

1950s

The *Comic Duck Family* was designed by Robert Barlow. The original price for "Mr. Duck" and "Mrs. Duck" was 2/6d each. "Dack" and "Dilly" each sold for 1/6d.

The Comic Duck Father and Mother are also found marked "Szeilor." The "Szeilor" models are glazed in dark blue and beige colours with large blue and black eyes. (Previously listed as Wade now deleted), they are from the same mould as the Wade Comic Duck, Father and Mother. John Szeilor worked for the Wade Pottery in the late 1940s-early 1950s before starting his own pottery, which would account for the similarity of Wade and Szeilor models.

NOTE: An identical model of the "Duck With Head Back" (See *The Charlton Standard Catalogue of Wade General Issues*) in different colours than the Wade model has also been found with the "Szeilor Backstamp."

Duck Family

Backstamp: **A.** Unmarked (1a, 2)
B. Black transfer print "Wade England" (1b, 1c, 2, 3, 4)

No.	Name	Description	Size	U.S. $	Can. $	U.K.£
1a	Mr. Duck	White; beige beak, tail, feet; blue cap, tie; small eyes	70 x 38	190.00	250.00	125.00
1b	Mr. Duck	White; yellow beak, feet; orange-red cap; small eyes	70 x 38	190.00	250.00	125.00
2	Mrs. Duck	White; yellow beak, feet, bonnet; small eyes	70 x 37	190.00	250.00	125.00
3	Dack	White; yellow beak, feet; blue cap; small eyes	40 x 28	160.00	240.00	120.00
4	Dilly	White; yellow beak, feet; orange tam; small eyes	40 x 27	160.00	240.00	120.00

FROG FAMILY

Circa 1948-1952

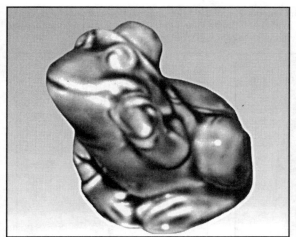

Mr. Frog

Mrs. Frog

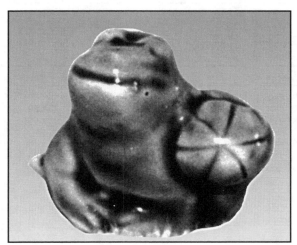

Boy Frog

Backstamp: Black ink stamp "Wade England"

No.	Name	Description	Size	U.S. $	Can. $	U.K.£
1	Mr. Frog	Dark green; bowler hat; cigar	40 x 58	180.00	240.00	120.00
2	Mrs. Frog	Dark green; bonnet; umbrella	40 x 58	180.00	240.00	120.00
3	Boy Frog	Dark green; football	28 x 38	180.00	240.00	120.00
4	Girl Frog	Dark green; bunch of flowers	28 x 38	180.00	240.00	120.00

PENGUIN FAMILY

Circa 1948-1955

The *Comic Penguin Family* was produced in pastels and in dark colours. Before the 1950s these models were stamped "Wade England" and afterwards were printed with a "Wade England" mark. "Mr. Penguin" and "Mrs. Penguin" are also found as salt and pepper pots. The original price of "Mr. Penguin" and "Mrs. Penguin" was 2/6d each. "Benny" and "Penny" each sold for 1/6d.

Mrs. Penguin, Benny and Mr. Penguin   **Penny**

Backstamp: **A.** Black ink stamp "Wade England" (1b, 3)
B. Black transfer "Wade England"s (1a, 4)
C. Unmarked (2, 5)

No.	Name	Description	Size	U.S. $	Can. $	U.K. £
1a	Mr. Penguin	White/grey; pale blue cap, scarf; black umbrella	90 x 40	180.00	240.00	120.00
1b	Mr. Penguin	White; blue cap, scarf; black umbrella	90 x 40	180.00	240.00	120.00
2	Mr. Penguin	Black/white; dark blue cap, scarf; yellow beak, hands, feet	65 x 40	180.00	240.00	120.00
3	Mrs. Penguin	White/grey penguin, shawl; black bag	85 x 40	180.00	240.00	120.00
4	Benny	White/grey; blue tam; black book	55 x 25	200.00	255.00	130.00
5	Penny	White/grey; blue bonnet; black penguin doll	50 x 25	200.00	255.00	130.00

Penguin Family Derivatives
Circa 1948

Salt and Pepper Pots

Backstamp: **A.** Black ink stamp "Wade England" (1, 2)
B. Black transfer "Wade England" (1, 2)
C. Unmarked (3, 4, 5)

No.	Name	Description	Size	U.S. $	Can. $	U.K. £
1	Mr. Penguin Pepper Pot	Black/white; maroon cap, scarf, umbrella	90 x 40	140.00	190.00	95.00
2	Mr. Penguin Pepper Pot	Black/white; blue cap, scarf	65 x 40	140.00	190.00	95.00
3	Mr. Penguin Pepper Pot	Pale green	75 x 40	180.00	240.00	120.00
4	Mrs. Penguin Salt Pot	Black/white; maroon shawl, handbag	85 x 40	140.00	190.00	95.00
5	Mrs. Penguin Salt Pot	Pale green	65 x 40	180.00	240.00	120.00

PIG FAMILY

"Mr. Pig" and "Mrs. Pig" were produced in cream with dark coloured clothing.

Photograph not available
at press time

Backstamp: Black ink stamp "Wade England"

No.	Name	Description	Size	U.S. $	Can. $	U.K. £
1	Mr. Pig	Cream; maroon tie, jacket	90 x 32	100.00	125.00	65.00
2	Mrs. Pig	Cream; dark yellow hat	80 x 30	100.00	125.00	65.00
3	Boy Pig	Unknown	Unknown		Rare	
4	Girl Pig	Unknown	Unknown		Rare	

Pig Family Derivatives

Circa 1948

The "Mr. Pig Salt Pot" and "Mrs. Pig Pepper Pot" were issued as a cruet set, both on an oval tray. The ink stamp on these models is a type used before the 1950s.

Salt and Pepper Pots

Backstamp: Black ink stamp "Wade England"

No.	Name	Description	Size	U.S. $	Can. $	U.K. £
1	Mr. Pig Salt Pot	Cream; maroon tie, jacket	90 x 32	125.00	160.00	78.00
2	Mrs. Pig Pepper Pot	Cream; dark yellow hat	90 x 32	125.00	160.00	78.00
—	Set (2) with Tray		90 x 32	235.00	300.00	155.00

RABBIT FAMILY

Circa 1948-1955

Before the 1950s these models were produced in cream with dark coloured clothing; in the 1950s they were made in white with pastel markings. The original prices were 2/6d each for "Mr. Rabbit" and for "Mrs. Rabbit" and 1/6d each for "Fluff" and for "Puff."

Rabbit Family

Backstamp: **A.** Black ink stamp "Wade England" (1a, 2a, 3a, 4a)
           B. Black transfer "Wade England" (1c, 2b, 3b, 4b)
           C. Unmarked (1b, 1d)

No.	Name	Description	Size	U.S. $	Can. $	U.K. £
1a	Mr. Rabbit	Cream; dark yellow jacket	90 x 40	185.00	250.00	125.00
1b	Mr. Rabbit	Cream; black jacket	90 x 40	140.00	200.00	100.00
1c	Mr. Rabbit	White; blue jacket	90 x 40	185.00	250.00	125.00
1d	Mr. Rabbit	Bright yellow all over	90 x 40	180.00	200.00	100.00
2a	Mrs. Rabbit	Cream; maroon bonnet; yellow basket	90 x 40	185.00	250.00	125.00
2b	Mrs. Rabbit	White; grey ear tips; blue bonnet, basket	90 x 40	185.00	250.00	125.00
3a	Fluff	Cream; dark blue shawl	40 x 30	160.00	200.00	100.00
3b	Fluff	White; grey ear tips; blue/grey shawl	40 x 30	160.00	200.00	100.00
4a	Puff	Cream; dark yellow jacket	40 x 30	160.00	200.00	100.00
4b	Puff	White; grey ear tips; blue jacket	40 x 30	160.00	200.00	100.00

Rabbit Family Derivatives
Circa 1948

The "Mr. Rabbit Salt Pot" and "Mrs. Rabbit Pepper Pot" were issued as a cruet set, both standing on an oval tray.

Salt and Pepper Pots

Backstamp: Black ink stamp "Wade England"

No.	Name	Description	Size	U.S. $	Can. $	U.K. £
1	Mr. Rabbit Salt Pot	Cream; black hat; yellow jacket	90 x 40	90.00	120.00	60.00
2	Mrs. Rabbit Pepper Pot	Cream; maroon hat; yellow ribbon	90 x 40	90.00	120.00	60.00
—	Set (2) with Tray				Rare	

RABBIT (LITTLE LAUGHING BUNNY)

Circa 1948-1952

There are a number of variations in the size of the "Little Laughing Bunny," due to the die being retooled when worn. The colour of the grey models is also not consistent because the models were decorated in two different potteries. The original price was 1/-.

A poem by one of the Wade Heath figure casters in a spring 1954 *Jolly Potter* magazine refers to the "Comic Rabbit" as the "Little Laughing Bunny."

NOTE: A "Comic Rabbit" with grey body, brown arms and feet has been found with a John Szeiler Backstamp.

Little Laughing Bunnies

Backstamp: **A.** Black ink stamp "Wade England" (1a, 1b, 1c)
B. Black transfer print "Wade England" (1d)
C. Blue transfer print "Wade England" (1d)
D. Brown ink stamp (1e, 1f, 1g, 1h, 1i, 1j)

No.	Description	Size	U.S. $	Can. $	U.K. £
1a	Beige; red mouth; black eyes; white stomach	65 x 40	85.00	110.00	55.00
1b	Dark grey; red mouth	63 x 38	85.00	110.00	55.00
1c	Dark grey; red mouth; black eyes	63 x 40	85.00	110.00	55.00
1d	Pale grey; brown ears, mouth; black eyes	63 x 38	85.00	110.00	55.00
1e	Pale grey; brown ears, mouth; red eyes	63 x 38	85.00	110.00	55.00
1f	Pale grey; brown striped ears; red mouth; black eyes	63 x 40	85.00	110.00	55.00
1g	Pale grey; red mouth; black eyes	63 x 40	85.00	110.00	55.00
1h	Pink; red mouth; black eyes	70 x 40	85.00	110.00	55.00
1i	White; brown ears, toes	63 x 38	85.00	110.00	55.00
1j	White; brown striped ears; red mouth; black eyes	65 x 40	85.00	110.00	55.00

Rabbit Derivatives

Circa 1948

This Art Deco shaped ashtray is similar in shape to a model produced by Sylvac in the late 1940s which would have an impressed "Sylvac" and a design No 1532 on the base. Although the illustrated model does not have a Wade mark, it has a registered design No of 827631.

Art Deco Ashtray

S-Shaped Ashtray

Backstamp: **A.** Ink stamp "Regd 827631 Made in England"
                B. Green-brown ink stamp "Wade England"

No.	Description	Size	U.S. $	Can. $	U.K. £
1	Beige rabbit; grey Art Deco ashtray	92 x 92	120.00	150.00	75.00
2	Dark grey rabbit; yellow S-shaped ashtray	110 x 110	120.00	150.00	75.00

Rabbit Posy Bowl

Backstamp: Green-brown ink stamp "Wade England"

No.	Description	Size	U.S. $	Can.$	U.K. £
1a	Blue; bramble-ware mustard pot	85 x 80	135.00	180.00	90.00
1b	Green; bramble-ware mustard pot	85 x 80	135.00	180.00	90.00
1c	Yellow; bramble-ware mustard pot	85 x 80	135.00	180.00	90.00

HAPPY FAMILIES

HAPPY FAMILIES

Circa 1961-1987

The *Happy Families* series was first issued from 1961 to 1965 and consisted of a mother animal and her two babies. The original five sets were sold in boxes with "Happy Families" printed in large letters in different colours on the front.

The first three *Happy Families* were the *Hippo Family* (3/11d), the *Tiger Family* (4/6d) and the *Giraffe Family* (4/11d). They were modelled by Leslie McKinnon and issued in the autumn and winter of 1961. They proved to be so popular that in spring 1962, Wade issued two more families, the *Rabbit Family* and the *Mouse Family*.

In 1978 four sets were reissued using the original moulds. *The Tiger Family* (which is the most sought after set) was not considered suitable for reissue. The only way to distinguish the reissued models from the earlier models is by a slight variation in colour. By 1984 four more families had been added — the *Frog Family, Pig Family, Elephant Family* and *Owl Family*. In spring 1987, the last year of the series, the *Dog Family* and *Cat Family* joined the series, making a total of eleven sets issued from 1961 to 1987.

The reissued *Happy Families* series were sold in blue-green boxes with giraffes, rabbits, mice and hippos printed on them. The boxes were changed again in 1984 to white with pastel-coloured jungle scenes.

At some time during the late 1980s, Wade sold off its remaining stock of *Happy Families* to Tesco Stores, a British discount company. The Tesco Stores box had a rigid cellophane top, front and sides; the base and back were cardboard. There is no reference to Wade on these boxes.

CAT FAMILY

1987

Backstamp: Black transfer "Wade Made in England"

No.	Name	Description	Size	U.S. $	Can. $	U.K. £
1	Mother	Grey/white; blue eyes; pink ear tips	45 x 35	40.00	55.00	28.00
2	Kitten, Lying	Grey/white; blue eyes; pink ears	30 x 35	25.00	35.00	18.00
3	Kitten, Sitting	Grey/white; blue eyes; pink ears	30 x 20	25.00	35.00	18.00
—	3 pce set	Boxed	—	90.00	120.00	65.00

DOG FAMILY

1987

Backstamp: A. Black transfer "Wade Made in England" (1-3)
B. Unmarked (1-3)

No.	Name	Description	Size	U.S. $	Can. $	U.K. £
1	Mother	Brown; white face, chest	55 x 35	40.00	55.00	28.00
2	Puppy, Lying	Brown; white face, chest	30 x 40	25.00	35.00	18.00
3	Puppy, Standing	Brown; white face, chest	30 x 35	25.00	35.00	18.00
—	3 pce set	Boxed	—	90.00	120.00	55.00

ELEPHANT FAMILY

1984-1987

Backstamp: Black transfer "Wade Made in England" (some with cricket in large C)

No.	Name	Description	Size	U.S. $	Can. $	U.K. £
1a	Mother	Blue; pink ears, mouth	35 x 70	20.00	25.00	12.00
1b	Mother	Grey; pink ears, mouth	35 x 70	20.00	25.00	12.00
2a	Baby, Trunk Down	Blue; pink ears, mouth	25 x 55	15.00	20.00	10.00
2b	Baby, Trunk Down	Grey; pink ears, mouth	25 x 55	15.00	20.00	10.00
3a	Baby, Trunk Up	Blue; pink ears, mouth	45 x 22	15.00	20.00	10.00
3b	Baby, Trunk Up	Grey; pink ears, mouth	45 x 22	15.00	20.00	10.00
—	3 pce set	Boxed	—	45.00	60.00	30.00

FROG FAMILY

1984-1987

Backstamp: **A.** Black transfer "Wade Made in England" (1-3)
B. Red transfer "Wade Made in England" (1-3)

No.	Name	Description	Size	U.S. $	Can. $	U.K. £
1	Mother	Brown; red-brown spots	25 x 45	20.00	25.00	12.00
3	Baby, Singing	Brown; red-brown spots	25 x 25	15.00	20.00	10.00
2	Baby, Smiling	Brown; red-brown spot	20 x 30	15.00	20.00	10.00
—	3 pce set	Boxed	—	45.00	60.00	30.00

GIRAFFE FAMILY

FIRST ISSUE

1961-1965

Except for a slight variation in eyelid and horn colour, the original and reissued models are hard to distinguish from each other.

Backstamp: **A.** Unmarked (1-3)
B. Black and gold label Genuine "Wade Porcelain Made in England" (1-3)
C. Brown ink stamp "Wade England" with cricket (1-3)

No.	Name	Description	Size	U.S. $	Can. $	U.K. £
1	Mother	Beige; light blue eyelids; light grey horns	60 x 45	20.00	25.00	12.00
2	Baby, Awake	Beige; light blue eyelids; light grey horns	40 x 28	15.00	20.00	10.00
3	Baby, Sleeping	Beige; light blue eyelids; light grey horns	15 x 30	15.00	20.00	10.00
—	3 pce set	Boxed	—	45.00	60.00	30.00

SECOND ISSUE

1978-1987

Photograph not available
at press time

Backstamp: **A.** Unmarked (1-3)
B. Brown transfer "Wade Made in England" (1-3)
C. Black transfer "Wade Made in England" (1-3)

No.	Name	Description	Size	U.S. $	Can. $	U.K. £
1	Mother	Beige; turquoise eyelids; dark grey horns	60 x 45	20.00	25.00	12.00
3	Baby, Awake	Beige; turquoise eyelids; dark grey horns	40 x 28	15.00	20.00	10.00
2	Baby, Sleeping	Beige; turquoise eyelids; dark grey horns	15 x 30	15.00	20.00	10.00
—	3 pce set	Boxed	—	43.00	60.00	30.00

HIPPO FAMILY

FIRST ISSUE

1961-1965

Backstamp: Unknown

No.	Name	Description	Size	U.S. $	Can. $	U.K. £
1	Mother	Dark blue/brown eyes	35 x 50	15.00	20.00	7.00
2	Baby, Asleep	Eyes shut	20 x 25	12.00	15.00	7.00
3	Baby, Awake	Dark blue/brown eyes	28 x 25	12.00	15.00	7.00
—	3 pce set	Boxed	—	43.00	60.00	30.00

SECOND ISSUE

1978-1987

Backstamp: Black transfer "Wade Made in England"

No.	Name	Description	Size	U.S. $	Can. $	U.K. £
1	Mother	Smoky blue; blue tear; brown eyes	35 x 50	15.00	20.00	10.00
2	Baby, Asleep	Smoky blue; blue tear; brown eyes	20 x 25	12.00	15.00	7.00
3	Baby, Awake	Smoky blue; blue tear; brown eyes	28 x 25	12.00	15.00	7.00
—	3 pce set	Boxed	—	38.00	50.00	25.00

Hippo Mother Blow Up

The hippo "Mother" is the only one of the *Happy Families* models reported in a blow-up size. Perhaps it was a prototype model, which was not issued because of high production costs.

Photograph not available
at press time

Backstamp: Unmarked

No.	Description	Size	U.S.$	Can.$	U.K.£
1	Pale blue; blue eyes	Unknown		Extremely rare	

MOUSE FAMILY

FIRST ISSUE

1962-1965

The *Mouse Family* was issued in spring 1962 and reissued from 1978 to 1984. The original models have yellow tails, compared with the pink tails of the later figures.

Backstamp: **A.** Unmarked (1-3)
                B. Brown ink stamp "Wade Made in England" (1-3)

No.	Name	Description	Size	U.S. $	Can. $	U.K. £
1	Mother	White; pink ears; yellow tail	50 x 28	40.00	60.00	20.00
2	Baby, Eyes Closed	White; pink ears, nose; yellow tail	28 x 28	35.00	50.00	20.00
3	Baby, Eyes Open	White; blue eyes; pink ears, nose; yellow tail	25 x 30	35.00	50.00	20.00
—	3 pce set	Boxed	—	100.00	125.00	50.00

SECOND ISSUE

1978-1987

Backstamp: **A.** Unmarked (1-3)
                B. Black transfer "Wade Made in England" (1-3)

No.	Name	Description	Size	U.S. $	Can. $	U.K. £
1	Mother	White; grey patch; pink ears, tail	50 x 28	20.00	25.00	12.00
2	Baby, Eyes Closed	White; grey patch; pink ears, tail	28 x 28	15.00	20.00	10.00
3	Baby, Eyes Open	White; grey patch; pink ears, tail	25 x 30	15.00	20.00	10.00
—	3 pce set	Boxed	—	45.00	60.00	30.00

OWL FAMILY

1984-1987

Backstamp: A. Black transfer "Wade Made in England" (1-3)
B. Red transfer "Wade Made in England" (1-3)

No.	Name	Description	Size	U.S. $	Can. $	U.K. £
1	Mother	Cream; beige head, back, wings	40 x 40	15.00	20.00	10.00
2	Baby, Wings Closed	Cream; beige head, back, wings	25 x 20	12.00	15.00	7.00
3	Baby, Wings Open	Cream; beige head, back, wings	25 x 32	12.00	15.00	7.00
—	3 pce set	Boxed	—	35.00	45.00	22.00

PIG FAMILY

1984-1987

Backstamp: A. Black transfer "Wade Made in England" (1-3)
B. Red transfer "Wade Made in England" (1-3)

No.	Name	Description	Size	U.S. $	Can. $	U.K. £
1a	Mother	Pink; black eyes; red mouth	28 x 65	20.00	25.00	12.00
1b	Mother	Reddish pink; white face; black eyes; red mouth	28 x 65	20.00	25.00	12.00
2	Baby, Asleep	Pink; blue eyelids	15 x 45	15.00	20.00	10.00
3a	Baby, Awake	Pink; black eyes; red mouth	18 x 40	15.00	20.00	10.00
3b	Baby, Awake	Reddish pink; white face; black eyes; red mouth	18 x 40	12.00	18.00	8.00
—	3 pce set	Boxed	—	45.00	60.00	30.00

RABBIT FAMILY
FIRST ISSUE
1963-1965

Backstamp: A. Unmarked (1-3)
B. Black and gold label "Genuine Wade Porcelain Made in England" (1-3)

No.	Name	Description	Size	U.S. $	Can. $	U.K. £
1	Mother	White; turquoise patches	55 x 30	30.00	50.00	25.00
2	Baby, Sitting	White; turquoise patches	34 x 28	25.00	45.00	20.00
3	Baby, Standing	White; turquoise patches	30 x 35	25.00	45.00	20.00
—	3 pce set	Boxed	—	80.00	150.00	60.00

SECOND ISSUE
1978-1984

Backstamp: A. Black transfer "Wade made in England" (1-3)
B. Unmarked (1-3)

No.	Name	Description	Size	U.S. $	Can. $	U.K. £
1	Mother	White; blue patches	55 x 30	20.00	25.00	12.00
2	Baby, Sitting	White; blue patches	34 x 28	15.00	20.00	10.00
3	Baby, Standing	White; blue patches	30 x 35	15.00	20.00	10.00
—	3 pce set	Boxed	—	45.00	60.00	30.00

TIGER FAMILY

1961-1965

This set was not reissued, so it is rare and highly sought after.

Backstamp: Unmarked

No.	Name	Description	Size	U.S. $	Can. $	U.K. £
1	Mother	Beige; brown stripes; green eyes; red tongue	40 x 40	80.00	105.00	40.00
2	Baby, Sleeping	Beige; brown stripes; green eyes; red tongue	10 x 30	50.00	65.00	30.00
3	Baby, Awake	Beige; brown stripes; green eyes; red tongue	10 x 30	50.00	65.00	30.00
—	3 pce set	Boxed	—	170.00	225.00	90.00

SMUDGER
1996-1997

LEPRECHAUNS AND PIXIES

LEPRECHAUNS AND PIXIES
BABY PIXIE
Circa 1978-1980s

The *Baby Pixie* models can be found free standing, on a circular pin tray or on a shamrock leaf dish. Some pin trays have a 1950s mark on the base, which means they may have been old stock reissued with pixies on them to create new products.

Baby Pixie

Backstamp: **A.** Black ink stamp "Made in Ireland" (1)
B. Embossed "Made in Ireland, Porcelain Wade, Eire Tir-Adheanta" (2, 3)
C. Impressed "Irish Porcelain Made in Ireland Co. Armagh" (3)

No.	Name	Description	Size	U.S. $	Can. $	U.K. £
1	Baby Pixie	Blue suit, cap, boots	35 x 10	30.00	45.00	12.00

Baby Pixie Derivatives

Baby Pixie on Shamrock Leaf Dish

No.	Name	Description	Size	U.S. $	Can. $	U.K. £
1	Baby Pixie Pin Tray	Blue suit; blue-green tray	40 x 75	25.00	35.00	10.00
2	Baby Pixie Shamrock Leaf Dish	Blue suit; blue-grey dish	40 x 75	25.00	35.00	10.00

LARGE LEPRECHAUNS

1974-1985

Although it appears that these models were in production for over ten years, they are rarely seen.

Backstamp: Unmarked

No.	Description	Size	U.S.$	Can.$	U.K.£
1a	Bright blue all over	70 x 30	45.00	55.00	25.00
1b	Brown all over	70 x 30	45.00	55.00	25.00
1c	Green hat; dark brown jacket; beige trousers	70 x 30	50.00	70.00	35.00
1d	Grey-green	70 x 30	35.00	45.00	20.00
1e	Turquoise blue	70 x 30	45.00	55.00	25.00
1f	Yellow hat; green jacket; beige trousers	70 x 30	50.00	70.00	35.00

Large Leprechaun Derivatives

Marble Bases

1974-1987

The model mounted on a square block of Connemara marble is the original 1974 model. It was intended for the tourist trade. The model on the circular resin base is designed to simulate Connemara marble.

On Connemara Marble Base   **On Simulated Marble Base**

Backstamp: **A.** Gold label "Real Connemara Marble Made in Ireland"
 B. Gold label "Lucky Irish Leprechaun Made in Ireland"
 C. None

No.	Description	Size	U.S.$	Can.$	U.K.£
1	Dark grey-green; gold label	90 x 55	75.00	100.00	50.00
2	Dark grey green; mottled grey resin base	85	35.00	50.00	25.00

Large Leprechaun Derivatives

Money Boxes

1987

In 1987 Wade issued three money boxes based on the earlier "Fawn," "Disney Kennel" and "Noddy Toadstool Cottage" money boxes. Because the original moulds were worn, Wade made new moulds, which produced larger, heavier and less delicate-looking models than the originals. New colours were also used. The "Large Leprechaun" was used on the "Toadstool Cottage." The moneyboxes were sold in plain, unmarked boxes. For the other two money boxes see *Whimsie-land* and Miscellaneous Models (pages 134 and 156).

Toadstool Cottage Money Box

Backstamp: Unmarked

No.	Name	Description	Size	U.S.$	Can.$	U.K.£
1	Toadstool Cottage	Brown roof, door and shirt; green hat	140 x 155	60.00	80.00	30.00

LARRY AND LESTER, THE LEPRECHAUN TWINS

1974-1985

Backstamp: Black ink stamp "Made in Ireland"

No.	Name	Description	Size	U.S.$	Can.$	U.K.£
1	Larry	Green hat; purple jacket; brown leggings	100 x 60	70.00	120.00	45.00
2	Lester	Yellow hat; green jacket; red leggings	100 x 60	70.00	120.00	45.00

Larry And Lester Derivatives

Bookends

1974-1985

The leprechaun twins were added to a heavy porcelain, L-shaped base to form a pair of bookends.

Larry and Lester Bookends

Backstamp: Purple ink stamp "Made in Ireland"

No.	Description	Size	U.S.$	Can.$	U.K.£
1	Larry on one base; Lester on the other; dark green bookends	115 x 75	250.00	325.00	125.00

LEPRECHAUN ON TOADSTOOL WITH CROCK O'GOLD

Circa 1975

This model is of a smiling leprechaun sitting on top of a toadstool with his hands resting on top of a crock o'gold.

Backstamp: Black ink stamp "Made in Ireland"

No.	Description	Size	U.S.$	Can.$	U.K.£
1	Grey/brown	125	65.00	85.00	30.00
2	Grey/brown leprechaun; blue toadstool	145	75.00	100.00	50.00

Crock O'Gold Derivative

Oak Leaf Dish

1957-1959

The George Wade Potterys 1957 oak leaf dish was issued with the 1956-1959 "Leprechaun Crock O'Gold" to produce this particular dish. The original selling price was 2/11d.

Backstamp: Embossed "Shamrock Pottery"

No.	Name	Description	Size	U.S. $	Can. $	U.K. £
1a	Crock O'Gold	Orange hat; blue jacket; brown boots; green leaf	40 x 100	30.00	40.00	10.00
1b	Crock O'Gold	Yellow hat; blue jacket; brown boots; green leaf	40 x 100	30.00	40.00	10.00
1c	Crock O'Gold	Maroon hat; blue jacket; brown boots; green leaf	40 x 100	30.00	40.00	10.00

LUCKY FAIRY FOLK

1956-1986

Lucky Fairy Folk, produced by Wade (Ulster) Ltd., is a set of three models sitting on the backs of a rabbit and a pig and on top of an acorn. Each figure was sold separately in a cylindrical-shaped acetate packet, with a multi-coloured string handle. On the end of the string was a black foil label, which read "Made in Ireland by Wade Co. Armagh" in gold lettering. The models themselves are not marked, so once removed from the packet, there is no indication of which pottery they were from. On the first issue models the colour of the face is beige brown and the snout and toes on the pigs was originally grey and was then changed to beige.

FIRST VERSION: BROWN FACES

1956-1960S

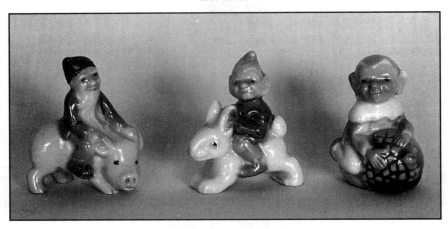

Backstamp: Unmarked

No.	Name	Description	Size	U.S. $	Can. $	U.K. £
1a	Leprechaun on Pig	Dark green hat; grey coat; blue trousers; white boots; pig has grey snout and toes	45 x 35	55.00	75.00	30.00
1b	Leprechaun on Pig	Orange hat; blue coat, boots; grey trousers; pig has grey snout and toes	45 x 35	55.00	75.00	30.00
1c	Leprechaun on Pig	Red hat; blue coat; grey trousers; white boots; pig has beige snout and toes	45 x 35	55.00	75.00	30.00
1d	Leprechaun on Pig	Red hat; blue coat, boots; grey trousers; pig has beige snout and toes	45 x 35	55.00	75.00	30.00
2a	Pixie on Acorn	Blue hat, boots; white trousers; grey coat	40 x 30	75.00	100.00	36.00
2b	Pixie on Acorn	Dark green hat; white trousers; grey coat	40 x 30	75.00	100.00	36.00
2c	Pixie on Acorn	Orange hat; white trousers; grey coat; blue boots	40 x 30	75.00	100.00	36.00
2d	Pixie on Acorn	Red hat; white trousers; grey coat; blue boots	40 x 30	75.00	100.00	36.00
2e	Pixie on Acorn	Dark yellow hat; white trousers; grey coat; blue boots	40 x 30	75.00	100.00	36.00
2f	Pixie on Acorn	White hat, trousers; grey coat; blue boots	40 x 30	75.00	100.00	36.00
3a	Pixie on Rabbit	Dark green hat; dark blue coat; grey trousers; blue boots; white rabbit	40 x 32	75.00	100.00	50.00
3b	Pixie on Rabbit	Red hat; dark blue coat; grey trousers; blue boots; white rabbit	40 x 32	75.00	100.00	50.00
3c	Pixie on Rabbit	Dark yellow hat; dark blue coat; grey trousers; blue boots; white rabbit	40 x 32	75.00	100.00	50.00

Lucky Fairy Folk First Version Derivative

Butter Dish

1970s

Pixie on Acorn Butter Dish

Backstamp: Embossed "Wade England"

No.	Description	Size	U.S.$	Can.$	U.K.£
1a	Green hat; yellow dish	65 x 80	75.00	100.00	30.00
1b	Yellow hat, dish	65 x 80	75.00	100.00	30.00
1c	Red hat; yellow dish	65 x 80	75.00	100.00	30.00
1d	Blue hat; yellow dish	65 x 80	75.00	100.00	30.00

SECOND VERSION: FLESH COLOURED FACE

1980-1986

The difference between the second version and the first version issued in 1956 is the colour of the Leprechaun's face. In this version the Leprechaun's faces are beige.

Backstamp: Unmarked

No.	Name	Description	Size	U.S. $	Can. $	U.K. £
1	Leprechaun on Pig	Red hat; flesh face, hands; blue coat, boots; beige trousers; pig has light beige snout and toes	45 x 35	55.00	75.00	30.00

LUCKY LEPRECHAUNS

1956-1980s

This set of three *Lucky Leprechauns* was first issued in 1956 by Wade (Ulster) Ltd. When the models were originally shipped to retailers, they were packaged in decorative display boxes of 24 models, with hat colours of white, yellow, orange, red, maroon, blue or green. Also included was a porcelain shamrock leaf to use as a price display. On it was printed "Lucky Leprechauns Made in Ireland By Wade Co. Armagh 1/11d each." Many of these shamrock plaques have survived and are sought by collectors. The *Lucky Leprechauns* set was reissued in the mid-1960s and again in the 1980s.

FIRST VERSION: BROWN FACES, PAPER LABEL

1956-1959

Originally the models each had a black and gold label on the base. The label is easily washed off and if it is missing it is difficult to tell which version the figure comes from. As a general guide, the 1956-1959 models have brown faces, whereas the faces of later figures are flesh coloured.

Backstamp: A. Black and gold label "Made in Ireland by Wade Co. Armagh" (1-3)
B. Unmarked (1-3)

No.	Name	Description	Size	U.S. $	Can. $	U.K. £
1a	Cobbler	Dark green hat; grey coat, boots; blue trousers	37 x 30	30.00	40.00	14.00
1b	Cobbler	Maroon hat; grey coat, boots; blue trousers	37 x 30	30.00	40.00	14.00
1c	Cobbler	Orange hat; grey coat, boots; blue trousers	37 x 30	30.00	40.00	14.00
1d	Cobbler	Red hat; grey coat, boots; blue trousers	37 x 30	30.00	40.00	14.00
1e	Cobbler	White hat; grey coat, boots; blue trousers	37 x 30	30.00	40.00	14.00
2a	Crock O'Gold	Maroon hat; blue coat; grey trousers; brown boots	34 x 25	30.00	40.00	14.00
2b	Crock O'Gold	Orange hat; blue coat; grey trousers; brown boots	34 x 25	30.00	40.00	14.00
2c	Crock O'Gold	Red hat; blue coat; grey trousers; brown boots	34 x 25	30.00	40.00	14.00
2d	Crock O'Gold	Dark yellow hat; blue coat; grey trousers; brown boots	34 x 25	30.00	40.00	14.00
2e	Crock O'Gold	Yellow hat; green coat; grey trousers; brown boots	34 x 25	30.00	40.00	14.00
3a	Tailor	Blue hat; white coat; blue trousers; grey boot	38 x 19	30.00	40.00	14.00
3b	Tailor	Dark green hat; white coat; blue trousers; grey boot	38 x 19	30.00	40.00	14.00
3c	Tailor	Red hat; white coat; blue trousers; grey boot	38 x 19	30.00	40.00	14.00

Lucky Leprechauns First Version Derivatives

Pintrays
1956-1959

The *Lucky Leprechauns* models used on these pin trays were issued by Wade (Ulster) Ltd. from 1956 to 1959. The pin tray in which the Lucky Leprechaun sits was originally produced as a "pin tray" (plain) and as a "butter pat" (with transfer printed decorations) see *The Charlton Standard Catalogue of Wade Decorative Ware, Vol. 2* and *The Charlton Standard Catalogue of Wade Tableware, Vol. 3*. There are two styles of pin trays: one with a recessed centre (Irish Wade Shape No I.P.619), and an early 1950s backstamp, the second with a flat centre, and 1971-1976 backstamps. The first version *Lucky Leprechauns* are found only on recessed trays.

There are no price differentials between the recessed and flat centre trays or between Version One, Two or Three Leprechauns.

Colour: Blue-green trays
Backstamp: Embossed Circular "Irish Porcelain Made in Ireland" around a central shamrock with letter T (early 1950s)

No.	Name	Description	Size	U.S. $	Can. $	U.K. £
1a	Cobbler	Dark green hat; grey coat, boots; blue trousers	45 x 75	27.00	32.00	10.00
1b	Cobbler	Orange hat; grey coat, boots; blue trousers	45 x 75	27.00	32.00	10.00
1c	Cobbler	Maroon hat; grey coat, boots; blue trousers	45 x 75	27.00	32.00	10.00
1d	Cobbler	White hat; grey coat, boots; blue trousers	45 x 75	27.00	32.00	10.00
2a	Crock O'Gold	Maroon hat; blue coat; grey trousers; brown boots	45 x 75	27.00	32.00	10.00
2b	Crock O'Gold	Orange hat; blue coat; grey trousers; brown boots	45 x 75	27.00	32.00	10.00
2c	Crock O'Gold	Dark yellow hat; blue coat; grey trousers; brown boots	45 x 75	27.00	32.00	10.00
3a	Tailor	Blue hat; white coat; blue trousers; grey boot	45 x 75	27.00	32.00	10.00
3b	Tailor	Dark green hat; white coat; blue trousers; grey boot	45 x 75	27.00	32.00	10.00
3c	Tailor	Maroon hat; white coat; blue trousers; grey boot	45 x 75	27.00	32.00	10.00

SECOND VERSION: FLESH COLOURED FACES, WITHOUT BACKSTAMPS

1960s

This boxed set of three *Lucky Leprechauns* had no labels and were unmarked. Once removed from their box, there is no indication of the year of issue or of the maker. The reissued models have flesh-coloured faces, which distinguish them from the original 1956-1959 version.

Backstamp: Unmarked

No.	Name	Description	Size	U.S. $	Can. $	U.K. £
1a	Cobbler	Green hat; light grey coat, boots; pale blue trousers	38 x 31	20.00	25.00	10.00
1b	Cobbler	Orange hat; light grey coat, boots; pale blue trousers	38 x 31	20.00	25.00	10.00
1c	Cobbler	Red hat; light grey coat, boots; pale blue trousers	38 x 31	20.00	25.00	10.00
1d	Cobbler	Yellow hat; light grey coat, boots pale blue trousers	38 x 31	20.00	25.00	10.00
2a	Crock O'Gold	Blue hat; pale blue grey coat; light grey trousers; brown boots with or without brown stripe	34 x 26	20.00	25.00	10.00
2b	Crock O'Gold	Green hat; pale blue grey coat; light grey trousers; brown boots with or without brown stripe	34 x 26	20.00	25.00	10.00
2c	Crock O'Gold	Red hat; pale blue grey coat; light grey trousers; brown boots with or without brown stripe	34 x 26	20.00	25.00	10.00
2d	Crock O'Gold	Yellow hat; pale blue grey coat; light grey trousers; brown boots with or without brown stripe	34 x 26	20.00	25.00	10.00
3a	Tailor	Pale blue hat, trousers; white coat; grey boot	39 x 20	20.00	25.00	10.00
3b	Tailor	Green hat; white coat; pale blue trousers; grey boot	39 x 20	20.00	25.00	10.00
3c	Tailor	Red hat; white coat; pale blue trousers; grey boot	39 x 20	20.00	25.00	10.00
3d	Tailor	Yellow hat; white coat; pale blue trousers; grey boot	39 x 20	20.00	25.00	10.00
—	3 pce set	Boxed		75.00	85.00	25.00

Lucky Leprechaun Second Version Derivatives

Butter Dish

1970s

The George Wade butter dish was first produced from 1955 to 1959, with a model of a squirrel, rabbit or the 1956 *Hat Box* "Jock" on the back rim. In the 1970s, the dish was combined with surplus Irish Wade, *Lucky Leprechauns* to produce novelty butter dishes.

Backstamp: Embossed "Wade England"

No.	Name	Description	Size	U.S. $	Can. $	U.K. £
1a	Cobbler	Blue hat; yellow dish	65 x 80	30.00	40.00	20.00
1b	Cobbler	Green hat; yellow dish	65 x 80	30.00	40.00	20.00
2a	Tailor	Blue hat; yellow dish	65 x 80	30.00	40.00	20.00
2b	Tailor	Green hat; yellow dish	65 x 80	30.00	40.00	20.00
2c	Tailor	Red hat; yellow dish	65 x 80	30.00	40.00	20.00

Lucky Leprechauns Second Version Derivatives

Marble Plinths

Circa 1975-1985

These models were taken from the reissued 1974-1985 *Lucky Leprechauns* set and mounted on a block of Connemara marble. They were intended for the tourist trade.

Lucky Leprechauns on Marble Plinthes

Backstamp: Gold label "Lucky Irish Leprechauns, Made in Ireland"

No.	Name	Description	Size	U.S. $	Can. $	U.K. £
1a	Cobbler	Light brown stool; beige shoe	58 x 52	15.00	20.00	10.00
2a	Crock O'Gold	Blue hat; yellow coins; grey jacket, trousers	58 x 52	15.00	20.00	10.00
2b	Crock O'Gold	Red hat; yellow coins; grey jacket, trousers	58 x 52	15.00	20.00	10.00
2c	Crock O'Gold	Yellow hat, coins; grey jacket, trousers	58 x 52	15.00	20.00	10.00
3a	Tailor	Blue hat; grey trousers, shoes	58 x 52	15.00	20.00	10.00
3b	Tailor	Yellow hat; grey trousers, shoes	58 x 52	15.00	20.00	10.00
4	Trio of models	Cobbler: red hat; tailor: blue hat; leprechaun: grey	82 x 79	20.00	25.00	15.00

Lucky Leprechauns Second Version Derivatives

Pin Trays

The second version of the *Lucky Leprechauns* are found on both styles of trays, recessed and flat centre.

Pin Trays

Colour: Blue-green trays
Backstamp: Embossed Circular "Irish Porcelain Made in Ireland" around a central shamrock with letter T (early 1950s)

No.	Name	Description	Size	U.S. $	Can. $	U.K. £
1a	Cobbler	Dark green hat; grey coat, boots; blue trousers	45 x 75	27.00	32.00	10.00
1b	Cobbler	Maroon hat; grey coat, boots; blue trousers	45 x 75	27.00	32.00	10.00
1c	Cobbler	Orange hat; grey coat, boots; blue trousers	45 x 75	27.00	32.00	10.00
1d	Cobbler	White hat; grey coat, boots; blue trousers	45 x 75	27.00	32.00	10.00
2a	Crock O'Gold	Dark yellow hat; blue coat; grey trousers; brown boots	45 x 75	27.00	32.00	10.00
2b	Crock O'Gold	Maroon hat; blue coat; grey trousers; brown boots	45 x 75	27.00	32.00	10.00
2c	Crock O'Gold	Orange hat; blue coat; grey trousers; brown boots	45 x 75	27.00	32.00	10.00
3a	Tailor	Blue hat; white coat; blue trousers; grey boot	45 x 75	27.00	32.00	10.00
3b	Tailor	Dark green hat; white coat; blue trousers; grey boot	45 x 75	27.00	32.00	10.00
3c	Tailor	Maroon hat; white coat; blue trousers; grey boot	45 x 75	27.00	32.00	10.00

THIRD VERSION: FLESH COLOURED FACES, WITH BACKSTAMP

1971-1976

Backstamp: **A.** Small black ink stamp "Made in Ireland" (1a)
B. Large black ink stamp "Made in Ireland" (1b, 2a, 2b, 3a, 3b, 3c)

No.	Name	Description	Size	U.S. $	Can. $	U.K. £
1a	Cobbler	Red hat; grey coat, boots; pale blue trousers	38 x 31	15.00	20.00	10.00
1b	Cobbler	White hat; dark grey coat, boots; dark blue trousers	38 x 31	15.00	20.00	10.00
2a	Crock O'Gold	Blue hat; blue coat; light grey trousers; brown boots with or without brown stripe	34 x 26	15.00	20.00	10.00
2b	Crock O'Gold	Green hat; blue coat; light grey trousers; brown boots with or without brown stripe	34 x 26	15.00	20.00	10.00
2c	Crock O'Gold	Red hat; blue coat; light grey trousers; brown boots with or without brown stripe	34 x 26	15.00	20.00	10.00
2d	Crock O'Gold	Yellow hat; blue coat; light grey trousers; brown boots with or without brown stripe	34 x 26	15.00	20.00	10.00
3a	Tailor	Blue hat / trousers; white coat; grey boot	39 x 20	15.00	20.00	10.00
3b	Tailor	Yellow hat; white coat; blue trousers; grey boot	39 x 20	15.00	20.00	10.00

Lucky Leprechauns Third Version Derivatives

Pin Trays
1980s

Backstamp: Embossed circular "Made in Ireland Irish Porcelain Wade Eire Tir A Dheanta" IP 619 with shamrock and crown in centre

No.	Name	Description	Size	U.S. $	Can. $	U.K. £
1a	Cobbler	Green hat; light grey coat, boots; pale blue trousers	45 x 75	27.00	32.00	14.00
1b	Cobbler	Orange hat; light grey coat, boots; pale blue trousers	45 x 75	27.00	32.00	14.00
1c	Cobbler	Red hat; light grey coat, boots; pale blue trousers	45 x 75	27.00	32.00	14.00
1d	Cobbler	Yellow hat; light grey coat, boots; pale blue trousers	45 x 75	27.00	32.00	14.00
2a	Crock O'Gold	Blue hat; pale blue grey coat; light grey trousers; brown boots with or without brown stripe	45 x 75	27.00	32.00	14.00
2b	Crock O'Gold	Green hat; pale blue grey coat; light grey trousers; brown boots with or without brown stripe	45 x 75	27.00	32.00	14.00
2c	Crock O'Gold	Red hat; pale blue grey coat; light grey trousers; brown boots with or without brown stripe	45 x 75	27.00	32.00	14.00
2d	Crock O'Gold	Yellow hat; pale blue grey coat; light grey trousers; brown boots with or without brown stripe	45 x 75	27.00	32.00	14.00
3a	Tailor	Pale blue hat, trousers; white coat; grey boot	45 x 75	27.00	32.00	14.00
3b	Tailor	Green hat; white coat; pale blue trousers; grey boot	45 x 75	27.00	32.00	14.00
3c	Tailor	Red hat; white coat; pale blue trousers; grey boot	45 x 75	27.00	32.00	14.00
3d	Tailor	Yellow hat; white coat; pale blue trousers; grey boot	45 x 75	27.00	32.00	14.00

LUCKY LEPRECHAUN SHAMROCK PLAQUE

1956-1959

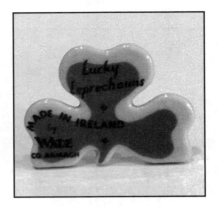

Backstamp: None

No.	Description	Size	U.S. $	Can. $	U.K. £
1	White/green; black lettering	100 x 48	200.00	265.00	100.00

SHAMROCK COTTAGE

1956-1984

The *Shamrock Cottage* was a slip cast, hollow model of an Irish cottage, produced by Wade (Ulster) Ltd. It was sold in a box decorated with a shamrock design and labeled "Shamrock Pottery" and "Ireland's own Pottery." The original selling price was 2/6d.

FIRST VERSION: LIGHT BROWN PEAT, GREEN BASE

1956-1961, 1977-Early 1980s

Backstamp: Impressed "Shamrock Pottery Made in Ireland"

No.	Description	Size	U.S. $	Can. $	U.K. £
1	Yellow roof; blue doors, windows; light brown peat; green base	45 x 40	45.00	60.00	25.00

SECOND VERSION: DARK BROWN PEAT, MOTTLED GREEN BASE

1977-1984

This reissued *Shamrock Cottage* is the same as the 1956-1961 model, except that the colour of the base is a mottled green and white and the peat pile at the back of the cottage is a darker shade of brown. It has also been found with names of places of interest printed in black letters on the front rim of the base.

Backstamp: Impressed "Shamrock Pottery Made in Ireland"

No.	Name	Description	Size	U.S. $	Can. $	U.K. £
1a	Bally Castle	Yellow roof; dark blue doors; dark brown peat; mottled green and white base; black lettering	45 x 40	45.00	60.00	25.00
1b	Belfast	Yellow roof; dark blue doors; dark brown peat; mottled green and white base; black lettering	45 x 40	45.00	60.00	25.00
1c	Cliftonville	Yellow roof; dark blue doors; dark brown peat; mottled green and white base; black lettering	45 x 40	45.00	60.00	25.00
1d	Conway	Yellow roof; dark blue doors; dark brown peat; mottled green and white base; black lettering	45 x 40	45.00	60.00	25.00
1e	Hawkshead	Yellow roof; dark blue doors; dark brown peat; mottled green and white base; black lettering	45 x 40	45.00	60.00	25.00
1f	Giants Causeway	Yellow roof; blue doors; dark brown peat; mottled green and white base; black lettering	45 x 40	45.00	60.00	25.00
1g	Guernsey	Yellow roof; dark blue doors; dark brown peat; mottled green and white base; black lettering	45 x 40	45.00	60.00	25.00
1h	Isle of Wight	Yellow roof; dark blue doors; dark brown peat; mottled green and white base; black lettering	45 x 40	45.00	60.00	25.00
1i	Jersey	Yellow roof; dark blue doors; dark brown peat; mottled green and white base; black lettering	45 x 40	45.00	60.00	25.00
1j	Shanklin	Yellow roof; dark blue doors; dark brown peat; mottled green and white base; black lettering	45 x 40	45.00	60.00	25.00
1k	Windermere	Yellow roof; blue doors; dark brown peat; mottled green and white base; black lettering	45 x 40	45.00	60.00	25.00
1l	Plain Cottage	Yellow roof; blue doors, windows; dark brown peat; mottled green and white base	45 x 40	45.00	60.00	25.00

THIRD VERSION: LIGHT BROWN PEAT, WHITE BASE

1977-Early 1980s

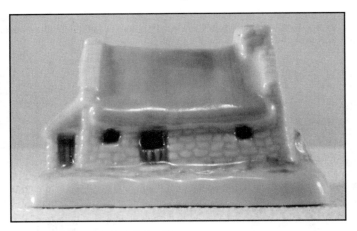

Backstamp: Impressed "Shamrock Pottery Made in Ireland"

No	Description	Size	U.S. $	Can. $	U.K. £
1	Yellow roof; blue doors, windows; light brown peat; white base	45 x 40	45.00	60.00	25.00

Shamrock Cottage Third Version Derivatives

Shamrock Cottage on Simulated Marble Plinth

This *Shamrock Cottage* is glued onto a simulated resin Connemara marble base. Attached to the base is a gold coloured piece of metal, the top of which is missing the original model, an unknown building or figure.

Backstamp: None

No.	Description	Size	U.S. $	Can. $	U.K. £
1	Yellow roof; blue door and windows; green and white base; on circular mottled olive green resin base	45 x 40 (plinth - 55 x 50)	20.00	30.00	15.00

Shamrock Cottage Third Version Derivatives
Cottage and Tailor on a Map of Ireland
1970s

The reissued "Tailor" and the reissued *Shamrock Cottage* (1974-1985) were combined by Wade Ireland and placed on a porcelain outline of the map of Ireland to form this unusual and sought-after souvenir model. It was discontinued in 1979.

Backstamp: Embossed "Made in Ireland"

No.	Name	Description	Size	U.S $	Can. $	U.K. £
1a	Tailor	Blue hat; grey trousers, shoes; grey-green base	65 x 140	120.00	160.00	90.00
1b	Tailor	Yellow hat; grey trousers, shoes; grey-green base	65 x 140	120.00	160.00	90.00
1c	Tailor	Blue hat, trousers; grey shoes; grey-green base	65 x 140	120.00	160.00	90.00

Shamrock Cottage Third Version Derivatives

Shamrock Cottage on Simulated Marble Plinth

1970s

In the late 1970s the "Cobbler," "Crock O'Gold" and "Tailor" *Leprechauns* and the reissued *Shamrock Cottage* (1974-1985) were combined and mounted on a rectangular marble base.

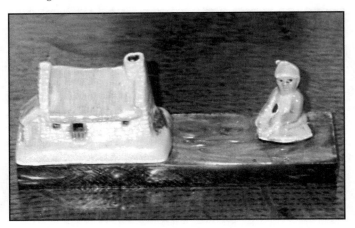

Backstamp: None

No.	Name	Description	Size	U.S. $	Can. $	U.K. £
1	Cobbler and Cottage	Beige stool; white shoes; yellow roof blue windows; dark brown peat	Unknown	20.00	25.00	15.00
2	Crock O'Gold and Cottage	Yellow hat; blue jacket; yellow roof blue windows; dark brown peat	Unknown	20.00	25.00	15.00
3	Tailor and Cottage	Yellow hat; grey trousers; yellow roof blue windows; dark brown peat	Unknown	20.00	25.00	15.00

NOVELTY ANIMALS AND BIRDS

NOVELTY ANIMALS AND BIRDS

Circa 1935-Circa 1949

BABY BIRD

Circa 1935

Backstamp: **A.** Black ink stamp "Flaxman Ware Hand Made Pottery By Wadeheath England" (1)
B. Black ink stamp "Wadeheath Ware England" (2)

No.	Name	Description	Size	U.S. $	Can. $	U.K. £
1a	Baby Bird, Large	Mottled green	200 x 165	160.00	190.00	95.00
1b	Baby Bird, Large	Pale orange	200 x 165	160.00	190.00	95.00
1c	Baby Bird, Large	Yellow	200 x 165	160.00	190.00	95.00
2a	Baby Bird, Small	Orange	90 x 65	65.00	90.00	45.00
2b	Baby Bird, Small	Yellow	90 x 65	65.00	90.00	45.00

CHEEKY DUCKLING

Backstamp: Black ink stamp "Flaxman Ware Hand Made Pottery by Wadeheath England"

No.	Name	Description	Size	U.S. $	Can. $	U.K. £
1	Cheeky Duckling, Large	Blue	180 x 115	145.00	190.00	95.00
2a	Cheeky Duckling, Small	Blue	150 x 85	110.00	145.00	70.00
2b	Cheeky Duckling, Small	Orange	150 x 85	110.00	145.00	70.00

DUCKLING

Circa 1937-1939

Backstamp: **A.** Ink stamp "Flaxman Wade Heath England" (1937-1939) (1a)
B. None (1b)

No.	Name	Description	Size	U.S. $	Can. $	U.K. £
1a	Duckling	Beige brown	95	120.00	150.00	75.00
1b	Duckling	Green	95	150.00	200.00	100.00

LAUGHING RABBIT

Backstamp: Black ink stamp "Flaxman Wade Heath England"

No.	Name	Description	Size	U.S. $	Can. $	U.K. £
1a	Laughing Rabbit, Large	Bright green	175 x 75	135.00	180.00	90.00
1b	Laughing Rabbit, Large	Orange	175 x 75	135.00	180.00	90.00
2a	Laughing Rabbit, Medium	Blue	160 x 70	110.00	150.00	75.00
2b	Laughing Rabbit, Medium	Brown	160 x 70	110.00	150.00	75.00
2c	Laughing Rabbit, Medium	Green	160 x 70	110.00	150.00	75.00
3a	Laughing Rabbit, Small	Beige	140 x 65	110.00	140.00	70.00
3b	Laughing Rabbit, Small	Blue	140 x 65	110.00	140.00	70.00
3c	Laughing Rabbit, Small	Green	140 x 65	110.00	140.00	70.00
4	Old Buck Rabbit	Brown	165 x 128	220.00	300.00	150.00

PONGO

1935-Circa 1949

Pongo was in production from 1935 to 1939 and was reissued for a short time in the late 1940s.

Backstamp: **A.** Black ink stamp "Flaxman Ware Hand Made Pottery By Wadeheath England"
B. Black ink stamp "Wadeheath Ware England"
C. Black ink stamp "Wade Heath England," 1938-1940s

No.	Name	Description	Size	U.S. $	Can. $	U.K. £
1a	Pongo, Large	Blue; mauve nose	140 x 128	120.00	170.00	85.00
1b	Pongo, Large	Green	145 x 150	120.00	160.00	80.00
1c	Pongo, Large	Lilac; mauve nose	140 x 128	120.00	170.00	85.00
1d	Pongo, Large	Mottled blue/orange	140 x 128	120.00	170.00	85.00
1e	Pongo, Large	Orange	145 x 150	120.00	170.00	85.00
1f	Pongo, Large	Orange; mauve nose	140 x 128	120.00	170.00	85.00
2a	Pongo, Medium	Blue; mauve nose	128 x 115	120.00	160.00	80.00
2b	Pongo, Medium	Lilac; mauve nose	128 x 115	120.00	160.00	80.00
2c	Pongo, Medium	Mottled blue/orange	128 x 115	120.00	160.00	80.00
2d	Pongo, Medium	Orange; mauve nose	128 x 115	120.00	160.00	80.00
2e	Pongo, Medium	Turquoise; black eyes, nose	128 x 115	120.00	160.00	80.00
3	Pongo, Miniature	Blue	105 x 95	100.00	125.00	65.00
4a	Pongo, Small	Blue; mauve nose	115 x 100	75.00	100.00	50.00
4b	Pongo, Small	Green; blue eyes, nose	120 x 110	75.00	100.00	50.00
4c	Pongo, Small	Lilac; mauve nose	115 x 100	75.00	100.00	50.00
4d	Pongo, Small	Mauve	120 x 110	75.00	100.00	50.00
4e	Pongo, Small	Orange; mauve nose	115 x 100	75.00	100.00	50.00

WADE BABY
1997-1998

STORYBOOK FIGURES

STORYBOOK FIGURES

At the end of World War II the giftware restrictions on potteries were lifted. Although there was plenty of work available to replace war-damaged industrial wares, a few novelty figurines were produced by the Wade Heath Royal Victoria Pottery and by the George Wade Pottery.

Before 1953 these models were produced in the Royal Victoria Pottery and were marked with a green ink stamp. Models produced in 1953 and after, in either the Royal Victoria Pottery or in the George Wade Pottery, were marked with black transfers.

The first nursery rhyme and fairy tale models produced by Wade were coloured in delicate shades of pastel blues, whites and greys. Because they were produced in both potteries, and dies were replaced when worn, there are slight variations in size and in hair colour on the earlier models. Models are listed in alphabetical order for ease of reference.

Alice and the Dodo was produced with a 1930s experimental cellulose glaze, which cracked and flaked when exposed to heat, damp and sunlight. It is rare to find cellulose models in mint condition.

Some models are marked with a 1935-1937 mark ("Flaxman Ware Hand Made Pottery by Wadeheath England") or any of the 1937-1939 marks ("Flaxman Wade Heath England or Wadeheath Ware England"). Most have an all-over, one-colour matt glaze. All the following storybook models are slip cast, and therefore hollow.

ALICE AND THE DODO

Circa 1935-1938

Alice and the Dodo was produced in the cellulose glaze described above. It is rare to find these models in perfect condition.

Backstamp: **A.** Black hand-painted "Wade Alice 2" with black ink stamp "Made in England" (1)
B. Black hand-painted "Wade Alice" with red ink stamp of leaping deer (2a, 2b, 2c)

No.	Description	Size	U.S. $	Can. $	U.K. £
1	Orange-yellow dress; black band; light brown bird; black beret	130 x 80	350.00	450.00	250.00
2a	Green dress; red band; dark brown bird; blue beret	130 x 80	350.00	450.00	250.00
2b	Pink dress; red band; dark brown bird; blue beret	130 x 80	350.00	450.00	250.00
2c	Blue dress; red band; dark brown bird; blue beret	130 x 80	350.00	450.00	250.00

ANDY CAPP FORTIETH ANNIVERSARY

1997

To celebrate the 40th anniversary of the *Daily Mirror* cartoon series *Andy Capp*, Wade Ceramics produced an *Andy Capp and Flo* cruet, teapot and toast rack. The complete set could be purchased for £35.00 ($58.00 U.S.).

Backstamp: A. Printed "Andy Capp © 1997 Mirror Group Newspapers Ltd, Wade" (3, 4)
B. Printed "Andy Capp Andy © 1997 Mirror Group Newspapers Ltd, Wade" (1)
C. Printed "Andy Capp Flo © 1997 Mirror Group Newspapers Ltd, Wade" (2)

No.	Name	Description	Size	U.S.$	Can.$	U.K.£
1	Andy Capp Salt	Light green cap and scarf; black suit; white base	93	17.00	20.00	10.00
2	Flo Pepper	Yellow hair; light green hairband, blouse; black skirt, shoes; white base	103	17.00	20.00	10.00
3	Andy Capp Teapot	Green cap; flesh coloured face; black pot;	132	30.00	40.00	20.00
4	Toast Rack	Black; gold line; multi-coloured print of Flo and Andy Capp	70	24.00	30.00	15.00

ANDY CAPP MONEY BOX

1998

Reg Smythe, the creator of *Andy Capp*, died of cancer in 1998, as a mark of respect Wade Ceramics donated £1.00 from the sale of the Andy Capp money box model to cancer research. Original cost direct from the Wade Club was £22.00.

Backstamp: Printed "Andy Capp © 1998 Mirror Group Newspapers LTD Andy Capp Wade England"

No.	Name	Description	Size	U.S.$	Can.$	U.K.£
1	Andy Capp Money Box	Green cap and scarf; Black suit and shoes; brown suitcase; grey stool; white base	181	40.00	55.00	28.00

BENGO AND HIS PUPPY FRIENDS, TV PETS

1959-1965

TV Pets was based on a popular British television cartoon series called "Bengo and his Puppy Friends."

The issue date for "Bengo," "Simon," "Pepi" and "Fifi" was May 1959; "Mitzi" and "Chee-Chee" came into production in September 1959; and "Bruno" and "Droopy" were issued in February 1961. At the beginning of 1965, the last two puppies "Percy" and "Whisky" joined the series, the same year the series came to an end, making a total of ten models in the set. The last two models are difficult to find, as they were only in production for a few months at most. The original price was 3/11d each.

Backstamp: A. Unmarked (1-10)
B. Black and gold label "Genuine Wade Porcelain Made in England" (1-10)

No.	Name	Description	Size	U.S. $	Can. $	U.K. £
1	Bengo (Boxer)	Light brown/white; grey muzzle	55 x 50	70.00	90.00	35.00
2	Bruno Junior (Saint Bernard)	Brown rump, head, ears; red tongue	55 x 35	100.00	135.00	45.00
3	Chee-Chee (Pekinese)	Beige; white face, chest, paws	60 x 35	65.00	85.00	32.00
4	Droopy Junior (Basset Hound)	Light brown; white chest; grey ear tips	55 x 40	95.00	125.00	50.00
5	Fifi (Poodle)	Grey-blue head, ears, legs; red bow	55 x 35	55.00	75.00	24.00
6	Mitzi (Kitten)	Blue-grey/white; pink mouth	50 x 50	75.00	95.00	35.00
7	Pepi (Chihuahua)	Tan patches; large black eyes; red mouth	55 x 35	90.00	120.00	35.00
8	Percy (Afghan)	Beige; orange patches; grey face	65 x 30	105.00	140.00	50.00
9	Simon (Dalmatian)	White; black spots	60 x 40	75.00	95.00	28.00
10	Whisky (Corgi)	Beige; white face, chest, paws; red tongue	55 x 65	200.00	265.00	90.00

BENGO MONEY BOX

1965

Only one model from the *TV Pets* series was remodeled as a money box. Because the original model is standing and had no bulk in which to hold coins, it was unsuitable. A new model of a sitting Bengo was created with a round body to contain the money.

Backstamp: Unmarked

No.	Description	Size	U.S. $	Can. $	U.K. £
1	Beige; white on face, feet; yellow basket	150 x 140	450.00	600.00	300.00

THE BUTCHER, THE BAKER AND THE CANDLESTICK MAKER

1953-Circa 1958

The Butcher, the Baker and the Candlestick Maker is a set of three characters, from a 1940s children's rhyme.

Backstamp: A. Black transfer "Wade England [name of model]" (1, 2a, 2b, 3)
B. Blue transfer "Wade England [name of model]" (2a, 2b)

No.	Name	Description	Size	U.S. $	Can. $	U.K. £
1	The Butcher	Blue/white apron; grey trousers	95 x 40	300.00	400.00	200.00
2a	The Baker	Blue/white shirt; blue trousers	95 x 30	300.00	400.00	200.00
2b	The Baker	White shirt; blue trousers	95 x 30	300.00	400.00	200.00
3a	The Candlestick Maker	Black coat; grey trousers; yellow candlestick	110 x 25	400.00	500.00	275.00
3b	The Candlestick Maker	Black coat; grey trousers; beige candlestick	110 x 25	400.00	500.00	275.00
3c	The Candlestick Maker	Green coat; grey trousers; beige candlestick	110 x 25	400.00	500.00	275.00
3d	The Candlestick maker	White coat; grey trousers; brown candlestick	110 x 25	400.00	500.00	275.00

DISMAL DESMOND

Circa 1935

This model of "Dismal Desmond," a weeping Dalmatian, is based on a British children's comic character who featured in *Deans Rag Books* during the mid 1930s.

Backstamp: Ink stamp "Wadeheath England" with lion (1934-1935)

No.	Description	Size	U.S. $	Can. $	U.K. £
1	White; black markings; brownish red tears, collar	165	620.00	825.00	360.00

GOLDILOCKS AND THE THREE BEARS

FIRST VERSION

1953-Circa 1958

Goldilocks and the Three Bears is a set of four models based on the children's fairy tale. It is believed that these models were intended for export only, because they are named "Poppa Bear" and "Mama Bear," which are North American expressions, instead of "Father Bear" and "Mother Bear," as they would be called in Britain.

Backstamp: Black transfer "Wade England [name of model]"

No.	Name	Description	Size	U.S. $	Can. $	U.K. £
1	Goldilocks	Blonde; blue/white skirt; pink petticoat, bonnet	100 x 60	375.00	500.00	250.00
2	Poppa Bear	Light brown; blue jacket; grey waistcoat	95 x 30	375.00	500.00	250.00
3	Mama Bear	Light brown; blue-grey dress	100 x 65	375.00	500.00	250.00
4	Baby Bear	Brown; blue dungarees	50 x 30	375.00	500.00	250.00

GOLDILOCKS AND THE THREE BEARS
SECOND VERSION
1996

The first figurine in this series was "Mummy Bear," and originally the production was intended to be 1,500 of each model but because of increasing club membership numbers the production was increased to 2,750. The cost of each figurine was £15. Two of the "Daddy Bear" models in a one-of-a-kind decoration were given as door prizes at the Trentham Gardens Wade Fair and at the Wisconsin, U.S.A. Wade/Jim Beam Fair held in July 1997.

Backstamp: Circular black and red printed "Official International Wade Collectors Club," Black printed "(name) 1996"

No.	Name	Description	Size	U.S. $	Can. $	U.K. £
1	Mummy Bear	Light brown; white cap, apron; dark blue dress; brown bowl	102	80.00	105.00	55.00
2	Daddy Bear	Light brown; dark blue suit; red bow tie; brown spoon, bowl	105	80.00	105.00	55.00
3	Goldilocks	Light brown chair; yellow hair; pink dress; white socks, porridge; brown spoon, bowl	85	80.00	105.00	55.00
4	Baby Bear	Light brown; dark blue dungarees; white shirt with yellow stripes; white hankie; brown spoon	80	45.00	60.00	30.00

JUMBO JIM

Circa 1930s-1940s

The shape number for *Jumbo Jim* is 331. *Jumbo Jim* is believed to have appeared in a 1930s/40s children's book

Backstamp: **A.** Black ink stamp "Flaxman Wade Heath England" (1a)
B. Ink stamp "Flaxman Wade Heath England" with impressed No 331 (1b)

No.	Name	Description	Size	U.S. $	Can. $	U.K. £
1a	Jumbo Jim	Light brown	180 x 105	350.00	450.00	200.00
1b	Jumbo Jim	Turquoise blue	180 x 105	350.00	450.00	200.00

THE NODDY SET

FIRST VERSION

1958-1961

The *Noddy* set consists of four characters created by the English childrens writer Enid Blyton. Only four models were issued, with an original price of 3/11d each. Production was discontinued in autumn 1961.

Backstamp: Unmarked

No.	Name	Description	Size	U.S. $	Can. $	U.K. £
1	Noddy	Red shirt, shoes; blue hat, trousers, bows	70 x 35	375.00	500.00	225.00
2	Big Ears	Blue jacket; yellow trousers; red hat	70 x 35	265.00	350.00	135.00
3	Mr. Plod	Blue uniform, helmet; yellow buttons	60 x 35	170.00	225.00	95.00
4	Miss Fluffy Cat	Brown coat, collar; yellow hat; red bag	60 x 35	110.00	150.00	55.00

Note: See page 358 for the second version of Noddy.

Noddy First Version Derivatives

Toadstool Cottage Money Boxes

Circa 1961

Following Wade's policy of using up unsold stock by converting it into better-selling lines (as with *First Whimsies* on candleholders and *Whimtrays*), "Big Ears" and "Noddy" from the *Noddy* set were placed on toadstool cottage money boxes, with a coin slot in the back rim of the roof. This series had a very limited production run and is extremely rare. The issue date is unknown, but it was probably soon after the *Noddy* set was finished in 1961. These models originally had black and gold foil labels.

Backstamp: A. Black and gold foil label "Genuine Wade Porcelain made in England"
B. Unmarked

No.	Name	Description	Size	U.S. $	Can. $	U.K. £
1a	Big Ears	Brown roof with white spots; yellow chimney, flowers; blue windows, door; green grass	110 x 120	375.00	500.00	185.00
1b	Big Ears	Brown roof with white spots; yellow chimney, flowers; blue windows; brown door; green grass	110 x 120	375.00	500.00	185.00
2	Noddy	Brown roof with white spots; yellow chimney, flowers; blue windows, door; green grass	110 x 120	400.00	525.00	200.00

NURSERY FAVOURITES

1972-1981

Nursery Favourites is a series of 20 large nursery rhyme and storybook characters. It was issued in four sets of five models, and each set was sold in a different coloured box. The original selling price for each figure was 7/6d. In 1990 and 1991, five *Nursery Favourites* were commissioned and reissued for Gold Star Gifthouse (see page 284).

SET ONE: DARK GREEN BOXES

1972

Backstamp: Embossed "Wade England"

No.	Name	Description	Size	U.S. $	Can. $	U.K. £
1	Jack	Brown hair, waistcoat; green trousers	75 x 30	45.00	58.00	22.00
2	Jill	Green bonnet, dress	75 x 40	45.00	58.00	22.00
3	Little Miss Muffett	Yellow hair; grey-green dress	60 x 50	45.00	58.00	22.00
4	Little Jack Horner	Green jacket; yellow trousers; brown hair	70 x 40	40.00	50.00	22.00
5	Humpty Dumpty	Honey brown; green suit; red tie	65 x 43	35.00	45.00	22.00

SET TWO: BLUE BOXES

1973

Backstamp: Embossed "Wade England"

No.	Name	Description	Size	U.S. $	Can. $	U.K. £
6	Wee Willie Winkie	Yellow hair; grey nightshirt	75 x 35	30.00	40.00	20.00
7	Mary Had a Little Lamb	Blue bonnet, skirt; grey-blue jacket	75 x 40	50.00	65.00	30.00
8	Polly Put the Kettle On	Brown; pink cap, kettle	75 x 35	60.00	80.00	35.00
9	Old King Cole	Yellow/grey hat; blue-grey cloak	65 x 50	48.00	62.00	30.00
10	Tom Tom the Pipers Son	Grey hat, kilt; brown jacket	65 x 55	45.00	60.00	30.00

SET THREE: YELLOW BOXES

1974

Backstamp: Embossed "Wade England"

No.	Name	Description	Size	U.S. $	Can. $	U.K. £
11	Little Boy Blue	Blue cap, jacket, trousers	75 x 30	45.00	60.00	30.00
12	Mary Mary	Yellow hair; blue dress; pink shoes	75 x 45	55.00	75.00	35.00
13	The Cat and the Fiddle	Brown/grey cat; yellow fiddle	70 x 50	55.00	70.00	35.00
14	The Queen of Hearts	Pink crown, hearts; beige dress	75 x 48	55.00	75.00	35.00
15	Little Tommy Tucker	Yellow hair; blue pantaloons	75 x 30	50.00	65.00	30.00

SET FOUR: PURPLE BOXES

1976

Backstamp: Embossed "Wade England"

No.	Name	Description	Size	U.S. $	Can. $	U.K. £
16	The Three Bears	Grey; green base	70 x 60	68.00	90.00	45.00
17	Little Bo Peep	Beige bonnet, dress; pink ribbon	70 x 40	125.00	170.00	85.00
18	Goosey Goosey Gander	Beige; pink beak; blue-brown steps	66 x 55	140.00	180.00	90.00
19	Old Woman in a Shoe	Blue bonnet, dress; brown roof, door	60 x 55	135.00	170.00	80.00
20	Puss in Boots	Beige; blue boots	70 x 30	68.00	90.00	45.00

NURSERIES MINIATURES

Circa 1979-1980

The *Nurseries* is a boxed set of five models from the Canadian Red Rose Tea *Miniature Nurseries*. For some reason these figures did not sell well to British collectors, so Wade discontinued the intended series with only five models issued. When these figures are out of their boxes, they are hard to distinguish from the Red Rose Tea models. As the *Nurseries* were advertised after the Corgies and Yorkshire terriers from the *Whimsies Dogs and Puppies* series (issued in 1979), the issue date for this series is set during late 1979.

Backstamp: Embossed "Wade England"

No.	Name	Description	Size	U.S.$	Can.$	U.K.£
1	Old Woman in a Shoe	Honey; red-brown roof	40	6.00	4.00	6.00
2a	Old King Cole with Blue Hem	Beige; blue hat; pink sleeves; blue hem	40	6.00	4.00	4.00
2b	Old King Cole without Blue Hem	Beige; blue hat; pink sleeves	40	6.00	4.00	4.00
3	Little Jack Horner	Beige; blue plum; pink cushion	40	6.00	4.00	6.00
4	Little Bo-Peep	Light brown; blue apron; green base	45	4.00	3.00	3.00
5	The Cat and the Fiddle	Beige; yellow fiddle	45	30.00	15.00	9.00
—	5 pce set	Boxed	—	50.00	35.00	30.00

NURSERY RHYMES

1953 - Circa 1958

Although Wade may have intended to add to this series each year, only two *Nursery Rhymes* characters were produced.

Backstamp: Black transfer "Wade [name of model] England"

No.	Name	Description	Size	U.S. $	Can. $	U.K. £
1a	Little Jack Horner	Blue trousers; dark blue braces	70 x 42	550.00	600.00	300.00
1b	Little Jack Horner	Grey trousers, braces	70 x 42	550.00	600.00	300.00
1c	Little Jack Horner	White shirt, trousers	70 x 42	550.00	600.00	300.00
2	Little Miss Muffett	Blonde hair; blue dress; pink petticoat	72 x 66	550.00	600.00	300.00

POGO

1959

"Pogo" is based on a 1940s possum character featured in American children's books, newspapers and comics. The model was produced by Wade (Ulster) Ltd. and modelled by William Harper, who worked for the George Wade Pottery during the 1950s.

Backstamp: Black ink stamp "Pogo Copyright, Walt Kelly, Made in Ireland 1959"

No.	Description	Size	U.S. $	Can. $	U.K. £
1	Grey; blue jacket; blue/pink bird	85 x 30	550.00	725.00	350.00

SAM AND SARAH
(MABEL LUCIE ATTWELL FIGURES)
1959-1961

Manufactured under license to designs by Mabel Lucie Attwell, these two figures of "Sam" and "Sarah," with their pet dogs, were produced to test the publics reaction to a change of style. Apparently, they were not very popular at the time, perhaps due to the high retail price of 6/11d. Subsequently these models, which are sought after by Wade and by Mabel Lucie Attwell collectors, are in high demand.

The issue date for "Sam" and "Sarah" was October 1959, and they were discontinued in summer 1961. Their original price was 6/11d each.

Backstamp: Embossed Raised "Wade Porcelain-Mabel Lucie Attwell © Made in England"

No.	Name	Description	Size	U.S. $	Can. $	U.K. £
1	Sam	Ginger hair; yellow shirt; grey dog	78 x 85	270.00	350.00	175.00
2a	Sarah	Blue shoes; blue/white dress; white/black dog	75 x 100	270.00	350.00	175.00
2b	Sarah	Green shoes; blue/white dress; white/black dog	75 x 100	270.00	350.00	175.00
2c	Sarah	Red shoes; blue/white dress; white/black dog	75 x 100	270.00	350.00	175.00

THOMAS THE TANK ENGINE

1986

Thomas the Tank Engine, based on the storybooks by Reverend Wilbert Awdry and on the British television cartoon, was a very short-lived series due to complicated copyright laws. Only two models were produced, "Thomas" and "Percy." They came in two forms, a money box train and a miniature train. A prototype of "The Fat Controller" has been seen, but the model was not put into production. These four models are very rare.

Backstamp: **A.** Unmarked (1, 3)
B. Black transfer "Wade Made in England" (1-4)

No.	Name	Description	Size	U.S.$	Can.$	U.K.£
1	Thomas the Tank Engine Money Box	Blue; red markings	110 x 165	285.00	375.00	165.00
2	Thomas the Tank Engine Miniature	Blue; red markings	28 x 40	130.00	175.00	75.00
3	Percy the Small Engine Money Box	Green; red markings	110 x 173	280.00	375.00	165.00
4	Percy the Small Engine Miniature	Green; red markings	28 x 38	130.00	175.00	75.00

TINKER, TAILOR, SOLDIER, SAILOR

1953-Circa 1958

Tinker, Tailor, Soldier, Sailor is a series of eight little boys dressed in adult clothes, depicting the characters from a 1940s children's rhyme.

Backstamp: Black transfer "Wade [name of model] England"

No.	Name	Description	Size	U.S. $	Can. $	U.K. £
1a	Tinker	Blue suit; white/grey cap; grey base	55 x 45	265.00	350.00	175.00
1b	Tinker	Pale blue suit; grey checkered cap; grey base	55 x 45	265.00	350.00	175.00
2	Tailor	Blue suit; grey trousers, base	55 x 45	265.00	350.00	175.00
3	Soldier	Blue suit, base; white/grey hat	80 x 45	265.00	350.00	175.00
4a	Sailor	Blue suit, base; white/grey hat	90 x 45	265.00	350.00	175.00
4b	Sailor	Pale blue suit; white/grey hat	90 x 45	265.00	350.00	175.00
5	Rich Man	Blue coat; grey hat, trousers; blue-green base	90 x 45	265.00	350.00	175.00
6a	Poor Man	Blue suit, base; grey hat	75 x 45	265.00	350.00	175.00
6b	Poor Man	Pale blue suit; grey hat	75 x 45	265.00	350.00	175.00
7	Beggar Man	Blue suit; white/blue scarf; blue-green base	65 x 45	265.00	350.00	175.00
8a	Thief	Blue suit; grey mask; blue-green base	80 x 45	265.00	350.00	175.00
8b	Thief	Pale blue suit; grey mask; blue-green base	80 x 45	265.00	350.00	175.00

TOM AND JERRY

1973-1979

Only two models were issued in the *Tom and Jerry* series, courtesy of Metro-Goldwyn-Mayer. The original price for the set of two cartoon character models was 95p.

Backstamp: Embossed "Wade England © M.G.M."

No.	Name	Description	Size	U.S. $	Can. $	U.K. £
1	Tom	Blue; yellow/black eyes; pink ears	90 x 55	95.00	125.00	55.00
2	Jerry	Beige; pink ears; green base	50 x 30	95.00	125.00	45.00
—	Set (2)		—	225.00	275.00	85.00

WYNKEN, BLYNKEN, NOD AND I'VE A BEAR BEHIND

Circa 1948-1958

This set of four nursery rhyme characters was based on the poem "Wynken, Blynken and Nod," by American writer Eugene Field: "Wynken, Blynken and Nod one night; sailed off in a wooden shoe; Sailed on a river of crystal light into a sea of dew."

The poem does not include the character "I've a Bear Behind"; this was purely a whim of the Wade modeler. Green moss covers the feet of some models, so their slippers cannot be seen.

FIRST VERSION: FLOWER BASE

Backstamp: **A.** Green ink stamp "[Name of model] Wade England" (1a, 1b, 2, 3, 4)
B. Black transfer print "Wade England" and green ink stamp "Wade England [model name]" (4)

No.	Name	Description	Size	U.S. $	Can. $	U.K. £
1a	Wynken	Blond hair; blue suit	71 x 38	200.00	266.00	145.00
1b	Wynken	Brown hair; blue suit	75 x 40	200.00	266.00	145.00
2a	Blynken	Blond hair; blue suit	58 x 40	200.00	266.00	145.00
2b	Blynken	Brown hair; blue suit	58 x 40	200.00	266.00	145.00
3	Nod	Blond hair; blue suit	70 x 40	200.00	266.00	145.00
4	I've a Bear Behind	Blond hair; blue suit	70 x 40	200.00	266.00	145.00

SECOND VERSION: GREEN BASE

Backstamp: Black transfer "Wade England [name of model]" 8

No.	Name	Description	Size	U.S. $	Can. $	U.K. £
1	Wynken	Blond hair; blue suit	75 x 40	185.00	250.00	125.00
2a	Blynken	Blond hair; blue suit	58 x 40	185.00	250.00	125.00
2b	Blynken	Light brown hair; blue suit	58 x 40	185.00	250.00	125.00
3	Nod	Light brown hair; blue suit	70 x 40	205.00	270.00	135.00
4	I've a Bear Behind	Light brown hair; blue suit	70 x 40	205.00	270.00	135.00

YOGI BEAR AND FRIENDS

1962-1963

Yogi Bear and Friends is a set of three Hanna-Barbera cartoon characters that were popular on television in the late 1950s/early 1960s. Their original price was 3/6d each.

Backstamp: Unmarked

No.	Name	Description	Size	U.S. $	Can. $	U.K. £
1	Yogi Bear	Beige; yellow/black hat; red tie	62 x 30	130.00	170.00	85.00
2a	Mr. Jinks	Pink; white/yellow/black face; blue bow tie	63 x 30	150.00	200.00	120.00
2b	Mr. Jinks	Yellow; white/yellow/black face; blue tie	63 x 30	150.00	200.00	75.00
3	Huckleberry Hound	Blue; white face; yellow bow tie	60 x 28	125.00	165.00	75.00

WALT DISNEY FIGURES

WALT DISNEY FIGURES

1937 -1984

A small number of Walt Disney character models were produced by Wade Heath Ltd. for approximately three years before giftware production ceased at the onset of World War II. In the early 1960s, Wade again produced Disney figures under license to Walt Disney.

BULLDOGS

Circa 1968

Two model bulldogs have been found, possibly representing Pluto's arch enemy "Butch" and his nephew "Bull." The models are slip cast (hollow). Both bulldogs are sitting and smiling; "Butch" scratches his ribs with his hind leg.

Backstamp: Black printed "Wade Porcelain Copyright Walt Disney Productions Made in England"

No.	Name	Description	Size	U.S. $	Can. $	U.K. £
1	Bull	Cream; grey muzzle, nose	85 x 100	300.00	400.00	150.00
2	Butch	Beige; grey muzzle, nose	90 x 110	300.00	400.00	150.00

DISNEY BLOW UPS

1961-1965

Disney Blow Ups is a set of ten characters from the Disney films *Lady and the Tramp* and *Bambi*. They are referred to as blow-ups because they are larger slip cast versions of the miniature *Hat Box Series* that preceded them. "Tramp," "Jock," "Thumper" and "Dachie" are the hardest of these models to find.

Name	Issue Price	Issue Date
Tramp	17/6d	January 1961
Lady	15/-	January 1961
Bambi	13/6d	January 1961
Scamp	12/6d	January 1961
Si	15/-	Autumn 1961
Am	15/-	Autumn 1961
Thumper	12/6d	Autumn 1961
Trusty	17/6d	Autumn 1961
Jock	13/6d	Autumn 1962
Dachie	15/-	Autumn 1962

Backstamp: **A.** Black transfer "Wade Porcelain—Copyright Walt Disney Productions—Made in England" (1-10)
B. Black transfer "Wade Porcelain—Copyright Walt Disney Productions—Made in Ireland" (7)

No.	Name	Description	Size	U.S. $	Can. $	U.K. £
1	Tramp	Grey; white face, neck, chest; red tongue	160 x 105	450.00	600.00	295.00
2	Lady	Beige; honey ears; blue collar	110 x 140	275.00	350.00	175.00
3	Bambi	Beige; white spots; pink ears; red tongue	110 x 120	190.00	255.00	125.00
4	Scamp	Grey; pink ears; white/maroon paws	110 x 115	225.00	300.00	140.00
5	Si	Brown; black/lilac ears; blue eyes; red mouth	140 x 110	245.00	325.00	150.00
6	Am	Brown; black/lilac ears; black nose, tail, legs	147 x 85	265.00	350.00	165.00
7	Thumper	Blue; white/yellow, white/red flowers	130 x 80	500.00	665.00	300.00
8	Trusty	Beige; red-brown ears; gold medallion	135 x 80	300.00	375.00	165.00
9	Jock	Grey; pink/mauve ears; gold medallion	100 x 115	1,050.00	1,400.00	700.00
10	Dachie	Beige; brown ears, eyes; red tongue	125 x 105	1,050.00	1,400.00	700.00

DONALD DUCK

1937

Backstamp: Black ink stamp "WadeHeath England with lion" (1934-1937)

No.	Description	Size	U.S. $	Can. $	U.K. £
1	White body; yellow beak/legs; blue hat and coat; red bow tie	127	1,200.00	1,600.00	800.00

DOPEY

1939

This cellulose model of Dopey is a different model than the one used for the 1938 *Snow White* set. He was the only model produced in an intended *Snow White* set for FW Woolworth, England during Christmas 1939, but with the onset of World War II, the order for the rest of the models was cancelled.

Backstamp: None

No.	Description	Size	U.S. $	Can. $	U.K. £
1	Mauve hat; yellow coat; brown shoes	110 x 53	400.00	525.00	200.00

HAPPY CLOCK

CIRCA 1938

A rare find is a *Happy Clock* in the cellulose glaze used by the Wade Heath pottery during the mid-late 1930s. The eyes move from side to side as the clock ticks. Although not marked "Wade," this unusual piece has the same cellulose colours used on the 1930s *Snow White Dwarfs*. More interesting is that the paper label has a BCM/OWL mark which is a known backstamp used on a number of the early Wade Lady Figures.

Happy Clock, Front

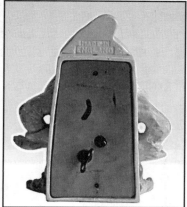
Happy Clock, Back

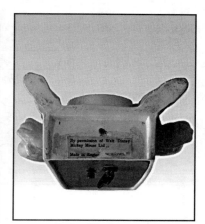
Happy Clock, Bottom

Backstamp: Impressed "Made in England" on back of hat, Paper Label on base with black printed "By permission Walt Disney Mickey Mouse Ltd., Made in England" BCM/OWL Foreign Movement is ink stamped on the wood back plate.

No.	Name	Description	Size	U.S. $	Can. $	U.K. £
1	Happy Clock	Yellow hat and jacket; orange trousers; green shoes	210		Extremely rare	

THE HAT BOX SERIES

These charming Walt Disney cartoon characters were sold in round, striped cardboard boxes which resemble hat boxes, from which this series takes its name. The boxes each had a colour print of the enclosed model on the lid. There are 26 models in this long-running series. The last ten models had only a short production run and are considered scarce. The hardest of all to find are the models from *The Sword in the Stone*, especially the Merlin models.

Three variations of "Jock" can be found. When first produced in 1956, he was not wearing a coat. After Wade was advised that he wore one in the film, he was produced with a blue tartan coat in early 1957. Later that year the coat was changed to green tartan.

The original price for all the models was 2/11d, except for the figures from *The Sword in the Stone*, which sold for 3/6d. The films from which the models were taken are as follows:

Film	Model	Date of Issue
Lady and the Tramp	Lady	January 1956
	Jock, No Coat	January 1956
	Jock, Blue Coat	Early 1957
	Jock, Green Coat	Late 1957
	Tramp	January 1956
	Trusty	January 1956
	Peg	February 1957
	Scamp	February 1957
	Dachie	January 1958
	Si	August 1958
	Am	August 1958
	Boris	February 1960
	Toughy	February 1960
Bambi	Bambi	December 1957
	Flower	December 1957
	Thumper	December 1957
Dumbo	Dumbo	December 1957
Fantasia	Baby Pegasus	January 1958
101 Dalmatians	The Colonel	September 1961
	Lucky	September 1961
	Rolly	September 1961
	Sergeant Tibbs	September 1961
The Sword in the Stone	Archimedes	Autumn 1962
	Madam Mim	Autumn 1962
	Merlin as a Caterpillar	Autumn 1962
	Merlin as a Hare	Autumn 1962
	Merlin as a Turtle	Autumn 1962
	The Girl Squirrel	Autumn 1962

FIRST ISSUE: SET ONE

1956-1965

Backstamp: **A.** Unmarked (1-6)
B. Black and gold "Wade England" label (1-6)
C. Blue transfer "Wade England" (1, 3, 6)

No.	Name	Description	Size	U.S. $	Can. $	U.K. £
1	Lady	Beige; light brown ears; blue collar	40 x 35	40.00	55.00	25.00
2a	Jock, No Coat	Blue-grey; purple mouth	40 x 25	55.00	75.00	35.00
2b	Jock, Blue Tartan	Blue coat; purple mouth	40 x 25	40.00	55.00	25.00
2c	Jock, Green Tartan	Green coat; purple mouth	40 x 25	40.00	55.00	25.00
3	Tramp, Standing	Grey/white; red tongue	50 x 50	80.00	110.00	45.00
4a	Trusty	Brown; brown nose	55 x 35	38.00	50.00	25.00
4b	Trusty	Brown; black nose	55 x 35	38.00	50.00	25.00
5	Peg	Yellow fringe; red nose, mouth	40 x 35	28.00	45.00	15.00
6	Scamp	Grey; mauve ears, mouth; brown toes	40 x 35	35.00	35.00	15.00

FIRST ISSUE: SET TWO

1956-1965

Backstamp: A. Unmarked (7-16)
B. Black and gold "Wade England" label (7-16)

No.	Name	Description	Size	U.S. $	Can. $	U.K. £
7	Bambi	Beige; tan/white patches; dark brown eyes	40 x 35	35.00	45.00	20.00
8	Flower	Black/white; blue eyes; red tongue	40 x 25	55.00	75.00	35.00
9a	Thumper	Blue-grey; pink cheeks; red mouth	60 x 35	55.00	75.00	35.00
9b	Thumper	Blue-grey; white cheeks; red mouth	60 x 35	55.00	75.00	35.00
10	Dumbo	Grey/white; pink ears	40 x 38	100.00	135.00	40.00
11	Baby Pegasus	Blue-grey; blue eyes; pink nose, mouth	40 x 30	80.00	105.00	40.00
12	Dachie	Brown; dark brown ears; red mouth	60 x 30	40.00	55.00	24.00
13	Si	Beige; black tail, legs, ears; blue eyes	60 x 30	55.00	70.00	35.00
14	Am	Beige; black tail, legs, ears; eyes closed	60 x 25	55.00	70.00	35.00
15	Boris	Grey; white chest, tail tip; pink in ears	60 x 28	80.00	105.00	40.00
16	Toughy	Brown; white chest, face; red tongue	55 x 30	95.00	130.00	55.00

FIRST ISSUE: SET THREE

1956-1965

Backstamp: **A.** Unmarked (17-26)
B. Black and gold "Wade England" label (17-26)

No.	Name	Description	Size	U.S. $	Can. $	U.K. £
17	The Colonel	Beige/white; black streak across eye	50 x 34	90.00	120.00	55.00
18	Sergeant Tibbs	Beige; white chest, nose, paws; blue in ears	55 x 30	95.00	130.00	65.00
19	Rolly	White; black spots; red collar; sitting	40 x 30	90.00	120.00	75.00
20	Lucky	White; black spots, ears; red collar; standing	30 x 35	140.00	185.00	75.00
21	Madam Mim	Honey/brown; black neck, wing tips	30 x 28	240.00	300.00	125.00
22	Merlin as a Turtle	Brown-grey; black/white eyes	30 x 45	300.00	400.00	175.00
23	Archimedes	Brown head, back, wings, log	50 x 35	150.00	200.00	80.00
24	Merlin as a Hare	Blue; white tail, chest	55 x 35	215.00	285.00	100.00
25	The Girl Squirrel	Beige; honey brown tail	50 x 30	100.00	135.00	95.00
26	Merlin as a Caterpillar	White/pink/mauve; black/yellow eyes	20 x 45	275.00	365.00	120.00

First Issue Derivatives

Butter Dish

Circa 1960

From 1955 to 1956, the George Wade Pottery produced a butter dish, to which "Jock" was later added on the back rim.

Jock Butter Dish

Backstamp: Embossed "Wade England"

No.	Name	Description	Size	U.S.$	Can.$	U.K.£
1a	Jock	No coat; blue dish	65 x 80	50.00	70.00	30.00
1b	Jock	No coat; grey dish	65 x 80	50.00	70.00	30.00
1c	Jock	No coat; white dish	65 x 80	50.00	70.00	30.00
1d	Jock	Blue coat, dish	65 x 80	50.00	70.00	30.00
1e	Jock	Green coat; blue dish	65 x 80	50.00	70.00	30.00

First Issue Derivatives
Candle Holders
Circa 1960

This set is similar in appearance to the 1959-1960 *Zoo Lights*, but the triangular base is much larger, thicker and heavier, and it has an original issue *Hat Box* model (style 9 has a *First Whimsies* "Panda") sitting on the front edge of the candle holder. The holders are all black and were made for cake-size candles, which stand in a hole on the back edge. These models are rarely found. Examples other than those listed below are believed to exist.

Flower Candle Holder

Lady Candle Holder

Backstamp: Embossed "Wade"

No.	Name	Description	Size	U.S. $	Can. $	U.K. £
1	Bambi	Beige; black holder	60 x 50	90.00	120.00	48.00
2	Dumbo	White/pink; black holder	60 x 50	120.00	150.00	75.00
3	Flower	Black/white; black holder	60 x 50	120.00	150.00	75.00
4	Jock	Blue-grey/white; green coat; black holder	60 x 50	90.00	120.00	48.00
5	Lady	Beige/white; black holder	60 x 50	90.00	120.00	48.00
6	Lucky	White; black spots, holder	50 x 50	120.00	150.00	75.00
7	Rolly	White; black spots, holder	60 x 50	120.00	150.00	75.00
8	Thumper	Blue-grey/white; black holder	80 x 50	90.00	120.00	48.00

First Issue Derivatives

Card Trumps

Circa 1960

These unusual pieces are of "Merlin as a Hare." One is glued onto a Bakerlite stand which has plastic playing card trumps hanging from the frame. The other is fixed to a Bouldray tray which has a brass card trump frame on it.

Merlin as Hare Card Trump

Backstamp: Raised "Bouldray Wade Porcelain 2 Made in England"

No.	Name	Description	Size	U.S. $	Can. $	U.K. £
1	Merlin as a Hare	Bakerlite brown stand/frame; blue/grey Merlin; white plastic cards	90 x 75	100.00	135.00	60.00
2	Merlin as a Hare	Brass frame; blue tray; blue/grey Merlin; white plastic cards	90 x 75	100.00	135.00	60.00

First Issue Derivatives

Money Boxes

1962

This series comprises a set of five money boxes in the shape of a dog kennel, with an original issue *Hat Box* figure standing in front of the entrance. The coin slot is in the kennel roof. The issue date for these money boxes was spring 1962, and they originally sold for 9/11d. Over time the glue breaks down holding the model on the base, and the money boxes can be found minus the dog model.

Backstamp: Unmarked

No.	Name	Description	Size	U.S. $	Can. $	U.K. £
1	Lady	Beige; blue kennel	95 x 105	145.00	190.00	95.00
2	Lucky	White; blue kennel	95 x 105	200.00	265.00	125.00
3	Jock, No Coat	Blue-grey; blue kennel	95 x 105	145.00	190.00	95.00
4	Rolly	White; blue kennel	95 x 105	200.00	265.00	125.00
5	Scamp	Grey; blue kennel	95 x 105	145.00	190.00	95.00

SECOND ISSUE

1981-1985

In spring 1981 George Wade and Son renewed its license with Walt Disney Productions Ltd. and reissued six models from the *Hat Box* series, using the original moulds. The new series was named "Disney's."

At first glance the reissues are hard to distinguish from the earlier figures, as the original moulds were used, some of which were worn, the model features are flat compared to the originals which is most noticeable on the "Scamp" model. There is only a slight variation in colour on the re-issued models. The name of "Dachie" was changed to "Dachsie."

Four new models from the Disney film, *The Fox and the Hound* "Tod," "Copper," "Chief" and "Big Mama" were added in February 1982. In 1985 the last two models in the seta new shape "Tramp" and a reissued "Peg" were issued.

When first issued the models were sold in round plastic hat box-shaped containers, later the plastic boxes were discontinued and the Disneys were then sold in oblong cardboard boxes. "Tramp" and "Peg," were issued in cardboard boxes only.

Backstamp: Black and gold label "Walt Disney Productions Wade England"

No.	Name	Description	Size	U.S. $	Can. $	U.K. £
1	Lady	Dark brown ears; light blue collar	40 x 35	25.00	35.00	16.00
2	Jock, Green Tartan	Green coat; pink mouth; orange collar	40 x 25	32.00	42.00	18.00
3	Scamp	Pink mouth, ears; facial markings flat	40 x 35	35.00	45.00	20.00
4	Dachsie	Light brown ears; pink mouth	60 x 30	30.00	40.00	16.00
5	Bambi	Light brown eyes	40 x 35	30.00	40.00	16.00
6	Thumper	Light grey; pink mouth, cheeks; pale orange flower	60 x 35	50.00	65.00	30.00
7	Tod	Red-brown; dark brown paws	45 x 50	70.00	90.00	55.00
8	Copper	Beige; brown patch, ears; white chest, paws	45 x 50	38.00	50.00	25.00
9	Chief	Grey; white chest; black eyes; red tongue	50 x 20	30.00	40.00	16.00
10	Big Mama	Beige head, back, wings; orange beak	45 x 45	95.00	130.00	45.00
11	Tramp, Sitting	Grey; red tongue	47 x 30	50.00	65.00	25.00
12	Peg	Beige fringe; brown nose; pink mouth	40 x 35	26.00	35.00	16.00

Note: Prices listed are for pieces only or pieces in cardboard boxes. Models that are found in their original round plastic boxes will command a premium of 10-20% above list price.

HIAWATHA

1937

"Hiawatha" was produced with a cellulose glaze, so it is difficult to find in mint condition.

Backstamp: Black hand-painted "'Hiawatha' Wade England"

No.	Description	Size	U.S. $	Can. $	U.K. £
1a	Yellow feather; red trousers	100 x 50	260.00	350.00	175.00
1b	Red feather; blue trousers	100 x 50	260.00	350.00	175.00

MICKEY MOUSE

1935

A rare model of *Mickey Mouse* was produced by the Wadeheath Pottery at the same time as a children's toy Mickey Mouse tea set. This model was first advertised along with the toy tea set in March 1935.

John Szeilor worked for the Wade Pottery in the late 1940s-early 1950s before starting his own pottery, which would account for the similarity of "Wade" and "Szeilor" models.

Backstamp: Black ink stamp "Wadeheath Ware by Permission Walt Disney Mickey Mouse Ltd Made in England" (1935)

No.	Description	Size	U.S. $	Can. $	U.K. £
1a	Black and white body; yellow gloves; blue shorts; orange shoes; brown suitcase	90	1,900.00	2,600.00	1,300.00
1b	Black and white body; yellow gloves; green shorts; orange shoes; brown suitcase	90	1,900.00	2,600.00	1,300.00
1c	Black and white body; yellow gloves; orange shorts and shoes; brown suitcase	95	1,900.00	2,600.00	1,300.00
1d	Black and white body; yellow gloves and shoes; blue shorts; brown suitcase	90	1,900.00	2,600.00	1,300.00

PLUTO

1937-1938

Some *Pluto* models may have the impressed shape number 205.

Backstamp: Black ink stamp "Wadeheath by permission of Walt Disney, England"

No.	Description	Size	U.S.$	Can.$	U.K.£
1a	Grey; black ears, nose, eyes	100 x 162	300.00	375.00	185.00
1b	Orange-brown; black ears, nose, eyes	100 x 162	300.00	375.00	185.00
1c	White; black ears, nose and eyes	100 x 162	300.00	375.00	185.00

PLUTO'S PUPS

1937

Pluto's quintuplet puppies, the "Quinpuplets," were from the Walt Disney cartoon film of the same name. In the film they were not given names, but one pup reappeared in a 1942 Disney cartoon as "Pluto Junior."

Backstamp: **A.** Black ink stamp "Flaxman Wadeheath England"(3a)
B. Black ink stamp "Wadeheath by permission of Walt Disney, England" (1a, 1b, 1c, 2a, 2b, 3b, 3c, 3d, 3e, 3f, 4a, 4b, 5)

No.	Name	Description	Size	U.S. $	Can. $	U.K. £
1a	Pup Lying on Back	Beige	62 x 112	360.00	400.00	200.00
1b	Pup Lying on Back	Green	62 x 112	360.00	400.00	200.00
1c	Pup Lying on Back	Orange	62 x 112	360.00	400.00	200.00
2a	Pup Sitting	Grey; blue ears, eyes, nose	100 x 62	360.00	400.00	200.00
2b	Pup Sitting	Orange	100 x 62	360.00	400.00	200.00
3a	Pup Sitting, Front Paws Up	Beige	95 x 85	360.00	400.00	200.00
3b	Pup Sitting, Front Paws Up	Grey; blue ears, eyes, nose	95 x 85	360.00	400.00	200.00
3c	Pup Sitting, Front Paws Up	Light blue; dark blue ears, eyes	95 x 85	360.00	400.00	200.00
3d	Pup Sitting, Front Paws Up	Light grey; dark blue ears, eyes	95 x 85	360.00	400.00	200.00
3e	Pup Sitting, Front Paws Up	Orange	95 x 85	360.00	400.00	200.00
3f	Pup Sitting, Front Paws Up	Orange; blue ears, eyes, nose	95 x 85	360.00	400.00	200.00
4a	Pup Lying, Head on Paws	Beige	62 x 112	360.00	400.00	200.00
4b	Pup Lying, Head on Paws	Orange	62 x 112	360.00	400.00	200.00
5	Pup Standing, Licking	Grey; blue ears, eyes, nose	100 x 62	360.00	400.00	200.00

SAMMY SEAL

1937

Sammy Seal is believed to have appeared in a Disney Short in which *Mickey Mouse* carries him home unknowingly in his picnic basket after a visit to the zoo. A miniature model of *Sammy* has been found which is approximately the same height size as the *Arundel Chick*. The miniature version has no backstamp.

Backstamp: Black ink stamp "Wadeheath England by permission Walt Disney"

No.	Description	Size	U.S. $	Can. $	U.K. £
1a	Beige	150 x 150	360.00	400.00	200.00
1b	Beige; black eyes, nose	85 x 70	300.00	350.00	150.00
1c	Grey; black eyes, nose	150 x 150	360.00	400.00	200.00
1d	Off white; brown eyes	150 x 150	360.00	400.00	200.00
1e	Orange	150 x 150	360.00	400.00	200.00
1f	Orange; black eyes, nose	150 x 150	360.00	400.00	200.00
1g	Pink; black eyes, nose	150 x 150	360.00	400.00	200.00
1h	White; black eyes, nose	150 x 150	360.00	400.00	200.00
2	Orange; black eyes, nose	110 x 110	300.00	350.00	150.00

SNOW WHITE AND THE SEVEN DWARFS

STYLE ONE

1938

The George Wade Pottery held a Walt Disney license to produce Disney models, and the Wade Heath Royal Victoria Pottery issued this first *Snow White* set to coincide with the release of the Walt Disney film, *Snow White and the Seven Dwarfs*. These models were produced with a cellulose glaze.

Backstamp: **A.** Black hand-painted "Wade [name of model]," plus red ink stamp with a leaping deer and "Made in England" (1)

          B. Black hand-painted "Wade [name of model]," plus red ink stamp "Made in England" (2, 3, 4, 6, 7, 8, 9)

          C. Unmarked (5)

No.	Name	Description	Size	U.S. $	Can.$	U.K. £
1	Snow White	Yellow dress; red bodice	180 x 65	450.00	600.00	300.00
2	Bashful	Orange coat; blue trousers	100 x 45	235.00	240.00	170.00
3	Doc	Orange jacket; maroon trousers	110 x 55	235.00	240.00	170.00
4	Dopey	Red coat; green trousers	110 x 45	235.00	240.00	170.00
5	Grumpy	Maroon jacket; green trousers	100 x 60	235.00	240.00	170.00
6	Happy	Orange jacket; red trousers	125 x 55	235.00	240.00	170.00
7	Sleepy	Orange-brown jacket; blue trousers	100 x 35	235.00	240.00	170.00
8	Sneezy	Blue jacket; red trousers	100 x 35	235.00	240.00	170.00
—	8 pce set	Boxed	—	3,500.00	4,000.00	2,000.00

SNOW WHITE AND THE SEVEN DWARFS

STYLE TWO

1981-1984

This issue of *Snow White and the Seven Dwarfs*, modelled by Alan Maslankowski, was first offered through mail order by Harper's Direct Mail Marketing just before Christmas 1981, then distributed in stores during the next spring.

Snow White, First Version

Snow White, Second Version

Backstamp: **A.** Black and gold label "© Walt Disney Productions Wade England" (1a, 8)
B. Black transfer "© Walt Disney Productions Wade England" (1b, 2-8)
C. Black transfer "Wade Made in England" (1a, 2, 4, 6)

No.	Name	Description	Size	U.S. $	Can. $	U.K. £
1a	Snow White	Head straight; smiling; pink spots on sleeves; light blue bodice; pale yellow skirt	95 x 100	250.00	350.00	175.00
1b	Snow White	Head back; pink stripes on sleeves; light blue bodice with pink heart; pale yellow skirt	95 x 100	250.00	350.00	150.00
2	Bashful	Orange coat; grey hat; beige shoes	80 x 45	190.00	235.00	110.00
3	Doc	Blue coat; grey trousers; beige hat, shoes	80 x 50	200.00	255.00	125.00
4	Dopey	Beige coat; red hat; pale blue shoes	80 x 50	190.00	235.00	110.00
5	Grumpy	Red coat; beige hat; brown shoes	75 x 45	200.00	255.00	125.00
6	Happy	Brown vest; beige hat; blue trousers	85 x 50	190.00	235.00	125.00
7	Sleepy	Pale green coat, shoes; orange hat	80 x 50	190.00	235.00	110.00
8	Sneezy	Navy coat; blue trousers; brown hat, shoes	80 x 45	190.00	235.00	110.00
—	8 pce set	Boxed	—	1,600.00	2,000.00	1,000.00

SNOW WHITE AND THE SEVEN DWARFS BROOCHES

Circa 1938

Miniature lapel brooches were produced in the cellulose glaze used by the Wadeheath pottery during the mid-late 1930s, one of Snow White's face and full figure brooches of the dwarfs. The brooches have only been found in Canada and the USA. They were probably produced for Walt Disney staff during the North American promotion of the film *Snow White and the Seven Dwarfs*. They have an unusual "Wade Burslem England" backstamp, which adds to the belief that they were a special promotion.

Backstamp: Embossed "[name of character] Made in England Wade Burslem England"

No.	Name	Description	Size	U.S. $	Can. $	U.K. £
1	Snow White	Black hair and eyes; red bow and mouth	40	Very Rare		
2	Bashful	Green hat; orange coat; blue trousers; brown shoes	35	Very Rare		
3	Doc	Green hat; orange coat; maroon trousers; yellow belt buckle; blue shoes	35		Very Rare	
4	Dopey	Unknown	35		Very Rare	
5	Grumpy	Orange hat; orange-brown coat; blue trousers; orange brown shoes	37		Very Rare	
6	Happy	Light blue hat; brown coat; green trousers; red-brown shoes	35		Very Rare	
7	Sleepy	Green hat; brown coat; purple trousers; red shoes	35		Very Rare	
8	Sneezy	Green hat; blue coat; orange-red trousers; orange shoes	35		Very Rare	

WHIMSIES
1954-1993

BALLY-WHIM IRISH VILLAGE

1984-1987

Due to the success of the *English Whimsey-on-Why* models, Wade Ireland introduced a set of eight Irish village houses. Because the Wade Ireland pottery ceased production of giftware in August 1987, only one *Bally-Whim Irish Village* set was made. Each model is marked in a hollow under the base. The model number is on the side.

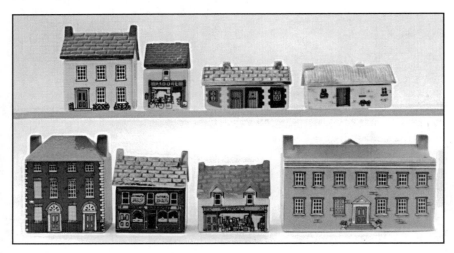

Backstamp: Embossed "Wade Ireland"

No.	Name	Description	Size	U.S.$	Can.$	U.K.£
1	Undertaker's House	Beige; brown roof, door	50 x 38	20.00	30.00	10.00
2	Moore's Post Office	Cream; brown roof	38 x 25	20.00	30.00	10.00
3	Barney Flynn's Cottage	Grey roof; red windows, door	28 x 45	20.00	30.00	10.00
4	Kate's Cottage	Yellow-brown roof	23 x 45	15.00	20.00	10.00
5	The Dentist's House	Dark brown; grey roof; red door	50 x 45	15.00	20.00	10.00
6	Mick Murphy's Bar	Green/grey	35 x 38	25.00	35.00	10.00
7	W. Ryan's Hardware Store	Yellow/brown roof	35 x 38	25.00	35.00	10.00
8	Bally-Whim House	Grey; blue roof; honey door	40 x 82	25.00	35.00	10.00

DOGS AND PUPPIES

1969-1982

This *Dogs and Puppies* series was advertised and labeled on the boxes as *Whimsies*. The models are of a mother dog and her two puppies, which were produced intermittently between 1969 and 1982. The mother dog was sold in one box and her two puppies in another. The boxes resemble books, and the inside of the lid has a description of the dogs breed printed on it. The first three sets were packaged in blue boxes, the last two sets in red. The original price was 7/6d per box.

SET ONE: ALSATIAN

1969-1982

Backstamp: Black and gold label "Genuine Wade Porcelain Made in England"

No.	Name	Description	Size	U.S. $	Can. $	U.K. £
1	Mother	Brown/honey brown	60 x 75	25.00	35.00	8.00
2	Puppy, Sitting	Brown/honey brown	40 x 45	15.00	20.00	6.00
3	Puppy, Lying	Brown/honey brown	35 x 45	15.00	20.00	6.00

SET TWO: CAIRN

1969-1982

Backstamp: Black and gold label "Genuine Wade Porcelain Made in England"

No.	Name	Description	Size	U.S. $	Can. $	U.K. £
1	Mother	Honey brown; brown ears, nose	65 x 70	25.00	35.00	8.00
2	Puppy, Standing	Honey brown; brown ears, nose	40 x 50	15.00	20.00	8.00
3	Puppy, Lying	Honey brown; brown ears, nose	35 x 50	15.00	20.00	10.00

SET THREE: RED SETTER

1973-1982

Backstamp: Black and gold label "Genuine Wade Porcelain Made in England"

No.	Name	Description	Size	U.S. $	Can. $	U.K. £
1	Mother	Red-brown	60 x 75	28.00	37.00	12.00
2	Puppy, Lying Facing Left	Red-brown	40 x 45	15.00	20.00	6.00
3	Puppy, Lying Facing Right	Red-brown	40 x 45	15.00	20.00	6.00

SET FOUR: CORGIES

1979-1982

Backstamp: Black and gold label "Genuine Wade Porcelain Made in England"

No.	Name	Description	Size	U.S. $	Can. $	U.K. £
1	Mother	Honey brown; brown ears, nose; green base	60 x 60	40.00	60.00	30.00
2	Puppy, Lying	Honey brown; brown ears, nose; green base	30 x 45	30.00	40.00	15.00
3	Puppy, Sitting	Honey brown; brown ears, nose; green base	45 x 40	30.00	40.00	15.00

SET FIVE: YORKSHIRE TERRIER

1979-1982

Backstamp: Black and gold label "Genuine Wade Porcelain Made in England"

No.	Name	Description	Size	U.S. $	Can. $	U.K. £
1	Mother	Black/brown; honey brown face, chest	55 x 70	50.00	70.00	35.00
2	Puppy, Sitting	Black/brown; honey brown face, chest	40 x 40	35.00	40.00	20.00
3	Puppy, Walking	Black/brown; honey brown face, chest	35 x 45	35.00	40.00	20.00

Dogs And Puppies Derivatives

Dog Pipe Stands

1973-1981

The *Dog Pipe Stands* have a mother dog from the 1969-1982 *Dogs and Puppies* series on the back rim of a stand. The original price was 72p each.

Backstamp: Embossed "Wade England"

No.	Name	Description	Size	U.S. $	Can. $	U.K. £
1	Alsatian	Brown/honey brown; green stand	60 x 115	30.00	40.00	15.00
2	Cairn	Honey brown; green stand	60 x 115	30.00	40.00	20.00
3	Red Setter	Red-brown; green stand	60 x 115	30.00	40.00	15.00
4	Corgi	Honey brown; green stand	60 x 115	35.00	45.00	20.00
5	Yorkshire Terrier	Black/brown; green stand	60 x 115	40.00	50.00	25.00

Cat And Puppy Dishes

1974-1981

The *Cat and Puppy Dishes* is a series of 11 basket dishes with the puppies from the 1969-1982 *Dogs and Puppies* series sitting in them. The only change is the addition of a new model and the first in the series, the "Tabby Cat." With the exception of style 1b, the baskets are coloured in mottled greys and browns. The puppy dishes were packaged in pastel boxes marked "Pup-in-a-Basket" in North America.

Backstamp: Embossed "Wade England"

No.	Name	Description	Size	U.S. $	Can. $	U.K. £
1a	Tabby Cat	Brown stripes	50 x 75	35.00	45.00	18.00
1b	Tabby Cat	Brown stripes; dark brown basket	50 x 75	35.00	45.00	18.00
2	Alsatian Puppy, Sitting	Brown/honey-brown	40 x 75	22.00	30.00	10.00
3	Alsatian Puppy, Lying	Brown/honey brown	35 x 75	22.00	30.00	10.00
4	Cairn Puppy, Standing	Honey brown	40 x 75	22.00	35.00	8.00
5	Cairn Puppy, Lying	Honey brown	35 x 75	22.00	35.00	8.00
6	Red Setter Puppy, Lying, Facing Left	Red-brown	40 x 75	22.00	30.00	10.00
7	Red Setter Puppy, Lying, Facing Right	Brown	40 x 75	22.00	30.00	10.00
8	Corgi Puppy, Sitting	Honey brown	45 x 75	30.00	40.00	15.00
9	Corgi Puppy, Lying	Honey brown	30 x 75	30.00	40.00	15.00
10	Yorkie Puppy, Sitting	Grey/brown	30 x 75	40.00	45.00	15.00
11	Yorkie Puppy, Standing	Grey/brown	35 x 75	40.00	45.00	15.00

ENGLISH WHIMSIES

1971-1984

In 1971, 25 of the original Red Rose Tea Canada models were individually boxed and sold by Wade as a retail line. Unlike their famous forerunners, *First Whimsies*, this series has five models per set, with each figure sold in its own numbered box. The boxes in each set were the same colour (for example, set 1 was dark blue, set 2 was red, etc.). An updated list of models was added to the back of the boxes each year.

A new set was usually issued annually, although on some occasions when demand was strong, two sets were issued per year. A further 35 new models were added to the 25 original Canadian models, making an English series of 60 models.

Note that the "Trout" as it was first issued was unmarked, and the back of the base differs slightly from the second issue, which is marked "Wade England" on the back rim. The "Hippo," "Bison" and "Pig" come in more than one size, due to the replacement of broken dies. In fact, there can be slight size variations in all the models listed below.

The black "Zebra" was glazed dark grey with black stripes, but after the first production run through the kiln, it emerged looking black all over, with very few markings to show it was a zebra. The Wade management then decided to change the colour to beige. The black "Zebra" is rare. The "Bullfrog" is the same model as the Red Rose Tea "Frog," but has been changed from green-yellow to brown. The "Kitten" can be found with or without a backstamp.

English Whimsies was offered as a pocket-money line to children for a price of 2/2d each.

SET ONE: DARK BLUE BOX

1971

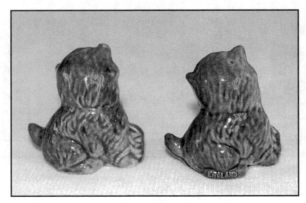

Backstamp: Embossed "Wade England"

No.	Name	Description	Size	U.S. $	Can. $	U.K. £
1	Fawn	Brown; blue ears	30 x 30	4.00	6.00	3.00
2	Rabbit	Beige; ears open	30 x 30	8.00	6.00	3.00
3	Mongrel	Dark brown back; light brown front	35 x 35	7.00	5.00	2.00
4a	Kitten	Dark/light brown; pink wool	30 x 30	7.00	9.00	3.00
4b	Kitten	Dark/light brown; red wool	30 x 30	6.00	8.00	3.00
5	Spaniel	Honey brown	35 x 35	8.00	5.00	2.00

SET TWO: RED BOX

1972

Backstamp: Embossed "Wade England"

No.	Name	Description	Size	U.S. $	Can. $	U.K. £
6	Duck	Blue/brown, yellow beak	30 x 40	9.00	7.00	3.00
7	Corgi	Honey brown	30 x 35	9.00	7.00	2.00
8	Beaver	Grey-brown; honey-brown face	35 x 45	8.00	6.00	2.00
9	Bushbaby	Brown; blue ears	30 x 30	6.00	4.00	2.00
10	Fox	Dark brown body, tail; fawn brown face, chest	30 x 30	7.00	7.00	3.00

SET THREE: DARK GREEN BOX

1972

Backstamp: A. Unmarked (15)
B. Embossed "Wade England" (11-15)

No.	Name	Description	Size	U.S. $	Can. $	U.K. £
11	Bear Cub	Grey; beige face	30 x 40	7.00	5.00	2.00
12	Otter	Beige; blue base	30 x 35	7.00	5.00	2.00
13	Setter	Brown; grey-green base	35 x 50	7.00	5.00	2.00
14	Owl	Dark brown; light brown chest, face	35 x 20	8.00	6.00	4.00
15	Trout	Brown; black patch; red tail; grey-green base	30 x 30	8.00	6.00	3.00

108

SET FOUR: YELLOW BOX

1973

Large Hippo (left), Small Hippo (right)

Backstamp: Embossed "Wade England"

No.	Name	Description	Size	U.S. $	Can. $	U.K. £
16	Lion	Light brown; dark brown head, mane	35 x 45	8.00	6.00	2.00
17	Elephant	Grey; some may have black eyes	35 x 28	20.00	15.00	6.00
18	Giraffe	Beige	35 x 35	7.00	5.00	3.00
19	Chimpanzee	Dark brown; light brown face, patches	35 x 35	7.00	5.00	2.00
20a	Hippo	Large; honey brown	25 x 45	16.00	12.00	4.00
20b	Hippo	Small; honey brown	20 x 40	6.00	4.00	2.00

SET FIVE: DARK RED BOX

1974

Backstamp: A. Embossed "Wade England" (21, 23, 25)
B. Embossed in recessed base "Wade England" (22)

No.	Name	Description	Size	U.S. $	Can. $	U.K. £
21	Squirrel	Grey; light brown head, legs; yellow acorn	35 x 30	7.00	5.00	2.00
22	Hedgehog	Dark brown; light brown face; black nose	23 x 40	9.00	7.00	3.00
23	Pine Marten	Honey brown	30 x 30	6.00	5.00	2.00
24	Fieldmouse	Yellow/brown	35 x 25	12.00	11.00	4.00
25	Alsatian	Grey; tan face	30 x 40	9.00	7.00	3.00

SET SIX: LIGHT BLUE BOX

1975

Large and Small Pigs

Backstamp: Embossed "Wade England"

No.	Name	Description	Size	U.S. $	Can. $	U.K. £
26	Collie	Golden brown; green base	35 x 35	10.00	8.00	4.00
27	Cow	Honey brown	35 x 35	12.00	12.00	4.00
28a	Pig	Large; beige; green base	27 x 44	25.00	20.00	10.00
28b	Pig	Medium; beige; green base	25 x 40	15.00	10.00	5.00
28c	Pig	Small; beige; green base	25 x 35	15.00	10.00	5.00
29	Horse	Dark grey; green base	38 x 30	15.00	12.00	4.00
30	Lamb	Fawn brown; green base	35 x 28	8.00	10.00	4.00

SET SEVEN: ORANGE BOX

1976

Black Zebra, Faint Stripes (left); Light Brown Zebra (right)

Backstamp: Embossed "Wade England"

No.	Name	Description	Size	U.S. $	Can. $	U.K. £
31	Rhino	Grey; green base	25 x 35	8.00	6.00	4.00
32	Leopard	Yellow/brown; green base	17 x 45	6.00	8.00	4.00
33	Gorilla	Grey; grey-green base	35 x 25	8.00	8.00	4.00
34	Camel	Light brown; green base	35 x 35	9.00	11.00	4.00
35a	Zebra	Black; faint stripes	40 x 35	75.00	100.00	24.00
35b	Zebra	Light brown; green base	40 x 35	9.00	11.00	4.00

SET EIGHT: MAGENTA BOX

1977

Backstamp: Embossed "Wade England"

No.	Name	Description	Size	U.S. $	Can. $	U.K. £
36	Donkey	Light brown; green base	30 x 30	14.00	18.00	7.00
37	Barn Owl	Light brown; dark brown head, back; blue base	35 x 20	20.00	25.00	7.00
38	Cat	Light brown/ginger; grey-green base	40 x 17	20.00	25.00	7.00
39	Mouse	Beige; grey-blue base	40 x 25	12.00	16.00	7.00
40	Ram	White; grey face; green base	30 x 30	12.00	16.00	5.00

SET NINE: MID BLUE BOX

1978

Backstamp: **A.** Embossed "Wade England" (41, 42, 43, 45)
B. Embossed "Wade England" in recessed base (44)

No.	Name	Description	Size	U.S. $	Can. $	U.K. £
41	Dolphin	Grey-brown; blue base	30 x 40	25.00	35.00	15.00
42	Pelican	Brown; yellow beak; green base	45 x 40	20.00	25.00	10.00
43	Angel Fish	Dark grey; blue base	35 x 30	15.00	12.00	8.00
44	Turtle	Greenish grey	15 x 50	9.00	12.00	6.00
45	Seahorse	Yellow; grey base	50 x 17	20.00	25.00	12.00

SET TEN: LIGHT GREEN BOX

1979

Backstamp: Embossed "Wade England"

No.	Name	Description	Size	U.S. $	Can. $	U.K. £
46	Kangaroo	Dark brown; light brown base	45 x 25	18.00	24.00	5.00
47	Orang-Outan	Ginger	30 x 30	5.00	7.00	5.00
48	Tiger	Yellow; green base	35 x 25	15.00	20.00	7.00
49	Koala Bear	Yellow-brown; black nose; green base	35 x 25	20.00	25.00	9.00
50	Langur Type 1	Light brown; dark brown stump; green leaves	35 x 30	5.00	7.00	4.00

SET ELEVEN: DARK BROWN BOX

1979

Large Bison (left), Small Bison (right)

Backstamp: **A.** Embossed "Wade England" (51a, 51b, 54, 55)
     B. Embossed in recessed base "Wade England" (52, 53)

No.	Name	Description	Size	U.S. $	Can. $	U.K. £
51a	Bison	Large; honey brown; dark brown head, mane	32 x 45	14.00	10.00	4.00
51b	Bison	Small; honey brown; dark brown head, mane	28 x 40	7.00	5.00	4.00
52	Bluebird	Beige body, tail; blue wings, head	15 x 35	10.00	8.00	4.00
53	Bullfrog	Brown	15 x 30	25.00	32.00	15.00
54	Wild Boar	Light brown; green base	30 x 40	9.00	12.00	4.00
55	Raccoon	Brown; grey-green base	25 x 35	15.00	12.00	4.00

SET TWELVE: DEEP BLUE BOX

1980

Backstamp: Embossed "Wade England"

No.	Name	Description	Size	U.S. $	Can. $	U.K. £
56	Penguin	Grey; white face, chest; yellow beak, feet	38 x 19	25.00	35.00	12.00
57	Seal Pup	Beige; blue base	25 x 37	20.00	30.00	7.00
58	Husky	Grey; grey/green base	35 x 30	20.00	30.00	9.00
59	Walrus	Light brown; grey base	30 x 30	12.00	15.00	3.00
60	Polar Bear	White; black nose; blue base	30 x 30	20.00	30.00	7.00

English Whimsies Derivatives

English Whimtrays

1971-1984

These *Whimtrays* were made with models from the *English Whimsies* series.

Photograph not available
at press time

Backstamp: Embossed "Whimtrays Wade Porcelain Made in England"

No.	Name	Description	Size	U.S. $	Can. $	U.K. £
1	Duck	Blue/brown; yellow beak; black tray	50 x 75	20.00	30.00	12.00
2	Fawn	Brown; blue ears; black tray	50 x 75	20.00	30.00	12.00
3	Trout	Brown; black patch; red tail; black tray	50 x 75	20.00	30.00	12.00

WHOPPAS

1976-1981

Whoppas are the big brothers of *Whimsies* and were in production from 1976 to 1981. They were issued in three sets of five models. The original price was 65p each.

SET ONE: RED BOX

1976-1981

Backstamp: Embossed "Wade England"

No.	Name	Description	Size	U.S.$	Can.$	U.K.£
1a	Polar Bear	Beige brown; blue base	35 x 55	25.00	35.00	7.00
1b	Polar Bear	White; grey-blue base	35 x 55	25.00	35.00	7.00
2	Hippo	Grey; green base	35 x 50	25.00	35.00	7.00
3	Brown Bear	Red-brown; brown base	35 x 45	20.00	28.00	7.00
4	Tiger	Yellow/brown; green base	30 x 60	20.00	28.00	7.00
5	Elephant	Grey; green base	55 x 50	25.00	35.00	7.00

SET TWO: GREEN BOX

1977-1981

Backstamp: Embossed "Wade England"

No.	Name	Description	Size	U.S. $	Can. $	U.K. £
6	Bison	Brown; green base	40 x 50	25.00	35.00	12.00
7	Wolf	Grey; green base	60 x 45	30.00	40.00	12.00
8	Bobcat	Light brown; dark brown spots; green base	55 x 50	30.00	40.00	12.00
9	Chipmunk	Brown; brown base	55 x 40	30.00	40.00	15.00
10	Racoon	Brown; black stripes; eye patches; green base	40 x 50	35.00	45.00	20.00

SET THREE: BROWN BOX

1978-1981

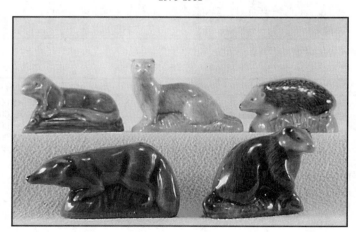

Backstamp: Embossed "Wade England"

No.	Name	Description	Size	U.S. $	Can. $	U.K. £
11	Fox	Red-brown; green base	30 x 60	45.00	55.00	25.00
12	Badger	Brown; cream stripe; green base	35 x 45	45.00	55.00	25.00
13	Otter	Brown; blue base	30 x 55	45.00	55.00	25.00
14	Stoat	Brown; green base	35 x 55	45.00	55.00	25.00
15	Hedgehog	Brown; green base	30 x 50	45.00	55.00	25.00

FIRST WHIMSIES

1954-1958

Following the end of World War II, the massive program to replace war-damaged houses and factories created a heavy demand for industrial ceramics. By the early 1950s, this demand had slackened, and new products had to be produced in order to avoid worker layoffs in the George Wade Potteries. With many years of experience, making small pressed articles for industrial use, coupled with a unique ability in specialist tool-making; it was decided to manufacture a range of miniature animals.

The first set of five models was produced in 1954 and was designed for children to spend their pocket money on. When Mr. Wade's secretary referred to the models as whimsical, the series was named *Whimsies* (and later referred to as the *First Whimsies*).

The original models were packaged and sold in sets of five pieces for 5/9d. Only those models on bases wide enough for a Wade stamp were marked; free-standing models with open-cast legs generally had no room for marks. All boxes were marked "Wade Whimsies," but once the unmarked figures were removed from their boxes, there was no way to tell that they were Wade.

Whimsies models had their first showing at the British Industries Fair in 1954. At first, the reaction of dealers and wholesalers to the five tiny models was discouraging. But the following day, when the public was allowed into the show, they quickly changed their attitude when they saw the growing numbers of children and parents queuing to buy *Whimsies*.

For the next six years, Wade produced and sold nine sets of five and one set of four miniature animal models. Today these *First Whimsies* are highly sought after by collectors all over the world.

SET ONE: ENGLISH ANIMALS

1954-1958

Backstamp: **A.** Embossed "Wade" (1, 2)
　　　　　　　B. Unmarked (3, 4, 5)

No.	Name	Description	Size	U.S. $	Can. $	U.K. £
1	Leaping Fawn	White; green base	40 x 40	45.00	40.00	20.00
2	Horse	Light brown; green/brown base	35 x 50	45.00	40.00	20.00
3	Spaniel with Ball	White; grey rump, tail	25 x 40	30.00	40.00	20.00
4	Poodle	Light brown; white markings	35 x 35	45.00	50.00	25.00
5	Squirrel	Light grey	25 x 50	25.00	35.00	18.00

Note: Whimsies animals are arranged in issue order.

SET TWO: ENGLISH ANIMALS

1954 -1958

Backstamp: **A.** Black and gold label "Genuine Wade Porcelain Made in England" (1, 3)
B. Unmarked (1, 2, 3, 4, 5)

No.	Name	Description	Size	U.S. $	Can. $	U.K. £
1	Bull	Brown legs; green base	45 x 55	80.00	100.00	50.00
2	Lamb	Brown muzzle, front legs; green base	45 x 25	50.00	65.00	25.00
3	Kitten	Grey face, paws, tail; blue bow	15 x 40	95.00	125.00	50.00
4	Hare	Light grey/white, white base	30 x 45	45.00	60.00	25.00
5	Dachshund	Beige	35 x 45	90.00	125.00	50.00

SET THREE: ENGLISH COUNTRY ANIMALS

1955-1958

Backstamp: **A.** Unmarked (1, 2, and 3)
B. Embossed "Wade" (4, 5)

No.	Name	Description	Size	U.S. $	Can. $	U.K. £
1	Badger	Grey; black/white face	30 x 40	35.00	45.00	22.00
2	Fox Cub	Light brown	35 x 35	75.00	100.00	40.00
3	Stoat	Grey tail; red eyes	20 x 35	55.00	70.00	35.00
4	Shetland Pony	Grey mane; green base	35 x 40	40.00	55.00	22.00
5	Retriever	Brown; white legs; green/white base	30 x 40	35.00	45.00	22.00

SET FOUR: AFRICAN JUNGLE ANIMALS

1955-1958

Backstamp: A. Unmarked (1, 5)
B. Black ink stamp "Wade Made in England" (2, 3, 4)

No.	Name	Description	Size	U.S. $	Can. $	U.K. £
1	Lion	Light brown	30 x 35	55.00	75.00	30.00
2	Crocodile	Green-brown	15 x 40	75.00	100.00	40.00
3	Monkey and Baby	Brown; green stump	45 x 25	40.00	55.00	25.00
4	Rhinoceros	Grey; green base	45 x 45	40.00	55.00	18.00
5	Baby Elephant	Grey	40 x 40	55.00	75.00	28.00

SET FIVE: HORSES

1956-1959

This is the only *First Whimsies* set of four figures and, despite its title, it includes a Beagle dog.

Backstamp: Embossed "Wade"

No.	Name	Description	Size	U.S. $	Can. $	U.K. £
1a	Mare	Light brown; brown tail, mane; green base	45 x 40	45.00	60.00	28.00
1b	Mare	White; brown mane, tail, hooves; green base	45 x 40	45.00	60.00	28.00
2a	Foal	Light brown; brown mane, tail; green base	40 x 40	45.00	60.00	28.00
2b	Foal	Dark brown; green base	40 x 40	45.00	60.00	28.00
2c	Foal	White; brown mane, tail, hooves; green base	45 x 40	45.00	60.00	28.00
3a	Colt	Light brown; brown mane, tail; green base	40 x 40	45.00	60.00	28.00
3b	Colt	White; brown mane, tail, hooves; green base	40 X 40	45.00	60.00	28.00
4	Beagle	Brown patches; green base	20 x 20	75.00	115.00	45.00

SET SIX: POLAR ANIMALS

1956-1959

The original price was 6/6d for the set.

Backstamp: Unmarked

No.	Name	Description	Size	U.S. $	Can. $	U.K. £
1	King Penguin	Black back, head, flippers; yellow beak, feet	35 x 20	45.00	60.00	28.00
2	Husky	Fawn/white; grey ears, muzzle	30 x 25	45.00	60.00	28.00
3	Polar Bear	Grey muzzle; blue base	45 x 45	45.00	60.00	25.00
4	Baby Seal	Light grey; white base	25 x 25	30.00	40.00	20.00
5a	Polar Bear Cub	White; brown eyes, nose, claws	20 x 30	40.00	50.00	25.00
5b	Polar Bear Cub	Pink; brown eyes, nose, claws	20 x 30	40.00	50.00	25.00

SET SEVEN: PEDIGREE DOGS

1957-1961

The original price was 6/6d for a box of five models.

Backstamp: Unmarked

No.	Name	Description	Size	U.S. $	Can. $	U.K. £
1	Alsatian	Grey/brown, green-brown base	35 x 40	30.00	40.00	20.00
2	West Highland Terrier	White	25 x 30	45.00	60.00	25.00
3	Corgi	Beige/white	25 x 30	45.00	60.00	25.00
4	Boxer	Brown; grey face; brown-green base	35 x 40	40.00	55.00	25.00
5	Saint Bernard	Brown/white	40 x 45	55.00	75.00	28.00

SET EIGHT: ZOO ANIMALS

1957-1961

Two "Panda" figures were issued by Wade, one larger than the other. The smaller one, with a black band across its chest, is the right model for this set; the larger, 35 by 25 millimetre figure is out of proportion to the other models in the set. The larger model may have been produced first, then found to be too large and was set aside for possible use in special offers or premiums. Whether or not it was actually used in a premium set or simply sold off is not known. The original price per box was 5/9d.

Backstamp: Unmarked

No.	Name	Description	Size	U.S. $	Can. $	U.K. £
1	Bactrian Camel	Light brown; dark brown humps; green base	40 x 40	45.00	55.00	25.00
2	Cockatoo	Yellow crest; grey base	30 x 30	55.00	75.00	25.00
3a	Giant Panda, Large	Black/white	35 x 25	35.00	45.00	20.00
3b	Giant Panda, Small	Black/white; black band on chest	30 x 18	40.00	55.00	22.00
4	Lion Cub	Brown; white chest	25 x 25	35.00	45.00	20.00
5	Llama	Grey face; brown-green base	45 x 30	45.00	55.00	22.00

SET NINE: NORTH AMERICAN ANIMALS

1958-1961

The "Grizzly Cub" (model 4a), is the figure issued as part of this set. Models 4b and 4c were issued at a later time. The original issue price was 6/6d per set.

Backstamp: **A.** Unmarked (1, 2, 4a, 4b, 4c, 5)
                B. Embossed "Wade" (3)
                C. Embossed "Wade England" (3)

No.	Name	Description	Size	U.S. $	Can. $	U.K. £
1	Snowy Owl	Brown eyes, claws	28 x 30	50.00	65.00	32.00
2	Raccoon	Grey/black, white base	30 x 30	40.00	50.00	22.00
3	Grizzly Bear	Brown/white; green base	50 x 25	65.00	85.00	35.00
4a	Grizzly Cub	Light brown, green base	25 x 25	35.00	45.00	20.00
4b	Grizzly Cub	Brown; pink ears	25 x 30	35.00	45.00	20.00
4c	Grizzly Cub	White; pink ears	25 x 25	45.00	55.00	28.00
5	Cougar	Brown; white face, feet	20 x 45	50.00	70.00	30.00

SET TEN: FARM ANIMALS

1959-1961

These are the hardest of all *First Whimsies* models to find. This was the last set made and was only in production for a short time.

The "Shire Horse" and "Swan" in this set have been unlawfully reproduced and sold as authentic *First Whimsies*. The "Shire Horse" fake is slightly larger, it leans backwards in an ungainly way (most will not stand) and its nose is longer. It does not have the appearance of a real horse, but looks more like a caricature. The counterfeit "Swan" has a thicker neck and shorter beak, and the detailing of the feathers is not as fine as on the original.

The original price was 5/9d per boxed set.

Backstamp: Unmarked

No.	Name	Description	Size	U.S. $	Can. $	U.K. £
1	Pig	Pink; green base	20 x 35	75.00	100.00	38.00
2	Italian Goat	Grey; white face, chest; green base	30 x 30	75.00	100.00	38.00
3a	Foxhound	Beige patches; green base	25 x 45	75.00	100.00	40.00
3b	Foxhound	Light brown patches; green/white base	25 x 45	75.00	100.00	40.00
4a	Shire Horse	Creamy beige; brown mane and tail	50 x 50	250.00	340.00	125.00
4b	Shire Horse	White; grey mane; brown hooves	50 x 40	245.00	325.00	115.00
4c	Shire Horse	Red brown; cream mane; cream / black hooves	50 x 50	240.00	320.00	135.00
5	Swan	Yellow beak; black tip	25 x 35	215.00	285.00	120.00

First Whimsies Derivatives Disney Lights, Candleholder

Circa 1960

A "Panda" model has been found on a Disney Light candle holder base, which is much thicker and heavier than the Zoo light candle holder base.

Photograph not available
at press time

No.	Name	Description	Size	U.S.$	Can.$	U.K.£
9	Panda, Large	Black/white; black base	55 x 50	68.00	80.00	30.00

First Whimsies Derivatives Irish Whimtrays

Circa 1985

In the mid-1980s, Wade Ireland reissued *Whimtrays*, but as the original mould for the tray was worn, a new one was designed. The plinth on which the figure sits is not gently rounded, as was that of the original George Wade model. Instead, it bends much farther out into the dish, making it easy to distinguish the two styles of trays. The figures attached to model numbers 1, 2, 3 and 4 are from the *First Whimsies* series; numbers 5, 6, and 7 were originally *English Whimsies*.

Duck (2)

King Penguin (5)

Backstamp: Embossed "Made in Ireland, Irish Porcelain, Wade 'Eire tir a dheanta'" in a circle around a crown and shamrock

No.	Name	Description	Size	U.S.$	Can.$	U.K.£
1	Cockatoo	Yellow crest; black tray	50 x 77	30.00	40.00	15.00
2a	Duck	Blue/brown; blue tray	50 x 77	15.00	20.00	8.00
2b	Duck	Blue/brown; green tray	50 x 77	15.00	20.00	8.00
3a	Fawn	Brown; black tray	50 x 77	15.00	20.00	8.00
3b	Fawn	Brown; green tray	50 x 77	15.00	20.00	8.00
4	Husky	Fawn/white; green tray	50 x 77	30.00	40.00	15.00
5a	King Penguin	Black/white; black tray	50 x 77	15.00	20.00	8.00
5b	King Penguin	Black/white; green tray	45 x 77	30.00	40.00	15.00
6a	Polar Bear Cub	White; black tray	40 x 77	30.00	40.00	15.00
6b	Polar Bear Cub	White; green tray	40 x 77	30.00	40.00	15.00
7a	Trout	Brown; black tray	50 x 77	15.00	20.00	8.00
7b	Trout	Brown; blue tray	50 x 77	15.00	20.00	8.00
7c	Trout	Brown; green tray	50 x 77	15.00	20.00	8.00

First Whimsies Derivatives Mare And Colt Dish

1963

The *Mare and Colt Dish* has two models from the *First Whimsies Horses,* set 5, on the rim of a figure-eight shaped dish. The original price was 6/6d. This dish is rare.

Backstamp: Embossed "Wade Porcelain Made in England"

No.	Description	Size	U.S. $	Can. $	U.K. £
1	Light brown horses; black dish	110 x 20	65.00	90.00	45.00

First Whimsies Deriviatives Whimtrays

1958-1965

Whimtrays are small round dishes with a *First Whimsies* animal on the back edge of the tray. The issue date was January 1958 (except for the Bactrian Camel, Cockatoo, Giant Panda, Llama and Lion Cub *Whimtrays*, which were issued in August 1958), and they originally sold for 2/6d each. The trays come in black, blue, yellow and pink.

The following *Whimtrays* are listed in alphabetical order.

Bactrian Camel (2)

Racoon (2)

Backstamp: Embossed "Whimtrays Wade Porcelain Made in England"

No.	Name	Description		Size	U.S. $	Can. $	U.K. £
1a	Alsatian	Grey/brown;	black tray	55 x 75	30.00	40.00	15.00
1b	Alsatian		blue tray	55 x 75	30.00	40.00	15.00
1c	Alsatian		pink tray	55 x 75	30.00	40.00	15.00
1d	Alsatian		yellow tray	55 x 75	30.00	40.00	15.00
2a	Bactrian Camel	Light brown;	black tray	60 x 75	30.00	40.00	15.00
2b	Bactrian Camel		blue tray	60 x 75	30.00	40.00	15.00
2c	Bactrian Camel		pink tray	60 x 75	30.00	40.00	15.00
2d	Bactrian Camel		yellow tray	60 x 75	30.00	40.00	15.00
3a	Baby Seal	Grey;	black tray	40 x 75	30.00	40.00	15.00
3b	Baby Seal		blue tray	40 x 75	30.00	40.00	15.00
3c	Baby Seal		pink tray	40 x 75	30.00	40.00	15.00
3d	Baby Seal		yellow tray	40 x 75	30.00	40.00	15.00
4a	Boxer	Brown;	black tray	45 x 75	30.00	40.00	15.00
4b	Boxer		blue tray	45 x 75	30.00	40.00	15.00
4c	Boxer		pink tray	45 x 75	30.00	40.00	15.00
4d	Boxer		yellow tray	45 x 75	30.00	40.00	15.00
5a	Cockatoo	Yellow crest;	black tray	50 x 75	30.00	40.00	15.00
5b	Cockatoo		blue tray	50 x 75	30.00	40.00	15.00
5c	Cockatoo		pink tray	50 x 75	30.00	40.00	15.00
5d	Cockatoo		yellow tray	50 x 75	30.00	40.00	15.00
6a	Corgi	Beige/white;	black tray	45 x 75	30.00	40.00	15.00
6b	Corg		blue tray	45 x 75	30.00	40.00	15.00
6c	Corgi		pink tray	45 x 75	30.00	40.00	15.00
6d	Corgi		yellow tray	45 x 75	30.00	40.00	15.00
7a	Giant Panda	Black/white;	black tray	50 x 75	30.00	40.00	15.00
7b	Giant Panda		blue tray	50 x 75	30.00	40.00	15.00
7c	Giant Panda		pink tray	50 x 75	30.00	40.00	15.00
7d	Giant Panda		yellow tray	50 x 75	30.00	40.00	15.00
8a	Giant Panda, Small	Black/white;	black tray	45 x 75	30.00	40.00	15.00
8b	Giant Panda, Small		blue tray	45 x 75	30.00	40.00	15.00
8c	Giant Panda, Small		pink tray	45 x 75	30.00	40.00	15.00
8d	Giant Panda, Small		yellow tray	45 x 75	30.00	40.00	15.00

First Whimsies Derivatives Whimtrays

1958-1965

No.	Name	Description		Size	U.S. $	Can. $	U.K. £
9a	Grizzly Bear	Brown/white;	black tray	65 x 75	30.00	40.00	15.00
9b	Grizzly Bear		blue tray	65 x 75	30.00	40.00	15.00
9c	Grizzly Bear		pink tray	65 x 75	30.00	40.00	15.00
9d	Grizzly Bear		yellow tray	65 x 75	30.00	40.00	15.00
10a	Grizzly Cub	Brown;	black tray	45 x 75	30.00	40.00	15.00
10b	Grizzly Cub		blue tray	45 x 75	30.00	40.00	15.00
10c	Grizzly Cub		pink tray	45 x 75	30.00	40.00	15.00
10d	Grizzly Cub		yellow tray	45 x 75	30.00	40.00	15.00
11a	Hare	Light grey/white;	black tray	50 x 75	30.00	40.00	15.00
11b	Hare		blue tray	50 x 75	30.00	40.00	15.00
11c	Hare		pink tray	50 x 75	30.00	40.00	15.00
11d	Hare		yellow tray	50 x 75	30.00	40.00	15.00
12a	Husky	Fawn/white;	black tray	50 x 75	30.00	40.00	15.00
12b	Husky		blue tray	50 x 75	30.00	40.00	15.00
12c	Husky		pink tray	50 x 75	30.00	40.00	15.00
12d	Husky		yellow tray	50 x 75	30.00	40.00	15.00
13a	King Penguin	Black/white;	black tray	50 x 75	30.00	40.00	15.00
13b	King Penguin		blue tray	50 x 75	30.00	40.00	15.00
13c	King Penguin		pink tray	50 x 75	30.00	40.00	15.00
13d	King Penguin		yellow tray	50 x 75	30.00	40.00	15.00
14a	Lion Cub	Brown;	black tray	45 x 75	30.00	40.00	15.00
14b	Lion Cub		blue tray	45 x 75	30.00	40.00	15.00
14c	Lion Cub		pink tray	45 x 75	30.00	40.00	15.00
14d	Lion Cub		yellow tray	45 x 75	30.00	40.00	15.00
15a	Llama	Grey face;	black tray	65 x 75	30.00	40.00	15.00
15b	Llama		blue tray	65 x 75	30.00	40.00	15.00
15c	Llama		pink tray	65 x 75	30.00	40.00	15.00
15d	Llama		yellow tray	65 x 75	30.00	40.00	15.00
16a	Mare	Light brown;	black tray	55 x 75	30.00	40.00	15.00
16b	Mare		blue tray	55 x 75	30.00	40.00	15.00
16c	Mare		pink tray	55 x 75	30.00	40.00	15.00
16d	Mare		yellow tray	55 x 75	30.00	40.00	15.00
17a	Monkey and Baby	Brown;	black tray	65 x 75	30.00	40.00	15.00
17b	Monkey and Baby		blue tray	65 x 75	30.00	40.00	15.00
17c	Monkey and Baby		pink tray	65 x 75	30.00	40.00	15.00
17d	Monkey and Baby		yellow tray	65 x 75	30.00	40.00	15.00
18a	Pig	Pink / green;	black tray	35 x 75	75.00	100.00	50.00
19a	Polar Bear	White;	black tray	65 x 75	30.00	40.00	15.00
19b	Polar Bear		blue tray	65 x 75	30.00	40.00	15.00
19c	Polar Bear		pink tray	65 x 75	30.00	40.00	15.00
19d	Polar Bear		yellow tray	65 x 75	30.00	40.00	15.00
20a	Polar Bear Cub	White;	black tray	40 x 75	30.00	40.00	15.00
20b	Polar Bear Cub		blue tray	40 x 75	30.00	40.00	15.00
20c	Polar Bear Cub		pink tray	40 x 75	30.00	40.00	15.00
20d	Polar Bear Cub		yellow tray	40 x 75	30.00	40.00	15.00
21a	Raccoon	Grey/black;	black tray	50 x 75	30.00	40.00	15.00
21b	Raccoon		blue tray	50 x 75	30.00	40.00	15.00
21c	Raccoon		pink tray	50 x 75	30.00	40.00	15.00
21d	Raccoon		yellow tray	50 x 75	30.00	40.00	15.00
22a	Snowy Owl	White;	black tray	44 x 75	30.00	40.00	15.00
22b	Snowy Owl		blue tray	44 x 75	30.00	40.00	15.00
22c	Snowy Owl		pink tray	44 x 75	30.00	40.00	15.00
22d	Snowy Owl		yellow tray	44 x 75	30.00	40.00	15.00
23a	Spaniel	White;	black tray	45 x 75	30.00	40.00	15.00
23b	Spaniel		blue tray	45 x 75	30.00	40.00	15.00
23c	Spaniel		pink tray	45 x 75	30.00	40.00	15.00
23d	Spaniel		yellow tray	45 x 75	30.00	40.00	15.00

First Whimsies Derivatives Whimtrays

1958-1965

No.	Name	Description		Size	U.S. $	Can. $	U.K. £
24a	Squirrel	Light grey;	black tray	45 x 75	30.00	40.00	15.00
24b	Squirrel		blue tray	45 x 75	30.00	40.00	15.00
24c	Squirrel		pink tray	45 x 75	30.00	40.00	15.00
24d	Squirrel		yellow tray	45 x 75	30.00	40.00	15.00
25a	Swan	White;	black tray	40 x 75	100.00	135.00	55.00
25b	Swan		blue tray	40 x 75	100.00	135.00	55.00
25c	Swan		pink tray	40 x 75	100.00	135.00	55.00
25d	Swan		yellow tra	40 x 75	100.00	135.00	55.00
26a	West Highland Terrier	White;	black tray	40 x 75	30.00	40.00	15.00
26b	West Highland Terrier		blue tray	40 x 75	30.00	40.00	15.00
26c	West Highland Terrier		pink tray	40 x 75	30.00	40.00	15.00
26d	West Highland Terrier		yellow tray	40 x 75	30.00	40.00	15.00

First Whimsies Derivatives Zoo Lights, Candle Holders

1957-1962

George Wade's policy of using unsold models by adding them to new items produced many different "Stick-em-on-Somethings," such as *Zoo Lights*, *Whimtrays* and *Disney Lights*. Luckily for collectors, single models of *First Whimsies* animals, which were eluding capture in their original form, were attached to an oval base with a candle holder on the back to become *Zoo Lights*. Almost all the *First Whimsies* animals are on *Zoo Lights*. The candle holders come in black, yellow, blue and pink, and all the animals are in their original colour glazes.

The *Zoo Lights* were first issued prior to Christmas 1957 as *Animal Candlesticks* (with the exception of the Camel, Llama and Panda, which were issued in August 1958), and were discontinued in January 1960. They are listed in alphabetical order.

Backstamp: Embossed "Wade Porcelain Made in England"

No.	Name	Description		Size	U.S. $	Can. $	U.K. £
1a	Alsatian	Grey/brown;	black holder	47 x 48	38.00	50.00	18.00
1b	Alsatian		blue holder	47 x 48	38.00	50.00	18.00
1c	Alsatian		pink holder	47 x 48	38.00	50.00	18.00
1d	Alsatian		yellow holder	47 x 48	38.00	50.00	18.00
2a	Baby Seal	Light grey;	black holder	35 x 48	38.00	50.00	18.00
2b	Baby Seal		blue holder	35 x 48	38.00	50.00	18.00
2c	Baby Seal		pink holder	35 x 48	38.00	50.00	18.00
2d	Baby Seal		yellow holder	35 x 48	38.00	50.00	18.00

First Whimsies Derivatives Zoo Lights Candleholders

1957-1962

No.	Name	Description		Size	U.S. $	Can. $	U.K. 3
3a	Bactrian Camel	Light brown;	black holder	52 x 48	38.00	50.00	18.00
3b	Bactrian Camel		blue holder	52 x 48	38.00	50.00	18.00
3c	Bactrian Camel		pink holder	52 x 48	38.00	50.00	18.00
3d	Bactrian Camel		yellow holder	52 x 48	38.00	50.00	18.00
4a	Badger	Grey/black/white;	black holder	40 x 48	38.00	50.00	18.00
4b	Badger		blue holder	40 x 48	38.00	50.00	18.00
4c	Badger		pink holder	40 x 48	38.00	50.00	18.00
4d	Badger		yellow holder	40 x 48	38.00	50.00	18.00
5a	Boxer	Brown;	black holder	45 x 48	38.00	50.00	18.00
5b	Boxer		blue holder	45 x 48	38.00	50.00	18.00
5c	Boxer		pink holder	45 x 48	38.00	50.00	18.00
5d	Boxer		yellow holder	45 x 48	38.00	50.00	18.00
6a	Cockatoo	Yellow crest;	black holder	44 x 48	38.00	50.00	18.00
6b	Cockatoo		blue holder	44 x 48	38.00	50.00	18.00
6c	Cockatoo		pink holder	44 x 48	38.00	50.00	18.00
6d	Cockatoo		yellow holder	44 x 48	38.00	50.00	18.00
7a	Corgi	Beige/white;	black holder	37 x 48	38.00	50.00	18.00
7b	Corgi		blue holder	37 x 48	38.00	50.00	18.00
7c	Corgi		pink holder	37 x 48	38.00	50.00	18.00
7d	Corgi		yellow holder	37 x 48	38.00	50.00	18.00
8a	Giant Panda, Small	Black/white;	black holder	40 x 48	38.00	50.00	18.00
8b	Giant Panda, Small		blue holder	40 x 48	38.00	50.00	18.00
8c	Giant Panda, Small		pink holder	40 x 48	38.00	50.00	18.00
8d	Giant Panda, Small		yellow holder	40 x 48	38.00	50.00	18.00
9a	Grizzly Bear	Brown/white;	black holder	60 x 48	38.00	50.00	18.00
9b	Grizzly Bear		blue holder	60 x 48	38.00	50.00	18.00
9c	Grizzly Bear		pink holder	60 x 48	38.00	50.00	18.00
9d	Grizzly Bear		yellow holder	60 x 48	38.00	50.00	18.00
10a	Hare	Light grey/white;	black holder	40 x 48	38.00	50.00	18.00
10b	Hare		blue holder	40 x 48	38.00	50.00	18.00
10c	Hare		pink holder	40 x 48	38.00	50.00	18.00
10d	Hare		yellow holder	40 x 48	38.00	50.00	18.00
11a	Husky	Fawn/white;	black holder	44 x 48	38.00	50.00	18.00
11b	Husky		blue holder	44 x 48	38.00	50.00	18.00
11c	Husky		pink holder	44 x 48	38.00	50.00	18.00
11d	Husky		yellow holder	44 x 48	38.00	50.00	18.00
12a	King Penguin	Black/white;	black holder	44 x 48	38.00	50.00	18.00
12b	King Penguin		blue holder	44 x 48	38.00	50.00	18.00
12c	King Penguin		pink holder	44 x 48	38.00	50.00	18.00
12d	King Penguin		yellow holder	44 x 48	38.00	50.00	18.00
13a	Lion Cub	Brown;	black holder	37 x 48	38.00	50.00	18.00
13b	Lion Cub		blue holder	37 x 48	38.00	50.00	18.00
13c	Lion Cub		pink holder	37 x 48	38.00	50.00	18.00
13d	Lion Cub		yellow holder	37 x 48	38.00	50.00	18.00
14a	Llama	Grey face;	black holder	55 x 48	38.00	50.00	18.00
14b	Llama		blue holder	55 x 48	38.00	50.00	18.00
14c	Llama		pink holder	55 x 48	38.00	50.00	18.00
14d	Llama		yellow holder	55 x 48	38.00	50.00	18.00
15a	Mare	Light brown;	black holder	55 x 48	38.00	50.00	18.00
15b	Mare		blue holder	55 x 48	38.00	50.00	18.00
15c	Mare		pink holder	55 x 48	38.00	50.00	18.00
15d	Mare		yellow holder	55 x 48	38.00	50.00	18.00
15e	Mare	White;	royal blue holder	55 x 48	38.00	50.00	18.00
16a	Polar Bear Cub	White;	black holder	35 x 48	38.00	50.00	18.00
16b	Polar Bear Cub		blue holder	35 x 48	38.00	50.00	18.00
16c	Polar Bear Cub		pink holder	35 x 48	38.00	50.00	18.00
16d	Polar Bear Cub		yellow holder	35 x 48	38.00	50.00	18.00

First Whimsies Derivatives Zoo Lights Candleholders

1957-1962

No.	Name	Description		Size	U.S. $	Can. $	U.K. £
17a	Poodle	Light brown;	black holder	44 x 48	38.00	50.00	18.00
17b	Poodle		blue holder	44 x 48	38.00	50.00	18.00
17c	Poodle		pink holder	44 x 48	38.00	50.00	18.00
17d	Poodle		black holder	40 x 48	38.00	50.00	18.00
18a	Retriever	Brown/white	black holder	40 x 80	38.00	50.00	18.00
18b	Retriever		blue holder	40 x 48	38.00	50.00	18.00
18c	Retriever		pink holder	40 x 48	38.00	50.00	18.00
18d	Retriever		yellow holder	40 x 48	38.00	50.00	18.00
19a	Spaniel	White;	black holder	35 x 48	38.00	50.00	18.00
19b	Spaniel		blue holder	35 x 48	38.00	50.00	18.00
19c	Spaniel		pink holder	35 x 48	38.00	50.00	18.00
19d	Spaniel		yellow holder	35 x 48	38.00	50.00	18.00
20a	Squirrel	Light grey;	black holder	35 x 48	38.00	50.00	18.00
20b	Squirrel		blue holder	35 x 48	38.00	50.00	18.00
20c	Squirrel		pink holder	35 x 48	38.00	50.00	18.00
20d	Squirrel		yellow holder	35 x 48	38.00	50.00	18.00
20a	West Highland Terrier	White;	black holder	35 x 48	38.00	50.00	18.00
21b	West Highland Terrier		blue holder	35 x 48	38.00	50.00	18.00
21c	West Highland Terrier		pink holder	35 x 48	38.00	50.00	18.00
21d	West Highland Terrier		yellow holder	35 x 48	38.00	50.00	18.00

NEW COLOURWAY WHIMSIES

1998

Wade re-issued six *Whimsie* models in new colourways. Four models, the "Gorilla," "Hippo," "Leopard" and "Racoon" are from the Red Rose Tea Canada and *English Whimsies* series, And two, the "Mole" and the "Safari Park Lion," are Tom Smith models. The "Safari Park Lion" is in identical colours to the original model, but the colour on the base is a brighter green. The cost direct from Wade Ceramics was £1.50 each. Listed in alphabetical order.

Backstamp: Embossed "Wade England" on rim

No.	Name	Description	Size	U.S. $	Can. $	U.K. £
1	Gorilla (RRC & EW)	Beige; blue base	25 x 35	4.00	5.00	2.00
2	Hippo (RRC & EW)	Light grey; blue base	23 x 35	4.00	5.00	2.00
3	Leopard (RRC & EW)	Pale honey; bright green base	17 x 45	4.00	5.00	2.00
4	Mole (TS)	Light grey; pale green base	25 x 40	4.00	5.00	2.00
5	Racoon (EW)	Light grey; black striped tail	25 x 35	4.00	5.00	2.00
6	Safari Park Lion (TS)	Honey brown; bright green base	30 x 45	4.00	5.00	2.00

Note: The following initials indicate the origin of the models.
EW: English Whimsies
TS: Tom Smith
RRC: Red Rose Tea

POLAR BLOW UPS

1962-1963

The *Polar Blow Ups* set is a series of slightly modified blow ups of three of the *First Whimsies Polar Animals*, set six. They are slip cast, hollow models, which because of high production costs, were never put into full production. Only a few hundred of these models are believed to exist. A blow up of the Polar set "Husky" has been seen and a description of colour and size has been reported; there are also unconfirmed reports of a "Dolphin," "Mermaid," and a "Penguin," but no written or visual evidence has been found.

Backstamp: **A.** Unmarked (1-8)
B. Black and gold label "Genuine Wade Porcelain Made in England" (1-3, 5-8)
C. Black and gold label "Made in Ireland by Wade Co. Armagh" (4)

No.	Name	Description	Size	U.S. $	Can. $	U.K. £
1	Polar Bear Mother	White/beige; pink tongue; blue/beige/white fish	150 x 120	375.00	500.00	185.00
2	Polar Bear Cub	White/beige; pink mouth	100 x 100	375.00	500.00	185.00
3	Seal	Greenish black; pink tongue	120 x 105	375.00	500.00	185.00
4	Walrus	Unknown	148 x 98	275.00	375.00	135.00
5	Husky	Beige/white	150 x 100	Unknown		
6	Mermaid	Unknown	Unknown	Unknown		
7	Penguin	Unknown	Unknown	Unknown		
8	Dolphin	Unknown	Unknown	Unknown		

WHIMSIE-LAND

1984-1988

Although the *English Whimsies* series was discontinued in 1984, George Wade and Son Ltd. continued to produce a range of inexpensive miniature animals, called the *Whimsie-land* series. Five sets of this series were issued between 1984 and 1988. There are five models per set, making a total of 25 figures.

All *Whimsie-land* models were issued in pastel coloured boxes with a complete numbered list of all the models in the series printed on the bottom. All these figures are marked on the back of the base. The original price was 49p each.

Note: The Elephant in this series is sometimes confused with the *English Whimsies* Elephant, as the pose is similar. However, the *Whimsie-land* Elephant has open-cast legs.

SET ONE: PETS

1984

Backstamp: Embossed "Wade England"

No.	Name	Description	Size	U.S.$	Can.$	U.K.£
1	Retriever	Beige; white face, underparts; green base	32 x 60	18.00	25.00	8.00
2	Puppy	Beige; white face, chest; pink tongue	35 x 36	15.00	20.00	8.00
3	Rabbit	Gold; brown front, base	50 x 25	25.00	35.00	12.00
4a	Kitten	Grey; blue wool	20 x 42	15.00	20.00	8.00
4b	Kitten	Grey; pink wool	20 x 42	12.00	16.00	8.00
5	Pony	Grey mane, tail; green base	37 x 47	20.00	27.00	12.00

SET TWO: WILDLIFE

1984

Backstamp: Embossed "Wade England"

No.	Name	Description	Size	U.S.$	Can.$	U.K.£
6	Lion	Brown; gold mane; honey base	30 x 50	15.00	20.00	8.00
7	Tiger	Orange-brown; black stripes, base	22 x 50	10.00	15.00	8.00
8	Elephant	Grey; green base	35 x 40	20.00	30.00	12.00
9	Panda	Grey/white; green base	37 x 20	20.00	30.00	8.00
10	Giraffe	Brown; green base	50 x 35	20.00	30.00	15.00

SET THREE: FARMYARD

1985

Backstamp: Embossed "Wade England"

No.	Name	Description	Size	U.S.$	Can.$	U.K.£
11	Cockerel	Grey wings, tail; pink comb; grey/green base	50 x 35	20.00	30.00	15.00
12	Duck	Grey back, tail; yellow beak; green base	45 x 35	25.00	35.00	15.00
13	Cow	Black patches; green base	30 x 45	33.00	45.00	20.00
14	Pig	Pink; green base	30 x 35	10.00	15.00	8.00
15	Goat	Grey patch; green base	35 x 35	22.00	30.00	12.00

SET FOUR: HEDGEROW

1986

Backstamp: Embossed "Wade England"

No.	Name	Description	Size	U.S.$	Can.$	U.K.£
16	Fox	Red-brown; honey face, chest, feet	35 x 35	30.00	40.00	20.00
17	Owl	White; yellow/black eyes	35 x 25	15.00	20.00	8.00
18	Hedgehog	Grey-brown; brown face, paws	25 x 35	10.00	15.00	8.00
19	Badger	Grey; black markings	25 x 35	18.00	25.00	8.00
20	Squirrel	Grey	35 x 25	10.00	15.00	8.00

SET FIVE: BRITISH WILDLIFE

1987

Backstamp: Embossed "Wade England"

No.	Name	Description	Size	U.S.$	Can.$	U.K.£
21	Pheasant	Honey; grey-blue markings	35 x 50	42.00	55.00	28.00
22	Fieldmouse	Brown; yellow corn	35 x 30	38.00	50.00	28.00
23	Golden Eagle	Brown; dark brown rock	35 x 40	38.00	50.00	28.00
24	Otter	Brown; blue base	40 x 40	15.00	20.00	18.00
25	Partridge	White; black beak; green base	35 x 35	25.00	35.00	18.00

Whimsie-land Derivatives

Money Box

1987

In 1987 Wade issued three money boxes based on the earlier "Fawn," "Disney Kennel" and "Noddy Toadstool Cottage" money boxes. Because the original moulds were worn, Wade made new moulds, which produced larger, heavier and less delicate-looking models than the originals. New colours were also used. The *Whimsie-land* Puppy was used on a newly modeled Disney Kennel money box. The money boxes were sold in plain, unmarked boxes. For the other two money boxes, see Leprechauns and Pixie models and Miscellaneous models (pages 27 and 156).

Kennel and Puppy

Backstamp: Unmarked

No.	Name	Description	Size	U.S.$	Can.$	U.K.£
1	Kennel and Puppy	Brown roof; honey walls	95 x 125	45.00	60.00	28.00

Whimsie-Land Derivatives Whimtrays

1987

During the summer of 1987, Wade produced a set of kidney-shaped trays it called *New Whimtrays*. Because the new *Whimsie-land* animals were used on them, they are often referred to as *Whimsie-land trays*.

Backstamp: Embossed "Wade England"

No.	Name	Description	Size	U.S.$	Can.$	U.K.£
1a	Duck	Black tray	90 x 110	27.00	35.00	15.00
1b	Duck	Blue tray	90 x 110	27.00	35.00	15.00
1c	Duck	Green tray	90 x 110	27.00	35.00	15.00
2a	Owl	Black tray	90 x 110	27.00	35.00	15.00
2b	Owl	Blue tray	90 x 110	27.00	35.00	15.00
2c	Owl	Green tray	90 x 110	27.00	35.00	15.00
3a	Pony	Black tray	90 x 110	27.00	35.00	15.00
3b	Pony	Blue tray	90 x 110	27.00	35.00	15.00
3c	Pony	Green tray	90 x 110	27.00	35.00	15.00
4a	Puppy	Black tray	90 x 110	27.00	35.00	15.00
4b	Puppy	Blue tray	90 x 110	27.00	35.00	15.00
4c	Puppy	Green tray	90 x 110	27.00	35.00	15.00
5a	Squirrel	Black tray	90 x 110	27.00	35.00	15.00
5b	Squirrel	Blue tray	90 x 110	27.00	35.00	15.00
5c	Squirrel	Green tray	90 x 110	27.00	35.00	15.00

Whimsie-land Derivatives Key Rings

1988

After the *Whimsie-land* series and the *New Whimtrays* were discontinued, surplus models were converted into key rings by adding a small chain and a ring. The *Whimsie-land* "Panda" was reglazed in black and white for this series.

Photograph not available
at press time

Backstamp: Embossed "Wade England"

No.	Name	Description	Size	U.S.$	Can.$	U.K.£
1	Badger	Grey; black markings	25 x 35	20.00	25.00	12.00
2	Duck	White/grey; yellow beak	45 x 35	20.00	25.00	12.00
3	Kitten	Grey/white; pink wool	20 x 42	20.00	25.00	12.00
4	Panda	Black/white	37 x 20	20.00	25.00	12.00
5	Puppy	Beige/white	35 x 36	20.00	25.00	12.00

WHIMSEY-IN-THE-VALE

1993

In 1993 two new sets of houses were produced in the *Whimsey-in-the-Vale* series. Each set consists of five models, boxed individually and not numbered.

The moulds from the *Whimsey-on-Why* houses were used to make the following models in the *Whimsey-in-the-Vale* series:

Whimsey-on-Why Models became Whimsey-in-the-Vale Models

Why Knott Inn	Antique Shop
Whimsey Service Station	Florist Shop
Briar Row	Jubilee Terrace
The Fire Station	St. Johns School
St. Sebastians Church	St. Lawrence Church
The Barley Mow	Boars Head Pub
The Antique Shop	Post Office
The Post Office	Rose Cottage
The Market Hall	Town Garage
The Stag Hotel	Vale Farm

SET ONE

Backstamp: Embossed "Wade England"

No.	Name	Description	Size	U.S.$	Can.$	U.K.£
1	Antique Shop	White; beige roof; green/yellow trim	33 x 39	15.00	20.00	7.00
2	Florist Shop	White; light brown roof; green/yellow trim	40 x 38	15.00	20.00	9.00
3	Jubilee Terrace	White; beige roof; yellow stonework	33 x 78	15.00	20.00	7.00
4	St. John's School	White; dark brown roof; green windows, doors	33 x 30	15.00	20.00	7.00
5	St. Lawrence Church	Grey; green doors	55 x 77	15.00	20.00	9.00

SET TWO

Backstamp: **A.** Embossed "Wade England" (1, 2, 3, 5)
B. Unmarked (4)

No.	Name	Description	Size	U.S.$	Can.$	U.K.£
1	Boar's Head Pub	White; brown roof, windows; yellow doors	35 x 77	15.00	20.00	9.00
2	Post Office	White; dark brown roof; blue doors	35 x 37	15.00	20.00	7.00
3	Rose Cottage	White; beige roof; yellow windows, doors	40 x 38	15.00	20.00	7.00
4	Town Garage	White; beige roof; blue doors, windows	35 x 50	15.00	20.00	9.00
5	Vale Farm	Light brown; grey roof; dark brown beams	42 x 66	15.00	20.00	9.00

WHIMSEY-ON-WHY

1980-1987

Whimsey-on-Why is a series of miniature porcelain houses based upon a mythical English village called Whimsey-on-Why. The highly accurate detail was achieved by the use of fired-on enamel transfers, which included the number of the model in an unobtrusive place. The original price for a set of eight models was £10, or the houses could be bought individually at prices ranging from 79p for a small model to £2.15 for a larger size.

SET ONE

1980-1981

Set One was issued in spring 1980. The original price for "Pump Cottage" was 79p. "Morgan's the Chemist," "Dr Healer's House" and the "Tobacconist's Shop" sold for 99p. "The Why Knott Inn" was 89p, "Bloodshott Hall" and "The Barley Mow" were £1.85 and "St. Sebastian's Church" was £2.15. All models are numbered.

Backstamp: Embossed "Wade England"

No.	Name	Description	Size	U.S.$	Can.$	U.K.£
1	Pump Cottage	Brown thatch, beams	28 x 39	20.00	25.00	6.00
2	Morgan's the Chemist	Grey roof; yellow windows	40 x 39	22.00	30.00	12.00
3	Dr. Healer's House	Brown roof, door	40 x 39	25.00	33.00	12.00
4	Tobacconist's Shop	Brown roof; red doors	33 x 39	20.00	25.00	6.00
5	Why Knott Inn	Beige thatch; black beams	33 x 39	20.00	25.00	6.00
6	Bloodshott Hall	Red-brown; grey roof	50 x 80	22.00	30.00	12.00
7	St. Sebastian's Church	Grey; brown door	55 x 77	30.00	40.00	15.00
8	The Barley Mow	Beige roof; black wood	35 x 77	30.00	40.00	15.00

SET TWO

1981-1982

This set was issued in spring 1981. "The Greengrocer's Shop" and "The Antique Shop" originally sold for 99p each. The price for the "Whimsey Service Station" and for "The Post Office" was £1.10. "The Whimsey School" cost £1.50, "The Watermill" and "The Stag Hotel" were £1.85 and "The Windmill" was £2.15.

Backstamp: **A.** Embossed "Wade England" (9-15)
             B. Unmarked (16)

No.	Name	Description	Size	U.S.$	Can.$	U.K.£
9	The Greengrocer's Shop	Grey roof; green windows	35 x 35	20.00	30.00	8.00
10	The Antique Shop	Purple-brown roof	35 x 37	25.00	33.00	12.00
11	Whimsey Service Station	Beige roof; green pumps	40 x 38	22.00	30.00	12.00
12	The Post Office	Beige roof; yellow/blue windows	40 x 38	20.00	25.00	10.00
13	Whimsey School	Brown; grey roof; blue window	38 x 51	45.00	60.00	20.00
14	The Watermill	Red-brown; beige thatch	42 x 66	25.00	35.00	10.00
15	The Stag Hotel	Grey roof; black wood	45 x 66	25.00	35.00	10.00
16	The Windmill	White; copper pin	60 x 30	90.00	120.00	50.00

SET THREE

1982-1983

Set Three was issued in spring 1982. "The Tinker's Nook" originally sold for 89p, the "Whimsey Station" cost 99p, "Merryweather Farm" was £2.15, "The Vicarage" was £1.65, "The Manor" was £1.85, "Briar Row" was £1.95 and "Broomyshaw Cottage" and "The Sweet Shop" were each £1.10. "Tinker's Nook" has been found with a Wade Ireland Backstamp.

Backstamp: **A**. Embossed "Wade England" (18-24)
B. "Wade Ireland" (17)

No.	Name	Description	Size	U.S.$	Can.$	U.K.£
17	Tinker's Nook	Red-brown roof; yellow/white windows	38 x 22	12.00	18.00	7.00
18	Whimsey Station	Red-brown; brown roof; yellow/blue windows	135 x 39	25.00	35.00	20.00
19	Merryweather Farm	Cream; brown roof; blue/yellow windows	48 x 55	55.00	70.00	35.00
20	The Vicarage	Pink; beige roof; blue/yellow windows	41 x 51	65.00	85.00	45.00
21	Broomyshaw Cottage	Beige; brown roof; blue/yellow windows	40 x 40	15.00	20.00	10.00
22	The Sweet Shop	Grey roof; black wood; blue windows	40 x 40	15.00	20.00	10.00
23	Briar Row	Beige thatch; yellow/blue windows	33 x 78	35.00	45.00	15.00
24	The Manor	Red-brown; brown roof; blue/yellow windows	42 x 66	25.00	35.00	12.00

SET FOUR

1984-1985

Only three new *Whimsey-on-Why* models were released during 1984. "The District Bank," "The Old Smithy" and "The Picture Palace" were issued the same year Wade Ireland introduced its *Bally-Whim Irish Village* (marketed by George Wade & Son Ltd.). The remaining five models of this set were produced in early 1985.

The original price for the "District Bank" was £1.75, "The Old Smithy" was £1.30 and "The Picture Palace" was £2.35. The original prices for the remaining models are not known.

Backstamp: **A.** Embossed "Wade England" (25-31)
B. Embossed "Wade Ireland" (On Old Smithy)
C. Unmarked (32)

No.	Name	Description	Size	U.S.$	Can.$	U.K.£
25	The District Bank	Red-brown; brown roof	43 x 40	15.00	20.00	10.00
26	The Old Smithy	Yellow thatch; black wood	25 x 45	18.00	25.00	12.00
27	The Picture Palace	Black wood; red lettering	45 x 65	25.00	35.00	20.00
28	The Butcher Shop	Brown roof; green/grey front	33 x 25	25.00	35.00	15.00
29	The Barber Shop	Grey roof; green/yellow front	33 x 25	25.00	35.00	20.00
30	Miss Prune's House	Grey roof; black wood; yellow door	38 x 38	10.00	15.00	10.00
31	The Fire Station	Brown roof; red fire engine	33 x 30	18.00	25.00	15.00
32	The Market Hall	Brown roof	35 x 50	18.00	25.00	15.00

SET FIVE

1987-Circa 1988

The last *Whimsey-on-Why* set, issued in 1987, comprises four models. This brought the series to a close with a total of 36 models. The original prices of this set are unknown. For similar models, see the section on *Whimsey-in-the-Vale*.

Backstamp: Embossed "Wade England"

No.	Name	Description	Size	U.S.$	Can.$	U.K.£
33	The School Teacher's House	Grey roof, walls	38 x 38	55.00	70.00	35.00
34	The Fishmonger's Shop	Brown roof	43 x 27	55.00	70.00	35.00
35	The Police Station	Blue; brown roof	43 x 27	55.00	70.00	35.00
36	The Library	Brown; grey roof	50 x 38	50.00	60.00	30.00

MISCELLANEOUS SETS

MISCELLANEOUS SETS
ALPHABET AND LONDON TRAINS
1958-1961

The *Alphabet Train* comprises a miniature engine pulling six carriages and was intended to be educational, as well as fun, for children to play with. The carriages have various numbers on their roofs and letters of the alphabet on both sides. The *London Train* has a single letter on the roof of each carriage (forming the name *London*), with scenes of Tower Bridge, St. Pauls Cathedral, Trafalgar Square, Piccadilly Circus, Big Ben or Westminster Abbey on each side.

The issue date for both sets was August 1958, and they originally sold for 6/11d. They were discontinued in January 1959. The trains are very rare. As they are only seen in complete sets, no individual prices are given below.

Alphabet Set

Backstamp: Unmarked

No.	Name	Description	Size	U.S. $	Can. $	U.K. £
1a	Alphabet Set: Engine, Tender, 6 Carriages	Blue engine	27 x 205	900.00	1,200.00	450.00

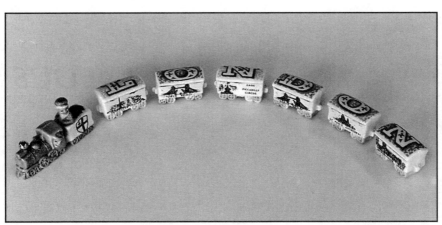

London Set

No.	Name	Description	Size	U.S. $	Can. $	U.K. £
1b	London Set: Engine, Tender, 6 Carriages	Grey engine	27 x 205	1,000.00	1,500.00	600.00

ANGELS

1963

The *Angels* is a small series of models which were only produced for a short time. They were modelled in three different positions standing, sitting and kneeling and coloured in pastel shades of pink, green, yellow and blue. These figures are also found on angel dishes and on angel candle holders. The *Angels* originally sold for 1/11 each.

Angels Kneeling, Sitting and Standing

KNEELING ANGEL

Backstamp: Unmarked

No.	Description	Size	U.S.$	Can.$	U.K.£
1a	Blue dress; brown hair	40 x 25	100.00	135.00	50.00
1b	Blue dress; yellow hair	40 x 25	100.00	135.00	50.00
1c	Green dress; brown hair	40 x 25	100.00	135.00	50.00
1d	Green dress; yellow hair	40 x 25	100.00	135.00	50.00
1e	Pink dress; brown hair	40 x 25	100.00	135.00	50.00
1f	Pink dress; yellow hair	40 x 25	100.00	135.00	50.00
1g	Yellow dress; brown hair	40 x 25	100.00	135.00	50.00
1h	Yellow dress; yellow hair	40 x 25	100.00	135.00	50.00

SITTING ANGEL

Backstamp: Unmarked

No.	Description	Size	U.S.$	Can.$	U.K.£
2a	Blue dress; brown hair	40 x 30	100.00	135.00	50.00
2b	Blue dress; yellow hair	40 x 30	100.00	135.00	50.00
2c	Green dress; brown hair	40 x 30	100.00	135.00	50.00
2d	Green dress; yellow hair	40 x 30	100.00	135.00	50.00
2e	Pink dress; brown hair	40 x 30	100.00	135.00	50.00
2f	Pink dress; yellow hair	40 x 30	100.00	135.00	50.00
2g	Yellow dress; brown hair	40 x 30	100.00	135.00	50.00
2h	Yellow dress; yellow hair	40 x 30	100.00	135.00	50.00

STANDING ANGEL

Backstamp: Unmarked

No.	Description	Size	U.S. $	Can. $	U.K. £
3a	Blue dress; brown hair	40 x 30	100.00	135.00	50.00
3b	Blue dress; yellow hair	40 x 30	100.00	135.00	50.00
3c	Green dress; brown hair	40 x 30	100.00	135.00	50.00
3d	Green dress; yellow hair	40 x 30	100.00	135.00	50.00
3e	Pink dress; brown hair	40 x 30	100.00	135.00	50.00
3f	Pink dress; yellow hair	40 x 30	100.00	135.00	50.00
3g	Yellow dress; brown hair	40 x 30	100.00	135.00	50.00
3h	Yellow dress; yellow hair	40 x 30	100.00	135.00	50.00

Angel Derivatives

Angel Candle Holders

The angel models were mounted on the front of triangular-shaped candle holders (the same candle holders that were used for the 1960 *Disney Lights*). All the candle holders are black, and they were sold with a candy-twist candle for an original price of 2/11d each.

Kneeling Angel Candle Holder

Backstamp: Embossed "Wade"

No.	Description	Size	U.S.$	Can.$	U.K.
1a	Blue dress; brown hair	58 x 50	120.00	160.00	60.00
1b	Blue dress; yellow hair	58 x 50	120.00	160.00	60.00
1c	Green dress; brown hair	58 x 50	120.00	160.00	60.00
1d	Green dress; yellow hair	58 x 50	120.00	160.00	60.00
1e	Pink dress; brown hair	58 x 50	120.00	160.00	60.00
1f	Pink dress; yellow hair	58 x 50	120.00	160.00	60.00
1g	Yellow dress; brown hair	58 x 50	120.00	160.00	60.00
1h	Yellow dress; yellow hair	58 x 50	120.00	160.00	60.00

Sitting Angel Candle Holder

Backstamp: Embossed "Wade"

No.	Description	Size	U.S.$	Can.$	U.K.£
2a	Blue dress; brown hair	58 x 50	120.00	160.00	60.00
2b	Blue dress; yellow hair	58 x 50	120.00	160.00	60.00
2c	Green dress; brown hair	58 x 50	120.00	160.00	60.00
2d	Green dress; yellow hair	58 x 50	120.00	160.00	60.00
2e	Pink dress; brown hair	58 x 50	120.00	160.00	60.00
2f	Pink dress; yellow hair	58 x 50	120.00	160.00	60.00
2g	Yellow dress; brown hair	58 x 50	120.00	160.00	60.00
2h	Yellow dress; yellow hair	58 x 50	120.00	160.00	60.00

Standing Angel Candle Holder

Backstamp: Embossed "Wade"

No.	Description	Size	U.S. $	Can. $	U.K. £
3a	Blue dress; brown hair	58 x 50	120.00	160.00	60.00
3b	Blue dress; yellow hair	58 x 50	120.00	160.00	60.00
3c	Green dress; brown hair	58 x 50	120.00	160.00	60.00
3d	Green dress; yellow hair	58 x 50	120.00	160.00	60.00
3e	Pink dress; brown hair	58 x 50	120.00	160.00	60.00
3f	Pink dress; yellow hair	58 x 50	120.00	160.00	60.00
3g	Yellow dress; brown hair	58 x 50	120.00	160.00	60.00
3h	Yellow dress; yellow hair	58 x 50	120.00	160.00	60.00

Angel Derivatives Dishes

The dishes, similar to the *Whimtrays*, are black and the angel figure is positioned on the back rim. They originally sold for 2/11d each.

Angel Dishes - Kneeling, Standing and Sitting

Kneeling Angel Dish

Backstamp: Embossed Angel Dish, "Wade Porcelain, Made in England"

No.	Description	Size	U.S. $	Can. $	U.K. £
1a	Blue dress; brown hair	40 x 75	80.00	100.00	40.00
1b	Blue dress; yellow hair	40 x 75	80.00	100.00	40.00
1c	Green dress; brown hair	40 x 75	80.00	100.00	40.00
1d	Green dress; yellow hair	40 x 75	80.00	100.00	40.00
1e	Pink dress; brown hair	40 x 75	80.00	100.00	40.00
1f	Pink dress; yellow hair	40 x 75	80.00	100.00	40.00
1g	Yellow dress; brown hair	40 x 75	80.00	100.00	40.00
1h	Yellow dress; yellow hair	40 x 75	80.00	100.00	40.00

Standing Angel Dish

No.	Description	Size	U.S.$	Can.$	U.K.£
2a	Blue dress; brown hair	40 x 75	80.00	100.00	40.00
2b	Blue dress; yellow hair	40 x 75	80.00	100.00	40.00
2c	Green dress; brown hair	40 x 75	80.00	100.00	40.00
2d	Green dress; yellow hair	40 x 75	80.00	100.00	40.00
2e	Pink dress; brown hair	40 x 75	80.00	100.00	40.00
2f	Pink dress; yellow hair	40 x 75	80.00	100.00	40.00
2g	Yellow dress; brown hair	40 x 75	80.00	100.00	40.00
2h	Yellow dress; yellow hair	40 x 75	80.00	100.00	40.00

Sitting Angel Dish

No.	Description	Size	U.S.$	Can.$	U.K.£
3a	Blue dress; brown hair	40 x 75	80.00	100.00	40.00
3b	Blue dress; yellow hair	40 x 75	80.00	100.00	40.00
3c	Green dress; brown hair	40 x 75	80.00	100.00	40.00
3d	Green dress; yellow hair	40 x 75	80.00	100.00	40.00
3e	Pink dress; brown hair	40 x 75	80.00	100.00	40.00
3f	Pink dress; yellow hair	40 x 75	80.00	100.00	40.00
3g	Yellow dress; brown hair	40 x 75	80.00	100.00	40.00
3h	Yellow dress; yellow hair	40 x 75	80.00	100.00	40.00

BEAR AMBITIONS

1995

The *Bear Ambitions* set of six named Teddy Bears was re-issued in 1996 for Tom Smith and Company (the British Christmas Cracker manufacturers) in three different glaze colours for their Christmas Time Crackers series (see page 348).

Backstamp: Embossed "Wade England"

No.	Name	Description	Size	U.S.$	Can.$	U.K.£
1	Admiral Sam	Honey	50	6.00	8.00	3.00
2	Alex the Aviator	Honey	45	6.00	8.00	3.00
3	Artistic Edward	Honey	40	6.00	8.00	3.00
4	Beatrice Ballerina	Honey	50	6.00	8.00	3.00
5	Locomotive Joe	Honey	50	6.00	8.00	3.00
6	Musical Marco	Honey	45	6.00	8.00	3.00

THE BRITISH CHARACTER SET

1959

The *British Character* set, also known to collectors as *London Characters,* includes four models: the "Pearly King," "Pearly Queen," "Lawyer" and the "Fish Porter," who in the famous Billingsgate Fish Market tradition, is carrying a basket of fish on his head. They were produced for only one year and are rarely seen and highly sought after.

Backstamp: **A.** Unmarked (1-4)
B. Black and gold label "Genuine Wade Porcelain" (1-4)

No.	Name	Description	Size	U.S. $	Can. $	U.K. £
1	Pearly King	White pearlised suit, cap: yellow brim	68 x 28	160.00	210.00	100.00
2a	Pearly Queen	White pearlised dress, jacket; yellow ribbon; lower hat brim black	68 x 38	200.00	265.00	100.00
2b	Pearly Queen	Blue/pink pearlised dress; lower hat brim pink	68 x 38	200.00	265.00	100.00
3	Lawyer	White wig; black gown, shoes; brown base	68 x 28	250.00	330.00	145.00
4a	Fish Porter	Pearlised fish; black hat, badge and shoes; green tie; blue trousers; and base	75 x 28	235.00	300.00	125.00
4b	Fish Porter	Pearlised fish; black hat, green tie; blue badge, trousers; and base; brown shoes	75 x 28	235.00	300.00	125.00

CHILD STUDIES

1962

Child Studies was a short-lived set of four children in national costumes, representing England, Ireland, Scotland and Wales. Each model stands on a circular base, which has an embossed flower design on it.

Their issue date was spring 1962, and they sold for an original price of 21/- each.

Backstamp: **A.** Unmarked (1-4)
B. Blue transfer "Wade England" (1-4)

No.	Name	Description	Size	U.S. $	Can. $	U.K. £
1	English Boy	Yellow hair; black hat; red jacket; blue waistcoat; grassy base	120 x 40	450.00	600.00	300.00
2	Irish Girl	Green kilt; shamrock base	115 x 40	775.00	1,000.00	520.00
3	Scots Boy	Blue kilt; black tam, jacket; thistle base	120 x 40	450.00	600.00	300.00
4	Welsh Girl	Striped skirt; chequered shawl; daffodil base	135 x 40	450.00	600.00	300.00

CHILDREN AND PETS

1993-1994

Children and Pets is a series comprising three figures modelled by Ken Holmes. Each is a limited edition of 2,500 and is numbered on its base. The first model, "Welcome Home," was issued in June 1993, "Fireside Friend" was produced in the latter half of 1993 and "Togetherness" was issued in late autumn 1994. The models have polished wood bases with recessed tops shaped in the same outline as the figure above.

Children and Pets was sold direct from the Wade pottery as a mail order and was limited to two models per customer. The original price was £25.00 each.

Backstamp: Black transfer "Wade Limited Editions [name of model] Modelled by Ken Holmes"

No.	Name	Description	Size	U.S.$	Can.$	U.K.£
1	Welcome Home	Yellow jacket; brown trousers; white/black dog	100 x 125	65.00	90.00	45.00
2	Fireside Friend	Pink blanket; brown or black ears	90 x 110	65.00	90.00	45.00
3	Togetherness	Green skirt, ribbon; white/grey dog	130 x 95	65.00	90.00	45.00

DINOSAUR COLLECTION

1993

The *Dinosaur Collection* was issued in the wake of a series of documentary films about dinosaurs and the popular movie, *Jurassic Park*, released in early 1993. The subject stirred the imagination of the public, and it sparked the revival of dinosaur exhibits and a subsequent flood of dinosaur toys and models. This set of five models was issued in July 1993.

Backstamp: Embossed "Wade England"

No.	Name	Description	Size	U.S.$	Can.$	U.K.£
1	Camarasaurus	Brown/honey	50 x 45	9.00	12.00	6.00
2	Euoplocephalus	Red-brown/beige	28 x 50	9.00	12.00	6.00
3	Spinosaurus	Beige; grey spines	45 x 60	9.00	12.00	6.00
4	Protoceratops	Brown	30 x 50	9.00	12.00	6.00
5a	Tyrannosaurus Rex	Brown/honey	50 x 60	9.00	12.00	6.00
5b	Tyrannosaurus Rex	Grey; greenish brown base	50 x 60	9.00	12.00	6.00
—	5 pce set	Boxed	—	45.00	60.00	30.00

DRUM BOX SERIES

1957-1959

In the advertising literature of the time, Wade called this set the *Animal Band*, later changing it to the *Drum Box* series. The set consists of five comical animals, four playing a musical instrument and the fifth, "Dora" the donkey, is the soprano. They were sold in round cardboard drum-design boxes, from which the series got its name. The original price for each model was 3/11d. They were issued in May 1957 and discontinued in spring 1959.

Backstamp: Unmarked

No.	Name	Description	Size	U.S. $	Can. $	U.K. £
1	Jem	Red collar; grey trousers; black tie, eye patch	45 x 25	100.00	135.00	50.00
2	Clara	White dress; yellow stripes; brown cello	50 x 25	100.00	135.00	50.00
3	Harpy	Blue dress; mauve/white harp	45 x 28	100.00	135.00	50.00
4	Trunky	White shirt, trousers; black tie	50 x 35	110.00	140.00	50.00
5	Dora	White dress; red hem; yellow base	55 x 25	160.00	210.00	80.00

FAWN MONEY BOX

FIRST VERSION

Circa 1963

This figure is different from "Bambi," a *Disney Blow Up*, and has a coin slot in the back. It is believed that a few other *Disney Blow Ups* were remodeled as money boxes. There are unconfirmed reports of a "Lady Money Box," "Jock Money Box" and "Thumper Money Box," but no visual or written evidence has been found. Because of high production costs, only a limited number of the "Fawn Money Box" were made.

Backstamp: A. Unmarked
B. Black transfer "Made in England"

No.	Name	Description	Size	U.S. $	Can. $	U.K. £
1	Fawn	Brown; orange-brown patches	120 x 105	100.00	130.00	65.00

FAWN MONEY BOX
SECOND VERSION
1987

In 1987 Wade issued three money boxes based on the earlier "Fawn Disney Kennel" and "Noddy Toadstool Cottage" money boxes. Because the original moulds were worn, Wade made new moulds, which produced larger, heavier and less delicate-looking models than the originals. New colours were also used. These models were sold in plain, unmarked boxes. For other moneyboxes see Leprechauns & Pixies and Whimsie-Land (see pages 27 and 134).

Backstamp: **A.** Black "Wade Made in England" (1)
B. Black "Wade England" on cap that covers hole in base (1)

No.	Name	Description	Size	U.S.$	Can.$	U.K.£
1	Fawn	Light brown; brown markings	130 x 125	45.00	60.00	30.00

FLYING BIRDS

1956-1961

Wade produced two sets in the *Flying Birds* series, "Swallows" and "Swifts." They were issued in white, with green, yellow, blue or beige wings and heads. These models were first produced in England, then their production was moved to Wade (Ulster) Ltd. The *Flying Birds* series was sold in boxed sets of three models of the same colour. The "Swifts" models were the last production run and are harder to find. The original price for a set of three "Swallows" was 5/9d, which was later increased to 5/11d.

FIRST ISSUE: WADE ENGLAND

SET ONE: SWALLOWS

1956-1960

Backstamp: Unmarked

No.	Description	Size	U.S. $	Can. $	U.K. £
1a	Beige wings, tail	65 x 68	20.00	26.00	12.00
1b	Blue wings, tail	65 x 68	20.00	26.00	12.00
1c	Green wings, tail	65 x 68	20.00	26.00	12.00
1d	Grey wings, tail	65 x 68	20.00	26.00	12.00
1e	Salmon pink wings, tail	65 x 68	20.00	26.00	12.00
1f	Yellow wings, tail	65 x 68	25.00	30.00	15.00
—	Boxed set (3)	65 x 68	45.00	60.00	35.00
—	Boxed set (3—yellow)	65 x 68	65.00	85.00	40.00

SET TWO: SWIFTS

1958-1959

The original price for three "Swifts" was 6/11d.

Backstamp: Unmarked

No.	Description	Size	U.S. $	Can. $	U.K. £
1a	Blue wings, tail	86 x 76	28.00	38.00	24.00
1b	Green wings, tail	86 x 76	28.00	38.00	24.00
1c	Grey wings, tail	86 x 76	28.00	38.00	24.00
1d	Yellow wings, tail	86 x 76	28.00	38.00	24.00
1e	Beige wings, tail	86 x 76	28.00	38.00	24.00
—	Boxed set (3)	86 x 76	80.00	100.00	60.00

SECOND ISSUE: WADE ULSTER

Following the production of the *Flying Birds* series in the George Wade Pottery, the models were made by Wade (Ulster) Ltd. As with the George Wade production, two sets were made. In this case, however, the numbers of the sets were reversed. Set 1 was now the "Swifts;" set 2 was the "Swallows."

SET ONE: SWIFTS

1960-1961

The original price for three "Swifts" was 6/11d.

Backstamp: Unmarked

No.	Description	Size	U.S. $	Can. $	U.K. £
1a	Blue head, wings	86 x 76	28.00	38.00	24.00
1b	Yellow head, wings	86 x 76	28.00	38.00	24.00
—	Boxed set (3)	—	90.00	120.00	55.00

SET TWO: SWALLOWS

1960-1961

On the front of the original box was printed, "Flying Birds Made in Ireland by Wade Co. Armagh, The Mourne Range of Porcelain Miniatures." "The Mourne Range of Wade Porcelain Miniatures" is on the end of the box and inside is "No. 2 The Mourne Range of Porcelain Miniatures, Made in Ireland by Wade Co. Armagh." The original price for a box of three "Swallows" was 5/11d per boxed set.

Backstamp: Unmarked

No.	Description	Size	U.S. $	Can. $	U.K. £
1a	Beige wings, tail	65 x 68	20.00	26.00	12.00
1b	Blue wings, tail	65 x 68	20.00	26.00	12.00
1c	Green wings, tail	65 x 68	20.00	26.00	12.00
1d	Grey wings, tail	65 x 68	20.00	26.00	12.00
1e	Yellow wings, tail	65 x 68	20.00	26.00	12.00
—	Boxed set (3)	—	80.00	100.00	50.00

THE FISH WAITER

June 1998

This model of a fish dressed as a Waiter and holding a plate in his left fin was first available from the Wade shop and was also sold at the Arundel and Buffalo shows. Original cost was £15.00.

Backstamp: Black Printed "Genuine Wade Porcelain"

No.	Name	Description	Size	U.S. $	Can. $	U.K. £
1	Fish Waiter	Grey fish; green eyes; black coat, bow tie; white vest; brown trousers; tan feet; orange base	140	35.00	50.00	25.00

GOODY BOXES

1998-1999

A *Goody Box* of randomly packed previously issued Wade models was offered to members of the O.I.W.C.C. in October 1998. Telephone orders only were accepted for the box which cost £35.00 and contained Wade models guaranteed to be a minimum value of £60.00. The first 500 purchasers of the *Goody Box* would receive a new model. Only available in the *Goody Box* was a model named "Rosie The Kitten": 400 were produced in honey glaze and 100 in white glaze.

ROSIE THE KITTEN

October 1998

Backstamp: Embossed "Wade England" in recessed base.

No.	Name	Description	Size	U.S. $	Can. $	U.K. £
1a	Rosie the Kitten	Honey; black eyes	115	60.00	90.00	40.00
1b	Rosie the Kitten	White; black eyes	115	300.00	400.00	195.00

FIZZY THE FAWN

October 1999

After the success of the 1998 *Goody Box*, Wade again offered one for 1999 that cost £35.00. The first 525 UK purchasers would receive a new model only available in the *Goody Box* called "Fizzy the Fawn." Four hundred and fifty of the models were in a honey glaze and 75 were in a white glaze.

Backstamp: Embossed "Wade England"

No.	Name	Description	Size	U.S. $	Can. $	U.K. £
1a	Fizzy the Fawn	Honey; black eyes, nose	95	45.00	60.00	30.00
1b	Fizzy the Fawn	White; black eyes, nose	95	150.00	200.00	95.00

THE HONEY BUNCH BEARS

1998

A set of three teddy bears named the *Honey Bunch* was introduced at the Trentham Gardens show on March 22nd 1998. The models were later available from the Wade Shop. The original cost was £18.00 for the set.

SET ONE

Backstamp: Embossed "Wade"

No.	Description	Colourways	Size	U.S. $	Can. $	U.K. £
1	Bear with arms raised with Bee on chest	honey; black / white Bee	55	10.00	18.00	9.00
2	Bear Sitting with Bee on Face	Honey; black/white Bee	57	10.00	18.00	9.00
3	Bear with Honey pot & Bee on Shoulder	Honey; black/ white Bee	57	10.00	18.00	9.00

SET TWO

A second set of *Honey Bunch Bears* was introduced at the combined Wade and Jim Beam Fair held in Buffalo on the weekend of July 18-19th 1998. The cost was £18.00 for the set.

No.	Description	Colourways	Size	U.S. $	Can. $	U.K. £
4	Bear Lying with Sunglasses	Honey; black sunglasses	55	10.00	18.00	9.00
5	Bear Sleeping with Bee	Honey; black/white Bee	55	10.00	18.00	9.00
6	Bear Sitting Waving with Bee on hip	Honey; black/white Bee	57	10.00	18.00	9.00

HORSE SETS

1974-1981

Two sets of horses were produced intermittently between 1974 and 1981. Each set comprised a "Mare" and her two foals. Although the models were sold with black and gold "Wade England" labels stuck on the bases, most of them either peeled off or wore off. But even without labels, the distinctive Wade glaze and their ribbed bases make these models easily recognizable.

SET ONE

1974-1981

Backstamp: **A.** Unmarked (1-3)
B. Black and gold label "Wade England" (1-3)

No.	Name	Description	Size	U.S.$	Can.$	U.K.£
1	Mare	Dark brown; light brown face	75 x 76	15.00	25.00	6.00
2	Foal, Lying	Dark brown; light brown face	32 x 55	15.00	25.00	6.00
3	Foal, Standing	Dark brown; light brown face	48 x 48	15.00	25.00	6.00
—	3 pce set	Boxed	—	45.00	60.00	22.00

SET TWO

1978-1981

Backstamp: A. Unmarked (1-3)
B. Black and gold label "Wade England" (1-3)
C. Embossed "Wade England" on rim (1-3)

No.	Name	Description	Size	U.S.$	Can.$	U.K.£
1	Mare	Honey; light brown mane	65 x 70	50.00	70.00	25.00
2	Foal, Lying	Honey; light brown mane	30 x 46	50.00	70.00	25.00
3	Foal, Sitting	Honey; light brown mane	38 x 38	50.00	70.00	25.00
—	3 pc set	Boxed	—	90.00	120.00	60.00

KISSING BUNNIES

Circa 1948-1950s

Care has to be taken when purchasing unmarked *Kissing Bunnies* models, as they were also produced by Sylvac and copied by other ceramic manufacturers including those in Japan.

Kissing Bunnies, large eyes

Kissing Bunnies, small eyes

Backstamp: Black transfer print "Wade England"

No.	Description	Size	U.S. $	Can. $	U.K. £
1a	White bunny; beige bunny; large eyes	64 x 80	135.00	180.00	90.00
1b	White bunny; grey bunny; large eyes	64 x 80	135.00	180.00	90.00
1c	White bunny; grey bunny; white tail; large eyes	64 x 80	135.00	180.00	90.00
1d	White bunny; grey ears, tail; brown bunny; white tail; small eyes	64 x 80	135.00	180.00	90.00
1e	White bunny; grey tail; grey bunny; large eyes	64 x 80	135.00	180.00	90.00

Kissing Bunnies Derivatives

Circa 1948

This ashtray is similar in design to a model produced by Sylvac in the late 1940s known as an "Angular ashtray with Kissing Rabbits," and carrying an impressed design No. of 1532.

Ashtray

Backstamp: Ink stamp "Made in England Reg No 824" (the rest of the numbers are missing)

No.	Name	Description	Size	U.S. $	Can. $	U.K. £
1	Kissing Bunnies	White and brown bunnies; light green tray	85	110.00	150.00	75.00

Posy Bowl

Backstamp: Green-brown ink stamp "Wade England"

No.	Name	Description	Size	U.S. $	Can. $	U.K. £
1a	Kissing Bunnies	Blue; bramble-ware mustard pot	70 x 87	110.00	150.00	75.00
1b	Kissing Bunnies	Cream; bramble-ware mustard pot	70 x 87	110.00	150.00	75.00
1c	Kissing Bunnies	Green; bramble-ware mustard pot	70 x 87	110.00	150.00	75.00
1d	Kissing Bunnies	White bunnies; black markings; large eyes; multi-coloured bramble-ware mustard pot, flower, base	70 x 87	145.00	170.00	85.00

MINIKINS

1955-1958

Minikins were issued in three separate series, with four different-shaped *Minikins* in each. They were sold to the retailer in boxes of 48 models (12 of each shape). *Minikins* were modelled by William Harper

The models are completely covered in white glaze, with decorative motifs on their bodies, different coloured ears and six eye styles. The combinations of eye expression, ear colour and body decoration could produce a total of 48 styles of *Minikins* in each set.

None of the *Minikins* was marked. Advertisements show that series B was offered for sale for Christmas 1956, and the demise of series C is mentioned in Wade's August 1958 "Wholesalers Newsletter." The original price was 1/- each.

MINIKINS SHOP COUNTER PLAQUE

1955-1958

These small half-circular plaques would have been used by the retailer in his shop display for *Minikins*, as they were not made for general sale. The wording on one plaque is "Porcelain Wade Minikins Made in England." On the other 1/- (One Shilling) each has been added to the plaque.

No Price

Price shown

Backstamp: None

No.	Description	Size	U.S. $	Can. $	U.K. £
1a	White; black lettering	28	300.00	400.00	150.00
1b	White; black lettering 1/- each	28	300.00	400.00	150.00

SERIES A: CATS AND RABBITS

1955-1958

Cat Walking (left), Cat Standing (right)

Cat Walking

Backstamp: Unmarked

No.	Description	Size	U.S. $	Can. $	U.K. £
1a	White; blue ears, tail; black/brown eyes	20 x 38	30.00	40.00	14.00
1b	White; blue ears, tail; green & black eyes; red nose	20 x 38	30.00	40.00	14.00
1c	White; yellow ears, tail; black/brown eyes	20 x 38	30.00	40.00	14.00
1d	White; yellow ears, tail; black/green eyes	20 x 38	30.00	40.00	14.00

Cat Standing

Backstamp: Unmarked

No.	Description	Size	U.S. $	Can. $	U.K. £
2a	Brown; black eyes, nose	30 x 17	30.00	40.00	14.00
2b	White; green ears; black eyes, nose; blue patches	30 x 17	30.00	40.00	14.00
2c	White; green ears; black eyes; blue patches	30 x 17	30.00	40.00	14.00
2d	White; green ears; black/green eyes; blue patches	30 x 17	30.00	40.00	14.00
2e	White; yellow ears; black eyes; green starburst	30 x 17	30.00	40.00	14.00
2f	White; yellow ears; black eyes; red starburst	30 x 17	30.00	40.00	14.00
2g	White; yellow ears; black/green eyes; blue starburst	30 x 17	30.00	40.00	14.00
2h	White; yellow ears; black/green eyes; green daisy	30 x 17	30.00	40.00	14.00

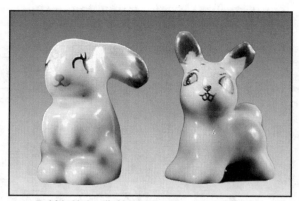

Rabbit Sitting (left), Narrow-Eared Rabbit (right)

Rabbit Sitting

Backstamp: Unmarked

No.	Description	Size	U.S. $	Can. $	U.K. £
3a	Brown; turquoise ears; black eyes, nose	30 x 18	30.00	40.00	14.00
3b	White; blue ears, nose; small black eyes	30 x 18	30.00	40.00	14.00
3c	White; green ears; eyes open; red nose; blue patch	30 x 18	30.00	40.00	14.00
3d	White; green ears; winking eyes; red nose; blue patch	30 x 18	30.00	40.00	14.00
3e	White; green/yellow ears; eyes open; red nose	30 x 18	30.00	40.00	14.00
3f	White; green/yellow ears; winking eyes; red nose	30 x 18	30.00	40.00	14.00
3g	White; turquoise ears, nose; small black eyes	30 x 18	30.00	40.00	14.00

Narrow-Eared Rabbit

Backstamp: Unmarked

No.	Description	Size	U.S. $	Can. $	U.K. £
4a	White; green ears; large black/brown eyes; black nose; blue patch	30 x 18	30.00	40.00	14.00
4b	White; yellow ears; large black eyes; red nose; blue patch;	30 x 18	30.00	40.00	14.00
4c	White; yellow ears; large black/brown eyes; black nose; blue patch	30 x 18	30.00	40.00	14.00
4d	White; yellow ears; large black eyes; red nose; blue OXO design	30 x 18	30.00	40.00	14.00
4e	White; yellow ears; large black eyes; red nose; green OXO design	30 x 18	30.00	40.00	14.00
4f	White; yellow ears; large black/brown eyes; red nose; green/red OXO design	30 x 18	30.00	40.00	14.00

SERIES B: BULL, COW, MOUSE AND RABBIT

1956-1958

Mouse   **Rabbit**   **Bull**   **Cow**

Bull

Backstamp: Unmarked

No.	Description	Size	U.S. $	Can. $	U.K. £
1a	Brown; small black eyes, nose; black spot (front and back)	20 x 25	30.00	40.00	14.00
1b	Brown; small black eyes, nose; black spot/yellow X (back and front)	20 x 25	30.00	40.00	14.00
1c	White; small black eyes, nose; black spot (front and back)	20 x 25	30.00	40.00	14.00
1d	White; large black/blue eyes; black nose; black spot/yellow X (front and back)	20 x 25	30.00	40.00	14.00
1e	White; green hair; large black eyes, nose; green daisy (front); red/green L-plate (back)	20 x 25	30.00	40.00	14.00
1f	White; green hair; black eyes, nose; green heart/blue arrow (front); orange heart/green arrow (back)	20 x 25	30.00	40.00	14.00
1g	White; green hair; large black eyes, nose; orange daisy (front); black daisy (back)	20 x 25	30.00	40.00	14.00
1h	White; green hair; black eyes, nose; red/blue notes (front); orange heart/blue arrow (back)	20 x 25	30.00	40.00	14.00
1i	White; green hair; large black eyes, nose; red/blue notes (front); red/green L-plate (back)	20 x 25	30.00	40.00	14.00
1j	White; green hair; large black eyes, nose; red/blue notes (front); red/blue L-plate (back)	20 x 25	30.00	40.00	14.00
1k	White; green hair; large black eyes, nose; red/blue notes (front); red L-plate (back)	20 x 25	30.00	40.00	14.00
1l	White; yellow hair; black eyes, nose; blue/green notes (front); blue heart/yellow arrow (back)	20 x 25	30.00	40.00	14.00
1m	White; yellow hair; black eyes, nose; blue/green notes (front); red/green L-plate (back)	20 x 25	30.00	40.00	14.00
1n	White; yellow hair; large black eyes; red heart / blue arrow front; red L back	20 x 25	30.00	40.00	14.00
1o	White; yellow hair; large brown eyes; blue and yellow flower;(front) red musical notes with green lines (back)	20 x 25	30.00	40.00	14.00

Cow

Backstamp: Unmarked

No.	Description	Size	U.S. $	Can. $	U.K. £
2a	White; green ears; black eyes; blue nose; orange daisy (front); blue daisy (back)	22 x 20	30.00	40.00	14.00
2b	White; green ears; black eyes; blue nose; orange/green notes (front) orange heart & blue arrow (back)	22 x 20	30.00	40.00	14.00
2c	White; pink ears; black eyes; red nose; red daisy (front); red heart/ green arrow (back)	22 x 20	30.00	40.00	14.00
2d	White; yellow ears; black eyes; blue nose; orange/blue notes (front); orange heart/green arrow (back)	22 x 20	30.00	40.00	14.00
2e	White; yellow ears; black eyes; blue nose; red heart/arrow (front);) yellow daisy (back	22 x 20	30.00	40.00	14.00
2f	White; yellow ears; black eyes; red nose; blue daisy (front); orange L (back)	22 x 20	30.00	40.00	14.00
2g	White; yellow ears; black eyes; red nose; blue daisy (front); red/ blue notes (back)	22 x 20	30.00	40.00	14.00
2h	White; yellow ears; black eyes; red nose; green daisy (front); red daisy (back)	22 x 20	30.00	40.00	14.00
2i	White; yellow ears; black eyes; red nose; blue heart/green arrow (front); blue daisy (back)	22 x 20	30.00	40.00	14.00
2j	White; yellow ears; black eyes; blue nose; red heart and green arrow (front); red & blue notes (back)	22 x 20	30.00	40.00	14.00

Mouse

Backstamp: Unmarked

No.	Description	Size	U.S. $	Can. $	U.K. £
3a	Brown; small black eyes, nose	25 x 23	30.00	40.00	14.00
3b	Brown; small black eyes, nose; dark blue patch	25 x 23	30.00	40.00	14.00
3c	White all over	25 x 23	25.00	35.00	12.00
3d	White; small black eyes, nose; blue patch	25 x 23	30.00	40.00	14.00
3e	White; green ears, nose; large black eyes; orange daisy (front); green daisy (back)	25 x 23	30.00	40.00	14.00
3f	White; green ears, nose; large black eyes; orange/green notes (front); orange daisy (back)	25 x 23	30.00	40.00	14.00
3g	White; green ears, nose; large black eyes; red/green L-plate (back and front)	25 x 23	30.00	40.00	14.00
3h	White; pink ears; large black eyes; green nose; blue/red notes (front); blue daisy (back)	25 x 23	30.00	40.00	14.00
3i	White; pink ears; large black eyes; green nose; blue heart/green arrow (front); blue daisy (back)	25 x 23	30.00	40.00	14.00
3j	White; yellow ears; large black eyes; orange nose; blue/green notes (front); red/blue notes (back)	25 x 23	30.00	40.00	14.00
3k	White; yellow ears; large black eyes; orange nose; green daisy front; green heart/blue arrow back	25 x 23	30.00	40.00	14.00
3l	White; yellow ears; large black eyes; blue nose; red L (front); orange L (back)	25 x 23	30.00	40.00	14.00
3m	White; yellow ears; large black eyes; orange nose; orange daisy (front); orange/blue notes (back)	25 x 23	30.00	40.00	14.00

Narrow-Eared Rabbit (left), Wide-Eared Rabbit (right)

Wide-Eared Rabbit

Backstamp: Unmarked

No.	Description	Size	U.S. $	Can. $	U.K. £
4a	White; green ears; blue nose; red/green flower (front); red heart/ blue arrow (back)	25 x 20	30.00	40.00	14.00
4b	White; green ears; red nose; red heart/green arrow (front); blue heart/ green arrow (back)	25 x 20	30.00	40.00	14.00
4c	White; pink ears; black nose; orange daisy (front); orange L (back)	25 x 20	30.00	40.00	14.00
4d	White; pink ears; black nose; red L-plate (front and back)	25 x 20	30.00	40.00	14.00
4e	White; yellow ears; blue/green notes (front); green heart/blue arrow (back)	25 x 20	30.00	40.00	14.00
4f	White; yellow ears; red heart/blue arrow (front and back)	25 x 20	30.00	40.00	14.00

SERIES C: DOG, DONKEY, FAWN AND PELICAN

1957-1958

Pelican   Fawn   Dog   Donkey

Dog

Backstamp: Unmarked

No.	Description	Size	U.S. $	Can. $	U.K. £
1a	White; blue ears; small black/blue eyes; blue collar	28 x 15	30.00	40.00	16.00
1b	White; blue/green ears; small black/blue eyes; orange flowers; blue collar	28 x 15	30.00	40.00	16.00
1c	White; green ears; large black/blue eyes; red/green collar	28 x 15	30.00	40.00	16.00
1d	White; green ears; small black/blue eyes; orange/red flowers; no collar	28 x 15	30.00	40.00	16.00
1e	White; green ears; small black/blue eyes; red/green collar	28 x 15	30.00	40.00	16.00
1f	White; pink ears; small black/blue eyes; orange/pink collar	28 x 15	30.00	40.00	16.00
1g	White; yellow ears; small black/blue eyes; orange/yellow collar	28 x 15	30.00	40.00	16.00

Donkey

Backstamp: Unmarked

No.	Description	Size	U.S. $	Can. $	U.K. £
2a	White; green ears; large black/blue eyes; pink/blue garland	35 x 20	30.00	40.00	16.00
2b	White; green ears; large black/blue eyes; red flower (front)	35 x 20	30.00	40.00	16.00
2c	White; pink ears; large black/blue eyes; red flower (front)	35 x 20	30.00	40.00	16.00
2d	White; pink ears; large black/blue eyes; red/yellow flower garland	35 x 20	30.00	40.00	16.00
2e	White; pink ears; large black/yellow eyes; red/yellow garland	35 x 20	30.00	40.00	16.00
2f	White; yellow ears; large black/blue eyes; red flower (front)	35 x 20	30.00	40.00	16.00
2g	White; yellow ears; large black/blue eyes; pink/blue garland	35 x 20	30.00	40.00	16.00
2h	White; yellow ears; large black/yellow eyes; red/yellow garland	35 x 20	30.00	40.00	16.00

Fawn

Backstamp: Unmarked

No.	Description	Size	U.S. $	Can. $	U.K. £
3a	White; green ears, tail; black/blue eyes; yellow flower	28 x 20	25.00	40.00	15.00
3b	White; green ears, tail; black/yellow eyes; yellow heart; red arrow	28 x 20	25.00	40.00	15.00
3c	White; pink ears, tail; black/blue eyes; blue flowers/heart/notes	28 x 20	25.00	40.00	15.00
3d	White; pink ears; black/blue eyes; yellow flower	28 x 20	25.00	40.00	15.00
3e	White; pink ears; black/yellow eyes; yellow flower	28 x 20	25.00	40.00	15.00
3f	White; yellow ears, tail; black/blue eyes; blue flowers/heart/notes	28 x 20	25.00	40.00	15.00
3g	White; yellow ears, tail; black/yellow eyes; red flower	28 x 20	25.00	40.00	15.00

Pelican

Backstamp: Unmarked

No.	Description	Size	U.S. $	Can. $	U.K. £
4a	White; black/blue eyes; blue wings, feet, anchor	30 x 15	30.00	40.00	15.00
4b	White; black/blue eyes; green wings, feet; blue anchor	30 x 15	30.00	40.00	15.00
4c	White; black/blue eyes; pink wings, feet; blue anchor	30 x 15	30.00	40.00	15.00
4d	White; black/blue eyes; yellow wings, feet; blue anchor	30 x 15	30.00	40.00	15.00
4e	White; black/blue eyes; green wings, feet; black waistcoat; red bowtie	30 x 15	30.00	40.00	15.00
4f	White; black/blue eyes; pink wings, feet; black waistcoat; red bowtie	30 x 15	30.00	40.00	15.00
4g	White; black/blue eyes; yellow wings, feet; black waistcoat; red bowtie	30 x 15	30.00	40.00	15.00
4h	White; black/blue eyes; yellow wings, feet; blue waistcoat; red bowtie	30 x 15	30.00	40.00	15.00

MR. & MRS. SNOWMAN CRUET

1997

The *Mr. and Mrs. Snowman Crue*t was available from the O.I.W.C.C. magazine in November 1997. The original price was £17.50

Backstamp: Gold printed "Wade England" between two gold lines

No.	Name	Description	Size	U.S.$	Can.$	U.K.£
1	Mr. Snowman	Black hat, buttons; green white striped scarf	100	12.00	17.00	9.00
2	Mrs. Snowman	Black hat; grey brown collar; brown muff	95	12.00	17.00	9.00

NENNIE SCOTTISH TERRIER

1996

Originally commissioned by Ms. F. Shoop (Ficol), "Nennie" was the first model in an intended series of Scottish dogs issued in a limited edition of 2,000 to raise funds for the STECS (Scottish Terrier Emergency Care Scheme). Unfortunately the series was cancelled and "Nennie," who was modelled on a rescued Scottish terrier, was sold by Wade Ceramics at the Wade Fair in Birmingham in April 1996 for £25.00.

Backstamp: White printed "Nennie produced exclusively for Ficol by Wade," print of 2 Scottie dogs and the edition No. in gold.

No.	Description	Size	U.S.$	Can.$	U.K.£
1	Black; grey streaks; pale blue collar; gold disc	125 x 165	65.00	90.00	45.00

POCKET PALS

October 1999

Pocket Pals, which were introduced in October 1999, are produced from the same moulds as the 1960s/1980s "Happy Families." The models used are the "Mother" animals from the Cat, Dog, Elephant, Frog, Giraffe, Hippo, Mouse, Owl, Pig, and Rabbit Happy Families. The models were sold attached by double sided tape on a card base at a cost of £5.50. For Cat model named "Tango" please see C&S Collectables page 260 for Frog model "Hopper" and Dog model "Woofit" please see *Collect It!* Magazine page 272.

Backstamp: Gold transfer print "Wade Pp" in shield

No.	Description		Size	U.S.$	Can.$	U.K.£
1	Cat Slinky	Dark brown body; honey face/chest; blue eyes	45 x 35	9.00	12.00	6.00
2	Dog Waggs	White; black patches; brown eyes	55 x 35	8.00	11.00	5.50
3	Elephant Tusker	Pale pink; pink ears; blue eyes	35 x 70	9.00	12.00	6.00
4	Frog Hip Hop	Dark green; green spots; blue eyes	25 x 45	9.00	12.00	6.00
5	Giraffe Stretch	Apricot; blue eyes	60 x 45	9.00	12.00	6.00
6	Hippo Paddles	Pink; blue eyes	35 x 50	9.00	12.00	6.00
7	Mouse Cheesy	Khaki; pink ears; blue eyes; brown tail	50 x 28	9.00	12.00	6.00
8	Owl Specs	Brown; off white; yellow eyes	40 x 40	9.00	12.00	6.00
9	Pig Truffle	White; tan brown patches; blue eyes	28 x 65	9.00	12.00	6.00
10	Rabbit Bounce	White; black patches; pink ears; brown eyes	55 x 30	9.00	12.00	6.00

RULE BEARTANNIA

1999

This nine-piece set of "Royal Teddy Bears" was produced by Wade and issued in the United States in early 1999 and were modelled by a well-known American artist Jerome Walker.

King Velveteen, Queen Beatrice, Queen Mum   Royal Guard

Prince Tedward, Princess Tedwina, Princess Plushette,Nanny   Rule Beartannia Plaque

Backstamp: Gold printed "© Jerome Walker Wade" with name of model

No.	Description	Colourways	Size	U.S.$	Can.$	U.K.£
1	King Velveteen	Red and gold crown; red cloak; pale blue and white edged robe; gold sceptre	165	75.00	110.00	50.00
2	Queen Beatrice	Green and gold crown; pearl earrings and necklace; green and white cloak; pale blue dress; gold sceptre; gold and white orb	150	75.00	110.00	50.00
3	Queen Mum	Pink hat, handbag and dress; dark blue and white cloak; gold spectacles	120	58.00	88.00	40.00
4	Prince Tedward	White sailor hat; dark blue and white sailor suit; gold telescope; white base	97	46.00	70.00	35.00
5	Princess Tedwina	Pale blue bonnet with dark red, pink and blue flowers; pale blue dress; pearl ribbon bow; white base	127	46.00	70.00	35.00
6	Princess Plushette	White bonnet with dark red and pink flowers; yellow dress; holding dark red and pink flower posy; white base	97	46.00	70.00	35.00
7	Nanny Fluffins and Baby Velveteena	Yellow hat with dark blue band; white dress with dark blue band; pale blue shawl; babies pram and base	130	70.00	105.00	55.00
8	Royal Guard	Black helmet and shoulder epaulettes with gold trim; dark red jacket; gold trim; gold trumpet; dark blue trousers; black shoes; white base	115	56.00	85.00	43.00
9	Rule Beartannia Plaque	White; multi coloured bears; bee and honey pot print; red and black lettering	125	17.00	25.00	12.00

SHAMROCK POTTERY

1956-1984

In 1956 Wade Ireland introduced a small series of models known as the *Shamrock Pottery Series*. It consisted of the "Irish Comical Pig," "The Pink Elephant," "Shamrock Cottage," "Pixie Dish" and the "Donkey and Cart Posy Bowl." The last three models were reissued between 1977 and the early 1980s. (For "Pixie Dish" and "Shamrock Cottage" see Leprechauns and Pixies section. For "Donkey and Cart Posy Bowl," see *The Charlton Standard Catalogue of Wade, Volume Two: Decorative Ware*).

IRISH COMICAL PIG

1956-1961

The *Irish Comical Pig*, made by Wade (Ulster) Ltd., is found in several different combinations of back patterns and nose and tail colours. The original selling price was 2/6d each. The places of interest named on the back are written in black lettering.

Backstamp: Green transfer print "Shamrock Pottery Made in Ireland"

No.	Name	Description	Size	U.S. $	Can. $	U.K. £
1a	Daisy Pattern	Green/orange daisy; orange nostrils; yellow tail	45 x 65	75.00	95.00	38.00
1d	Daisy Pattern	Green/orange daisy; yellow nostrils, tail	45 x 65	75.00	95.00	38.00
1b	Daisy Pattern	Green/orange daisy; green nostrils, tail	45 x 65	75.00	95.00	38.00
1c	Daisy Pattern	Green & orange daisy; yellow nostrils; orange tail	45 x 65	75.00	95.00	38.00
1d	Loop Pattern	Orange loops; green stars, lines; brown eyes; green nostrils, tail	45 x 65	75.00	95.00	38.00
1e	Shamrocks	Black Pig; green	45 x 65	75.00	95.00	38.00
1f	Shamrocks	White; green nostrils, tail, shamrocks	45 x 65	75.00	95.00	38.00

TOWN NAMES

No.	Name	Description	U.S.$	Can.$	U.K.£
1g	Canterbury	Green nostrils, tail; black lettering	75.00	95.00	38.00
1h	Eastbourne	Green nostrils; yellow tail; black lettering	75.00	95.00	38.00
1i	Henley on Thames	Green nostrils; yellow tail; black lettering	75.00	95.00	38.00
1j	Holy Island	Black pig; gold decal Holy Island	75.00	95.00	38.00
1k	Hunstanton	Green nostrils; yellow tail; black lettering	75.00	95.00	38.00
1l	Isle of Wight	Green nostrils; yellow tail; black lettering	75.00	95.00	38.00
1m	Llandudno	Green nostrils; yellow tail; black lettering	75.00	95.00	38.00
1k	Old Smithy Godshill	Green nostrils, tail; black lettering	75.00	95.00	38.00
1n	Penmaenmawr	Green nostrils yellow tail; black lettering	75.00	95.00	38.00
1o	Stratford-Upon-Avon	Green nostrils, tail; black lettering	75.00	95.00	38.00
1p	Stratford-Upon-Avon	Green nostrils; yellow tail; black lettering	75.00	95.00	38.00
1q	Windermere	Green nostrils; yellow tail; black lettering	75.00	95.00	38.00
1r	York	Green nostrils; yellow tail; black lettering	75.00	95.00	38.00

PINK ELEPHANT

1956-1961

The *Pink Elephant*, made by Wade (Ulster) Ltd., is found with several different slogans on its back associated with the consumption of too much alcohol. Some have names of places of interest. Originally, these models sold for 2/6d each.

Backstamp: Green transfer print "Shamrock Pottery Made in Ireland"

No.	Description	Size	U.S. $	Can. $	U.K. £
1a	Bournemouth; pink; orange nostrils, tail	40 x 80	65.00	85.00	38.00
1b	Devils Bridge; pink; green nostrils, tail	40 x 80	65.00	85.00	38.00
1c	Henley on Thames; pink; green nostrils, tail	40 x 80	65.00	85.00	38.00
1d	Isle of Wight; pink; orange nostrils, tail	40 x 80	65.00	85.00	38.00
1e	Never Again; pink; green nostrils, tail	40 x 80	65.00	85.00	38.00
1f	Never Again; pink; orange nostrils, tail	40 x 80	65.00	85.00	38.00
1g	Never Mix Em! pink; green nostrils, tail	40 x 80	65.00	85.00	38.00
1h	Oh! My Head; pink; green nostrils, tail	40 x 80	65.00	85.00	38.00
1i	Old Smithy Godshill pink; green nostrils, tail	40 x 80	65.00	85.00	38.00
1j	Pale pink	40 x 80	65.00	85.00	38.00
1k	Ramsgate; pink; orange nostrils, tail	40 x 80	65.00	85.00	38.00
1l	Salisbury; pink; green nostrils, tail	40 x 80	65.00	85.00	38.00
1m	Stick to Water; pink; green nostrils, tail	40 x 80	65.00	85.00	38.00

SNIPPETS

1956-1957

Snippets models are thin, flat outlines of a figure with a rectangular porcelain box on the back, which enables the model to stand. It was a new idea by Wade, one which was not very successful at the time. Only two sets of three models were produced. Because of this and the fact that they are easily broken, these models are rare.

Set One was a set of three 15th, 16th and 17th century sailing ships, modelled as an outline of the ships and enameled in bright colours. The three ships are in graduated sizes.

SET ONE: SAILING SHIPS

1956

Backstamp: A. Black transfer "Wade Snippet No. 1 Mayflower Carried 102 Pilgrims to North America 1620 Real Porcelain Made In England" (1)
B. Black transfer "Wade Snippet No. 2 Santa Maria Flag ship of Columbus 1492 Real Porcelain Made In England" (2)
C. Black transfer "Wade Snippet No. 3 Revenge Flag ship of Sir Richard Grenville 1591 Real Porcelain Made in England" (3)

No.	Name	Description	Size	U.S. $	Can. $	U.K. £
1	The Mayflower	Brown; yellow sails; red flags; blue/white waves	58 x 60	65.00	85.00	45.00
2	The Santa Maria	Brown; green sails; red/yellow flags; blue/white waves	45 x 50	65.00	85.00	45.00
3	The Revenge	Brown; red sails; yellow flags; blue/white waves	35 x 45	65.00	85.00	45.00
—	3 pce set	Boxed	—	200.00	250.00	130.00

SET TWO: HANSEL AND GRETEL

1957

Set Two comprises three characters from the fairy tale, "Hansel and Gretel."

Backstamp: A. Black transfer "Wade Snippet No. 4 Hansel Real Porcelain Made in England" (4a, 4b)
B. Black transfer "Wade Snippet No. 5 Gretel Real Porcelain Made in England" (5)
C. Black transfer "Wade Snippet No. 6 Gingy Real Porcelain Made in England" (6)

No.	Name	Description	Size	U.S. $	Can. $	U.K. £
1a	Hansel	Yellow stockings; grey-blue trousers, jacket; red shirt, toadstools	64 x 42	165.00	250.00	110.00
1b	Hansel	Green stockings; grey-blue trousers, jacket; red shirt, toadstools	64 x 42	165.00	250.00	110.00
2	Gretel	Yellow pigtail, apron; blue shoe; green grass; red toadstools	56 x 42	165.00	250.00	110.00
3	Gingy the Bear	Brown/beige; red toadstools	32 x 20	180.00	275.00	135.00
—	3 pce set	Boxed	—	500.00	700.00	350.00

COLOUR AND SHAPE VARIATIONS

Colour Variations

Few colour variations are seen in the older Wade giftware models. These modifications could be the result of a decorator's whim, colour substitutions, or not using a second coat of glaze colour over the base coat. In cases where an older model has been re-issued, the original glaze colours for the ears, mouth and eyes are no longer available and different colours were used.

There are many more colour variations to be found in the commissioned models, especially in the Red Rose and Tom Smith models. Some models may appear to be a lighter or darker colour, due to the number of coats of glaze applied before firing. True colour variations are difficult to discern: as a guide, they should be a totally different shade of colour, such as turquoise, blue and royal blue, and not just a lighter or darker version of the same shade. Some colours used are so close in shade that they are difficult to tell apart — i.e. light grey, pale grey and grey — yet when seen together there is a definite difference (see the colour plates for a wide selection of colour variations for different models.)

Shape Variations

Variations in model style are due to the replacement of worn or broken dies (moulds). The majority of these variations are found in the Red Rose Tea and Tom Smith models. Some typical shape variations concern the size of models (i.e. the Red Rose "Bison," "Hippo" and "Pig"), which can be impressed or embossed on the base or rim, and be a total backstamp such as "Wade England," or the partial "Wade Eng."

Variations also include slight shape changes of the models, for example the "Rabbit" with open ears or closed ears, or the "Queen of Hearts" with small or large hearts. All of these colour and shape variations help to make Wade collecting more exciting as collectors search for that elusive different coloured or shaped model.

Some common examples of shape variations are as follows:

Model	Shape Variation	Reason
Bear Cub	Type One - circular recessed base Type Two - flat base	——
Beaver	Type One - circular recessed base Type Two - flat base	——
Bison	Found in more than one size	Replacement of broken dies
Bushbaby	Type One - circular recessed base Type Two - flat base	——
Circus Tiger	Type One - mouth slightly open; less detail in fur of throat and chest Type Two - mouth open wider; more detail in fur of throat and chest (beard-like)	New mould
	Type One - "Wade England" backstamp Type Two - "Wade Eng" backstamp	New mould
Crocodile	Type One - circular recessed base Type Two - circular base slightly raised	——

Note: The following initials indicate the origin of the models used in the colour plates:

EW:	*English Whimsies*	RRU:	Red Rose Tea (USA)
RRC:	Red Rose Tea (Canada)	TS:	Tom Smith models

Model	Shape Variation	Reason
Hedgehog	Type One - deep recessed base with three pads around the rim Type Two - shallow recessed base with two pads, one at either end of the rim	———
Hippo	Found in more than one size	Replacement of broken dies
Kodiak Bear	Type One - no gap between legs Type Two - slightly smaller; gap between legs	———
Langur	Type One - no gap between the head and tree stump; space under left arm Type Two - gap between the head and tree stump; space under the left arm Type Three - gap betwen head and tree stump; no space under the left arm	New dies used
Old King Cole	Type One - v-shaped gap in base between feet Type Two - no gap in base	———
Owl	Type One - circular recessed base Type Two - flat base	
Pig	Found in more than one size	Replacement of broken dies
Queen of Hearts	Type One - two large hearts on dress Type Two - two small hearts on dress Type Three - eight small hearts on dress	———
Rabbit	Type One - ears closed Type Two - ears open	New dies used
Squirrel	Type One - circular recessed base Type Two - flat base	———
Tortoise - Father	Type One - open back; slotted projection on tail that fits into base; small pads on bottom of feet; embossed mould Nos. 1 and 5 Type Two - closed back; projection below tail; bottom of feet are smooth; embossed mould No.4	Possibly produced in two potteries (Type One - Wade England, Type Two - Wade Ireland)

MOULD VARIATIONS

CIRCUS TIGER

FRONT

Without Beard (TS)   With Beard (RRU)

BACK

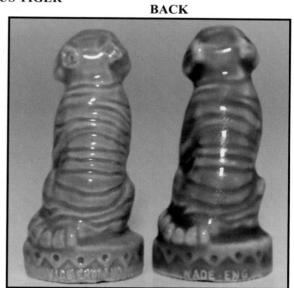

"Wade England" (TS)   "Wade Eng" (RRU)

OWL

Recessed Base (RRC)   Flat Base (RRU)   Ribbed Base (EW)

BEAR CUB

Recessed Base
(Unknown)   Ribbed Base (RRU)

COLOUR AND MOULD VARIATIONS

SCAMP

Hat Box Series   Disney

BAMBI

Hat Box Series   Disney

PEG

Hat Box Series   Disney

TRAMP

Standing, Hat Box Series   Sitting, Disney

DACHIE/DACHSIE

Dachie, Hat Box Series   Dachsie, Disney

JOCK

Hat Box Series   Disney

COLOUR AND MOULD VARIATIONS

LARGE FAWNS

Disney Blow Up "Bambi"   Fawn Money Box, First Version   Fawn Money Box, Second Version

LANGUR (REAR VIEW)

Neck Touches Stump, Space Under Arm (EW)   Gap Between Head and Stump, Space Under Arm (RRU)   Gap Between Head and Stump, No Space Under Arm (RRU)

HEDGEHOG

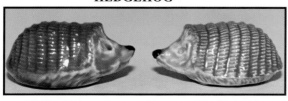

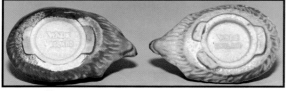

Shorter Snout, Two Pads on Base   Longer Snout, Three Pads on Base

OSCAR THE CHRISTMAS TEDDY BEAR

Red Hat (Trentham Gardens, 1997-1998)   Green Hat (Buffalo, 1998)

COLOUR AND MOULD VARIATIONS

RHINO

Grey/Green (EW)	Grey (TS)

WHELK

Honey Brown (King Aquariums Ltd.)	Blue (TS)

POODLE

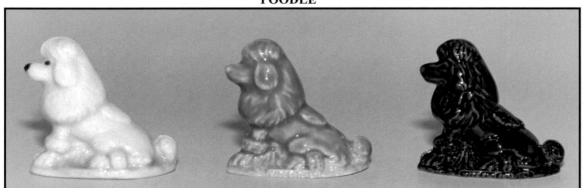

White (RRC)	Apricot (TS)	Black (Patty Keenan)

SEAL ON ROCK

Beige/Blue (RRC)	Blue (TS)	Dark Brown (TS)

PANDA

First Whimsies

Large	Small

COLOUR VARIATIONS

HUSKY

Grey/Green (EW)　　　　　　White (TS)

BLUEBIRD

Beige/Blue (RRC, EW)　　　　Beige (RRU)　　　　Blue (TS)

DUCK SWIMMING

White (TS)　　　　Blue (TS)　　　　Beige (TS)　　　　Light Blue (Unknown)

COLOUR VARIATIONS

FROG

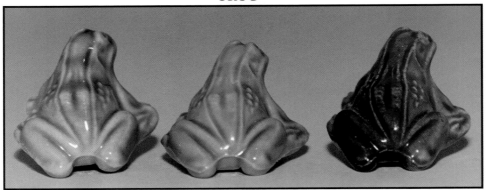

Green (RRC)   Yellow (RRC)   Brown (EW)

LANGUR

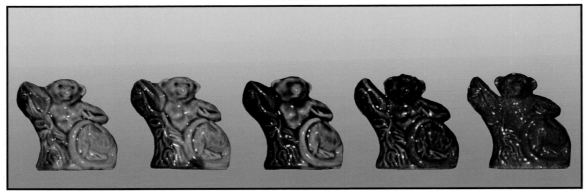

Beige/Brown/Green (EW)   Beige/Brown (RRC)   Light/Dark Brown (TS)   Dark Brown (RRU)   Brown (Unknown)

HARE

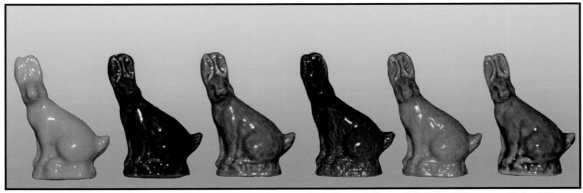

White (TS)   Dark Brown (RRU)   Honey (TS)   Light Brown (TS)   Pale Beige (TS)   Beige (TS)

COLOUR VARIATIONS

ZEBRA

Black (EW)   Beige/Green (EW)   Grey (TS)   Light Grey (RRU)

BISON

Brown/Honey - Large (RRC)   Brown/Honey - Small (RRC, EW)   Dark Brown (TS)   Honey (Unknown)

SQUIRREL

Dark Blue (RRU)   Red-Brown (TS)   Blue (TS)

WALRUS

Beige/Grey (EW)   Beige (TS)   Honey (TS)

COLOUR VARIATIONS

MONGREL

Dark/Light Brown (EW)   Grey/Blue (TS)

ORANG-UTAN

Ginger (EW)   Brown (TS)   Dark Brown
(RRC, RRU)

POLAR BEAR

Beige/Blue-Grey (TS)   White/Blue (EW)   White (TS)

GRIZZLY CUB

Light Brown (First Whimsies)   White (First Whimsies)   Brown (First Whimsies)

COLOUR VARIATIONS

MINIKINS

Narrow-Eared Rabbit

Pelican (left), Fawn (right)

Rabbit Sitting (right view)

Rabbit Sitting (left view)

COLOUR VARIATIONS

MINIKINS

Mouse (front view)

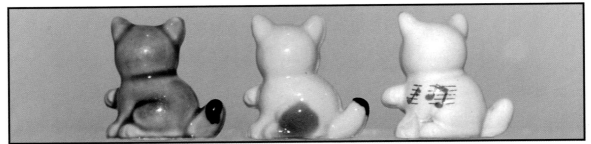

Mouse (rear view)

Mouse (front view)

Mouse (rear view)

COLOUR VARIATIONS

MINIKINS

Bull (front view)

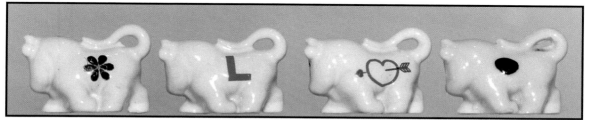

Bull (rear view)

Cow (front view)

Cow (rear view)

COLOUR VARIATIONS

MINIKINS

Wide-Eared Rabbit (front view)

Wide-Eared Rabbit (rear view)

Cat Walking

Cat Standing

Dog

COLOUR VARIATIONS

FROG

Mother Frog, Happy Families (left), Wade Pocket Pal "Hip Hop" (centre), Collect-It! Pocket Pal "Hopper" (right)

HIPPO

Mother Hippo, Happy Families — First Issue (left), Second Issue (centre), Wade Pocket Pal "Paddles" (right)

GIRAFFE

Mother Giraffe, Happy Families — First Issue (left), Second Issue (centre), Wade Pocket Pal "Stretch" (right)

COLOUR VARIATIONS

CAT

Variations of Mother Cat, Happy Families —
Wade Pocket Pal "Slinky" (left),
C&S Pocket Pal "Tango" (right)

DOG

Variations of Mother Dog, Happy Families —
Wade Pocket Pal "Waggs" (left),
Collect It! Pocket Pal "Woofit" (right)

OWL

Mother Owl, Happy Families (left),
Wade Pocket Pal "Specs" (right)

RABBIT

Mother Rabbit, Happy Families — First Issue (left),
Second Issue (centre), Wade Pocket Pal "Bounce" (right)

LUCKY LEPRECHAUNS

Brown and Flesh-Coloured Faces — Cobbler (left), Crock O'Gold (centre), Tailor (right)

COLOUR VARIATIONS

GORILLA

Beige/Blue (New Whimsies)

HIPPO

Light/Dark Blue (New Whimsies)

LEOPARD

Pale Honey/Green (New Whimsies)

Grey (EW)

Honey Brown (EW)

Yellow/Brown/Green (EW)

SAFARI PARK LION

Honey/Bright Green (New Whimsies)

MOLE

Light Grey/Green (New Whimsies)

RACOON

Light Grey/Black (New Whimsies)

Honey/Green (TS)

Dark Grey (TS)

Brown/Green-Grey (TS)

COLOUR VARIATIONS

ROCKING HORSE

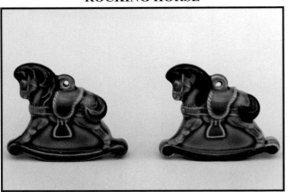

Patty Keenan — Grey (left), Honey (right)

SEAL PUP

English Whimsies (left), Wade Enrol A Friend Club (right)

FATHER, TORTOISE FAMILY

Brown/Blue   Green

BEAR CUB

Beige/Grey (RRC)   Beige/Grey (EW)   Honey (Unknown)   Beige (RRU)

THE TORTOISE FAMILY

1958-1988

Wades first tortoise, the "Large (Father)," was issued in January 1958, and it proved so popular that the following January Wade introduced two more, the "Medium (Mother)" and "Small (Baby)," which were sold as a pair. These three models were so successful that they were produced almost continuously for the next thirty years. Considered by Wade as their best-selling line, this family of tortoises is in plentiful supply. The original price for the "Large (Father)" was 4/6d the pair of "Medium (Mother)" and "Small (Baby)" cost 4/9d.

In 1973 the "Jumbo" tortoise was added to the family. It was modelled differently from the other tortoises, however, and resembles a turtle. Because it was not in production for as long as the rest of the *Tortoise Family*, it is harder to find. The "Large (Father)" and the "Jumbo" tortoises are the only ones in this series to have lift-off shells. The numbers 1 through 8 were embossed on the bases of model 3, which refer to the production tool used to press the model. Production tools usually lasted for one to three years before having to be replaced; therefore, the models with the lowest numbers should be the oldest.

Version One: Recessed Back   **Version Two: Full Back**

182

Baby, Mother and Father

Jumbo Turtoise

Backstamp: A. Embossed "Wade Porcelain Made in England No. 3" (1, 2, 3)
   B. Embossed "Wade Made in England" (4)

No.	Name	Description	Size	U.S. $	Can. $	U.K. £
1a	Small (Baby)	Brown/blue	25 x 45	10.00	15.00	8.00
1b	Small (Baby)	Green/blue	25 x 45	50.00	60.00	30.00
1c	Small (Baby)	Green	25 x 45	52.00	70.00	35.00
2a	Medium (Mother)	Brown/blue	35 x 75	15.00	25.00	10.00
2b	Medium (Mother)	Green/blue	35 x 75	45.00	60.00	30.00
2c	Medium (Mother)	Green	35 x 75	60.00	80.00	40.00
3a	Large (Father Type 1)	Beige; /blue	50 x 105	18.00	25.00	12.00
3b	Large (Father Type 2)	Brown/blue	50 x 105	15.00	20.00	8.00
3c	Large (Father)	Green/blue	50 x 105	60.00	80.00	40.00
3d	Large (Father)	Green	50 x 105	65.00	90.00	45.00
4	Jumbo	Beige/blue	65 x 150	75.00	100.00	45.00

The Tortoise Family Derivatives

1958-1984

The *Tortoise Ash Bowls* are large and round, with a scintillite, high-gloss finish. An embossed reptile-skin design covers the inside, and a model from the *Tortoise Family* set is fixed to the inside curve of the bowl. The ash bowl with the "Medium (Mother)" tortoise was issued in January 1958 for 12/6d. The ash bowl with the "Small (Baby)" tortoise was produced from 1975 to 1984.

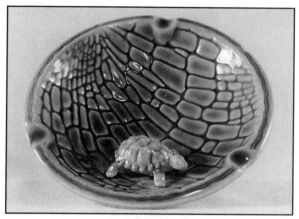

Ash Bowls

Backstamp: **A.** Impressed "Wade Porcelain Made in England" (1a, 1b)
B. Large embossed "Wade Made in England"(2a, 2b)

No.	Description	Size	U.S. $	Can. $	U.K. £
1a	Ash bowl with Medium (Mother) tortoise; brown/blue	55 x 183	55.00	70.00	30.00
1b	Ash bowl with Medium (Mother) tortoise; green/blue	55 x 183	55.00	70.00	30.00
2a	Ash bowl with Small (Baby) tortoise; brown/blue	45 x 145	45.00	60.00	28.00
2b	Ash bowl with Small (Baby) tortoise; green/blue	45 x 145	45.00	60.00	28.00

The Tortoise Family Derivatives

1976

The round tortoise ash bowls were such a successful line that Wade introduced a new oblong bowl in 1976. This bowl had feet and was embossed with a reptile-skin design and finished with a high-gloss finish. The "Medium (Mother)" tortoise figure was used on this bowl.

Footed Oblong Bowl

Backstamp: Large embossed "Wade Made in England"

No.	Description	Size	U.S. $	Can. $	U.K. £
1	Medium (Mother) tortoise; beige/blue	150 x 100	60.00	80.00	30.00

Souvenir Tortoises

Wade retooled the "Medium (Mother)" tortoise from the *Tortoise Family* series by cutting a recess in the back of the model and inserting the name of a British colony resort in embossed letters in the top shell.

Backstamp: Embossed "Wade Porcelain Made in England"

No.	Name	Description	Size	U.S.$	Can.$	U.K.£
1	Bahamas	Bahamas on shell; brown; blue markings	35 x 75	30.00	40.00	15.00
2	Bermuda	Bermuda on shell; brown; blue markings	35 x 75	30.00	40.00	15.00
3	Bermuda Triangle	Bermuda Triangle on shell; brown; blue markings	35 x 75	30.00	40.00	15.00
4	Devil's Hole, Bermuda	Devils Hole, Bermuda on shell; brown; blue markings	35 x 75	30.00	40.00	15.00

Note: See page 271 for a commissioned set of tortoises for *Ciba Geigy* that is another derivative of the *Tortoise Family*.

TREASURES SET

1957-1959

The *Treasures* set was the first in an intended series, but unfortunately for collectors, no more sets were put into production. It consists of a set of five white elephants in varying sizes, with bright pink blankets decorated with orange, yellow, blue and green flowers. Early advertising material calls the set *Elephant Chains* and *Elephant Train*.

The original price for a box of five elephants was 10/6d.

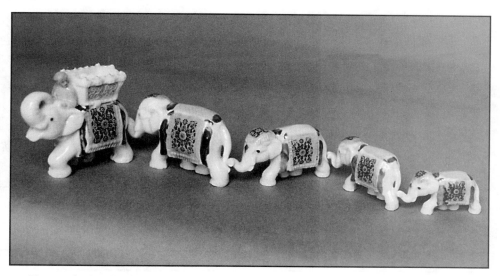

Backstamp: Blue transfer "Wade England"

No.	Name	Description	Size	U.S. $	Can. $	U.K. £
1	Large Elephant	White; pink blanket; howdah and mahout; blue turban	47 x 63	150.00	200.00	85.00
2	Medium Elephant	White; pink blanket; gold tassel	35 x 57	150.00	200.00	75.00
3	Small Elephant	White; pink blanket; gold tassel	28 x 54	135.00	180.00	65.00
4	Tiny Elephant	White; pink blanket; gold tassel	24 x 45	135.00	180.00	65.00
5	Miniature Elephant	White; pink blanket; gold tassel	20 x 39	135.00	180.00	65.00
—	5 pce set	Boxed	—	700.00	930.00	375.00

VARIOUS NOVELTY MODELS

1955-1960

The issue date for these models is late 1955. Although Wade advertisements suggest that they were in production for five years, they are hard to find and are considered rare.

Backstamp: **A.** Embossed "Wade" (1, 2)
B. Embossed "Wade Ireland" (on 2b Dustbin Cat)
C. Unmarked (3, 4, 5)
D. Black and gold label "Wade England" (3, 4, 5)

No.	Name	Description	Size	U.S. $	Can. $	U.K. £
1	Bernie and Poo	One white/brown; one white/blue	55 x 75	170.00	225.00	80.00
2a	Dustbin Cat	White cat; beige dustbin	45 x 25	200.00	260.00	100.00
2b	Dustbin Cat	White cat; grey dustbin	45 x 25	200.00	260.00	100.00
3	Jonah in the Whale	Blue jacket; white whale	40 x 40	1,200.00	1,600.00	800.00
4	Jumbo Jim	Blue hat, tears	45 x 25	180.00	240.00	90.00
5a	Kitten on the Keys	Grey cat; white blue spotted shirt; white trousers	30 x 35	235.00	310.00	130.00
5b	Kitten on the Keys	White cat	30 x 35	235.00	310.00	130.00

WATER LIFE COLLECTION

1997

Alligater, Goldfish, Whale

Backstamp: Black printed (on Whale) and red printed (on goldfish and alligator) "Wade Made in England"

No.	Name	Description	Size	U.S.$	Can.$	U.K.£
1	Alligator	Green	25 x 65	15.00	20.00	7.00
2	Goldfish	Orange fish; blue grey, orange streaked water	50 x 40	15.00	20.00	7.00
3	Whale	Light blue whale; blue waves	47 x 70	15.00	20.00	7.00

Hermit Crab, Octopus, Seahorse

Backstamp: Gold "Wade England" between two gold lines

No.	Name	Description	Size	U.S.$	Can.$	U.K.£
4	Hermit Crab	Orange crab; grey blue waves	30	15.00	20.00	7.00
5	Octopus	Grey octopus; sea green-blue waves	50	15.00	20.00	7.00
6	Seahorse	Beige seahorse; dark blue waves	30	15.00	20.00	7.00

ALICE IN WONDERLAND
1999

FAIRS AND EVENTS

ALTON TOWERS FAIR - 1998

Wade held their Extravaganza in a Marquee at Alton Towers, a "Theme Park" in Staffordshire, U.K., on November 22nd, 1998.

Bears Just Want To Have Fun

Size:	Unknown
Colour:	Amber bear; yellow shirt; red bow; dark blue dungarees; pale blue shoes; white base
Issued:	November 1998 in a limited edition of 500
Issue Price:	£25.00
Series:	Baby Bears
Backstamp:	"Bears Just Want To Have Fun Limited Edition of 500 Wade" with Alton Towers logo

Description	U.S. $	Can. $	U.K. £
Bears Just Want to Have Fun	65.00	90.00	45.00

Once Upon a Time Teddy Bears Money Box

Twenty of these models were held for the Wade/I.A.J.B.B.S.C. show held in San Antonio, Texas, in July 1999.

Size:	157mm
Colour:	Papa - brown; dark blue dressing gown; brown slippers; Boy - brown; light blue pyjamas
Issued:	Novemer 1998 in a limited edition of 120
Issue Price:	£150.00
Backstamp:	"Once Upon a Time-Wade England 1998 Limited Edition of 120"

Description	U.S. $	Can. $	U.K. £
Once Upon a Time Money Box	275.00	390.00	185.00

Panda Bear Plaque

Size:	195mm
Colour:	Black and white; white plaque with red lettering
Issued:	November 1998
Issue Price:	£20.00
Backstamp:	"Wade England Extravaganza 1998"

Description	U.S. $	Can. $	U.K. £
Panda Bear Plaque	35.00	50.00	28.00

ARUNDEL SWAP MEETS
ARUNDEL WADE SWAP MEET - 1997

GENERAL ISSUE
Arundel Duck

Size:	95mm
Colour:	1 Creamy white
	2 Dull yellow
Issued:	1 1997 in a limited edition of 100
	2 1997 in a limited edition of 1,400
Issue Price:	1 £20.00
	2 £15.00
Backstamp:	"O.I.W.C.C." (logo) and The Arundel Duck August 1997

Colourway	U.S. $	Can. $	U.K. £
1 Creamy white	225.00	300.00	175.00
2 Dull yellow	95.00	130.00	65.00

Creamy White Arundel Duck

ONE-OF-A-KIND
Various

Special one-of-a-kind coloured models were auctioned and given as prizes at the Wade Arundel Swap Meet in August 1997.

Size:	See below
Colour:	See below
Issued:	1997
Backstamp:	"Arundel Swap Meet" with O.I.W.C.C. logo

Pantomime Dame

	Name	Colourways	Size
1a	Arundel Duck	Blue duck; greenish base	95
1b	Arundel Duck	Green duck; greenish base	95
1c	Arundel Duck	Orange duck; greenish base	95
2	Christmas Teddy Bear	Red hat; white trim; brown bear; blue sack	110
3	Dick Whittington's Cat	Unknown	110
4	Felicity Squirrel	Orange	105
5	Mother Goose	White; green bonnet, ribbon; white bloomers; black shoes; yellow beak red/white striped socks	110
6	Pantomime Dame	Brown hair; green bow and shoes; blue dress with striped shoulders; striped handbag	110
7	Pantomime Dame	Green dress	Unknown
8	Rufus	Red brown dog; green cushion; gold trim	65 x 84
9	Water Life Goldfish and Whale	Goldfish: white face; orange body black tipped fin/tail; Whale: Unknown	50 x 40 47 x 70
10	Water Life Alligators	Unknown	25 x 65

Note: Since these are unique, or one-of-a-kind pieces, the price must be determined between the buyer and seller.

Betty Boop Wall Plaque

This one-of-a-kind model was the first prize in the Treasure Hunt.

Size:	95mm
Colour:	White moon; pearlized dress; yellow earrings and bracelet; brown dog"Pudgy"
Issued:	1997
Backstamp:	Gold printed "Wade England"

Daddy Bear - Arundel Bran Tub

Daddy Bear (Bran Tub Draw and Prize Draw)

Two one-of-a-kind *Daddy Bears* were prizes in the Bran Tub and Prize Draw held in Arundel. Other one-of-a-kind *Daddy Bears* were won at Trentham Gardens and Wisconsin.

Size:	1	105mm
	2	105mm
Colour:	1	Dark blue jacket; white bow tie with blue knot and lines; blue waistcoat; brown spoon/bowl; green and blue striped trousers
	2	Dark blue jacket; white bow tie; dark blue striped waistcoat; red spoon/bowl; dark and light blue striped trousers
Issued:		1997
Backstamp:		Unknown

Daddy Bear - Arundel 1997 Prize Draw

Note: Since these are unique, or one-of-a-kind pieces, the price must be determined between the buyer and seller.

GENERAL ISSUE
Arundel Bunny

Size:	55 x 110mm
Colour:	1 Honey brown; green ears; brown eyes/nose
	2 White; blue ears; black eyes/nose
Issued:	1 1998 in a limited edition of 1,400
	2 1998 in a limited edition of 100
Issue Price:	1 £25.00
	2 £25.00
Backstamp:	Embossed "Wade England" and printed "The Official International Wade Collectors Club the Arundel Bunny July 1998" with O.I.W.C.C. logo

Colourway	U.S. $	Can. $	U.K. £
1 Honey brown	65.00	90.00	45.00
2 White	285.00	350.00	175.00

Arundel Bunny - Honey Brown

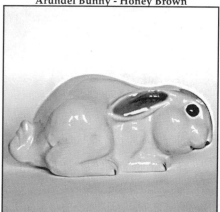

Arundel Bunny - White

Teddy Bear Plaque

The *Teddy Bear Plaque* was produced in four different colourways during 1998 for the Ripley Castle, Arundle, Buffalo and Wade Christmas Extravaganza shows.

Size:	195mm
Colour:	Caramel brown bear and plaque; dark green paw pads; black lettering
Issued:	1998 in a limited edition of 1,500
Issue Price:	£20.00
Backstamp:	Gold printed "Wade England Swap Meet 1998"

Description	U.S. $	Can. $	U.K. £
Teddy Bear Plaque	35.00	50.00	28.00

Toy Soldier, Camping Bear

Chuckles the Clown, Cornish Tin Mine

Emily the Doll

ONE-OF-A-KIND MODELS
Various

Size:	See below
Colour:	See below
Issued:	1998
Backstamp:	Unknown

	Name	Description	Size
1	Camping Bear (Teddy Bears Picnic)	Brown bear; light brown pack; pale blue jacket; black trousers; brown boots; white base	115
2	Chuckles the Clown (Toy Box)	Black hat, shoes and bow-tie; green coat; yellow spotted trousers; grey chair	115
3	Cornish Tin Mine Pixie	Brown hat; black eyebrows; dark green coat; brown trousers; gold hammer; black shoes with gold buckles	110
4	Emily the Doll (Toy Box)	White hat; yellow hair; green dress with pink bands; black shoes	85
5	Toy Soldier (Toy Box)	Red helmet and jacket; pale blue plume and epaulettes; green trousers; black boots; white base	110

Note: Since these are unique, or one-of-a-kind pieces, the price must be determined between the buyer and seller.

GENERAL ISSUE
Arundel Chick

Size:	78mm
Colour:	1 Honey
	2 White
Issued:	1 1999 in a limited edition of 900
	2 1999 in a limited edition of 100
Issue Price:	1 £15.00
Backstamp:	Printed "The Arundel Chick Arundel 1999" with the O.I.W.C.C. logo

	Colourway	U.S. $	Can. $	U.K. £
1	Honey	50.00	65.00	30.00
2	White	275.00	350.00	175.00

Arundel Honey Chick

Arundel White Chick

Puppy Love "Steino"

Size:	70 x 43mm
Colour:	White and brown; pink nose; blue ball; green base
Issued:	1999 in a limited edition of 500
Issue Price:	£20.00
Series:	Puppy Love (fourth in series)
Backstamp:	Black paw print with black and red lettering "Puppy L♥ve By Wade Puppy L♥ve Limited Edition 500 1999 Steino"

Description	U.S. $	Can. $	U.K. £
Steino	45.00	60.00	30.00

ONE-OF-A-KIND MODELS
Puck

Size:	114mm
Colour:	Black hair and hooves; brown tree stump with dark green top; flesh coloured body; gold flute and legs
Issued:	1999
Series:	Myths and Legends
Backstamp:	Unknown

Mummy and Daddy Bears

Size:	1 Mummy - 102mm
	2 Daddy - 105mm
Colour:	1 Honey bear; white and black cap, apron; pale blue dress
	2 Honey bear; black bow tie, trousers; white shirt with black cuffs; pale blue waistcoat
Issued:	1999
Backstamp:	Unknown

Bookend Bear

Given as the prize in the "Wade Word Search," this model was originally one of the Boots Bookends produced 1988-1989.

Size:	150mm
Colour:	Multi-coloured chintz on a white background
Issued:	1999
Backstamp:	Red printed "Wade England"

Note: Since these are unique, or one-of-a-kind pieces, the price must be determined between the buyer and seller.

BIRMINGHAM FAIRS

BIRMINGHAM FAIR - 1994

Spaniel

Commissioned by U.K. Fairs Ltd. for the first Official U.K. Wade Collectors Fair.

Size: 75 x 60mm
Colour: Honey brown
Issued: 1994 in a limited edition of 1,000
Issue Price: £12.50
Backstamp: Large embossed "Wade"

Description	U.S. $	Can. $	U.K. £
Spaniel	140.00	185.00	85.00

BIRMINGHAM FAIR - 1995

Grey-Haired Rabbit

Commissioned by U.K. Fairs Ltd. for the 1995 Official Wade Collectors Fair.

Size: 87 x 60mm
Colour: Grey-brown
Issued: 1995 in a limited edition of 1,250
Issue Price: £12.50
Backstamp: Embossed "Wade"

Description	U.S. $	Can. $	U.K. £
Grey-Haired Rabbit	110.00	150.00	70.00

BIRMINGHAM FAIR - 1996

Smiling Frog

Commissioned by U.K. Fairs Ltd. for the third Wade Collectors Fair.

Size: 60 x 80mm
Colour: Green
Issued: 1996 in a limited edition of 1,250
Issue Price: £12.50
Backstamp: Embossed "Wade"

Description	U.S. $	Can. $	U.K. £
Smiling Frog	80.00	105.00	50.00

COLLECT IT! FAIRS

NEWARK - 1998

Travelling Frog

Issued at Newark, August 1998.

Size: 135mm
Colour: Olive frog; red bag and cravat; green jacket; black belt; light grey base
Issued: 1998 in a limited edition of 2,500
Issue Price: £20.00
Backstamp: Black printed "Genuine Wade Porcelain Newark 1998"

Description	U.S. $	Can. $	U.K. £
Travelling Frog	45.00	60.00	30.00

STONELEIGH - 1998

Baby Bear In Pyjamas

Issued at the Royal Fairgrounds, Stoneleigh, Warwickshire, December 5th, 1998.

Size: 153mm
Colour: Brown bear; blue and white striped pyjamas; white base
Issued: 1998 in a limited edition of 1,000
Issue Price: £25.00
Backstamp: Gold printed "Baby Bear Collection, Baby Bear in Pyjamas-Limited edition of 1,000 Wade England"

Description	U.S. $	Can. $	U.K. £
Baby Bear in Pyjamas	42.00	60.00	30.00

Oops! The Bear
Version One

Two hundred and fifty models were sold at the Stoneleigh fair; the remaining 250 were sold at a Christmas Bonanza held by C&S Collectables in Arundel on December 6th, 1998.

Size: 60mm
Colour: Amber; pink plaster on knee
Issued: 1998 in a limited edition of 500
Backstamp: Printed "Oops! The Bear Wade England Ltd. Edition 500 1998"

Description	U.S. $	Can. $	U.K. £
Oops! the Bear (Version One)	65.00	80.00	40.00

Honey Bunch Bears

Approximately 40 of each of the six *Honey Bunch Bears* with the Bee transfer omitted were randomly decorated by freehand and sold at the *Collect It!* Fair wrapped in Christmas paper and shaped as Christmas Crackers. Some models were also available at the C & S Wade Bonanza (December 6th, 1998) and the San Antonio Wade Show (July 1999).

Size:	See below
Colour:	See below
Issued:	1998 in a limited edition of approximately 40 each
Issue Price:	£25.00
Backstamp:	Embossed "Wade"

Bear Sitting (two colourways)

	Name	Description	Size
1	Bear with Arms Raised	Honey; brown paw pads; blue pants	55
2	Bear with Honey Pot	Honey; brown paw pads; red vest gold honey pot	57
3	Bear with Honey Pot	Honey; gold collar and cuffs	57
4	Bear Sitting	Honey; gold collar and cuffs	57
5	Bear Sitting	Honey; red nose and mouth; red and blue spots	57
6	Bear Sleeping	Honey; pink night cap and collar	55

	Name	U.S. $	Can. $	U.K. £
1	Bear with Arms Raised	45.00	60.00	30.00
2	Bear with Honey Pot	45.00	60.00	30.00
3	Bear with Honey Pot	45.00	60.00	30.00
4	Bear Sitting	45.00	60.00	30.00
5	Bear Sitting	45.00	60.00	30.00
6	Bear Sleeping	45.00	60.00	30.00

Bear with Honey Pot (two colourways)

Bear with Arms Raised, Bear Sleeping

DUNSTABLE FAIRS

DUNSTABLE FAIR - 1996

Timid Mouse

Commissioned by U.K. Fairs Ltd.

Size:	60 x 100mm
Colour:	Light brown; black eyes and nose; green and brown base
Issued:	1996 in a limited edition of 1,750
Issue Price:	£18.00
Backstamp:	Embossed "Wade" with black printed "Limited Edition of 1,750 Exclusively for Dunstable Wade Fair 1996"

Description	U.S. $	Can. $	U.K. £
Timid Mouse	75.00	100.00	45.00

DUNSTABLE FAIR - 1997

Koala Bear

Size:	127mm
Colour:	Beige; black eyes and nose; brown tree; green leaves
Issued:	1 1997 in a limited edition of 1,500
	2 1997 in a limited edition of 150
Issue Price:	1 £20.00 2. £20.00
Backstamp:	A. Black printed "The Koala Bear 1 of 1,500 Exclusive Edition for Dunstable Wade Fair 1997 ©UK Fairs Ltd and WadeCeramics Ltd"
	B. Black printed "The Koala Bear 1 of 150 Exclusive Edition of Dunstable Wade Fair Special Produced Soley for Over-seas Wade Collectors ©UK Fairs Ltd & Wade Ceramics Ltd"
Series:	Australian Animals (second in series)

Description	U.S. $	Can. $	U.K. £
Koala Bear	65.00	90.00	45.00

DUNSTABLE FAIR - 1998

Cook Catkins

Size:	140mm
Colour:	1 Brown cat; blue dress; white apron; grey base
	2 Brown cat; blue dress; white apron with green lace/spots
Issued:	1 1998 in a limited edition of 1,500 (Comm. by UK Fairs Ltd and Wade Ceramics)
	2 1998 in a limited edition of 500 (Comm. by UK Fairs Ltd)
Issue Price:	1 £25.00 2. £25.00
Backstamp:	Printed "Cook Catkins 1 of 1,500 Eclusive Edition for the Dunstable Wade Fair 1998 UKWCO2 ©UK Fairs Ltd & Wade ®Ceramics Ltd
Series:	Catkins (second in series)

Colourway	U.S. $	Can. $	U.K. £
1 White apron	55.00	75.00	35.00
2 White/green apron	75.00	100.00	45.0

DUNSTABLE FAIR - 1999

British Lion

Commissioned by U.K. Fairs Ltd. This was a show special

Size:	160 x 120mm
Colour:	1 Tan; streaked brown mane; yellow/orange base
	2 Unknown (one-of-a-kind colourway)
Issued:	1 1999 in a limited edition of 340
	2 1999 in a limited edition of 10
Issue Price:	1 £30.00 2 £30.00
Backstamp:	Printed "Wade Limited Edition of 350 ©Wade Ceramics LTD ©UKI Ceramics LTD Produced Exclusively for UKI Ceramics LTD in an Exclusive World-wide Edition with Name of model and UKI Ceramics Tel No information."

Colourway	U.S. $	Can. $	U.K. £
1 Tan	55.00	75.00	35.00
2 Unknown		Unknown	

Puppy Love "Ella"

Size:	60 x 70mm
Colour:	White; black eyes and nose; tan patches
Issued:	1999 in a limited edition of 500
Issue Price:	£20.00
Series:	Puppy Love (fifth in series)
Backstamp:	Black paw print with black and red lettering "Puppy L♥ve By Wade Puppy L♥ve Limited Edition 500 1999 Ella"

Description	U.S. $	Can. $	U.K. £
Ella	40.00	55.00	25.00

Seals

Wade produced these two *Seals* using the original Jessie Van Hallen moulds (which she produced after her retirement from the Wade Pottery).

Size:	1 Curved Tail - 40 x 70mm
	2 Straight Tail - 30 x 70mm
Colour:	1 Grey; black eyes, whisker spots and nose
	2 Grey; black eyes and nose
Issued:	1999 in a limited edition of 750 (set of two)
Issue Price:	£30.00/set
Backstamp:	Printed "Wade England"

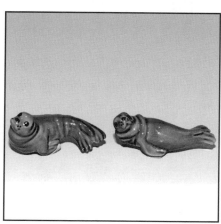

Description	U.S. $	Can. $	U.K. £
Seals - Set (2) (Boxed)	60.00	80.00	40.00

Shoal of Fish

Commissioned by U. K. Fairs Ltd. This was a show special.

Size:		140 x 130mm
Colour:	1	Orange; black eyes, gills and fins; white waves; blue base
	2	Unknown (one-of-a-kind colourway)
Issued:	1	1999 in a limited edition of 340
	2	1999 in a limited edition of 10
Issue Price:	1	£30.00
	2	£30.00
Backstamp:		Printed "Wade Limited Edition of 350 ©Wade Ceramics LTD ©UKI Ceramics LTD Produced Exclusively for UKI Ceramics LTD in an Exclusive World-wide Edition with Name of model and UKI Ceramics Tel No information."

Colourway	U.S. $	Can. $	U.K. £
1 Orange	55.00	75.00	35.00
2 Unknown		Unknown	

TRENTHAM GARDENS FAIRS

TRENTHAM GARDENS FAIR - 1997

GENERAL ISSUE- *Kangaroo*

Size:	127mm
Colour:	Orange-brown; green base
Issued:	1 1997 in a limited edition of 1,500
	2 1997 in a limited edition of 150
Issue Price:	£18.00
Series:	Australian Animals (first in series)
Backstamp:	**A.** Black printed "The Kangaroo 1 of 1,500 Exclusive Limited Edition For The Trentham Gardens Wade Fair 1997 ©UK Fairs LTD & Wade Ceramics LTD"
	B. Printed "The Kangaroo 1 of 50 Exclusive Edition of Trentham Gardens 1997 Wade Fair Special Produced solely for overseas Wade Collectors ©UK Fairs Ltd & Wade Ceramics Ltd"

Description	U.S. $	Can. $	U.K. £
Kangaroo	85.00	115.00	50.00

Rufus

Rufus was available at International Wade Collector Club venues throughout 1997.

Size:	65 x 84mm
Colour:	Red-brown; cobalt blue cushion
Issued:	1997
Issue Price:	£15.00
Series:	Wade on Tour (first in series)
Backstamp:	Printed "The Official International Wade Collectors Club Wade on Tour 1997"

Description	U.S. $	Can. $	U.K. £
Rufus	35.00	45.00	20.00

ONE-OF-A-KIND
Daddy Bear

This model was won at a prize draw at Trentham Gardens. Other one-of-a-kind *Daddy Bears* were won at Arundel and Wisconsin.

Size:	105mm
Colour:	Unknown
Issued:	1997
Backstamp:	Unknown

Note: Since this is a unique, or one-of-a-kind piece, the price must be determined between the buyer and seller.

Badges

CHRISTMAS EXTRAVAGANZA - 1997

Christmas Decorations and Badge Novelties

Wade Ceramics sold Christmas decorations and badge novelties at the Christmas Extravaganza held in Trentham Gardens in November 1997.

Badges

Wade Ceramics decorated plain white ceramic plaques with multi-coloured Christmas transfers, then added a pin on the back to convert them into Badges (pins).

Size:	50mm (diameter)
Colour:	See below
Issued:	1997
Issue Price:	£2.00
Backstamp:	Printed "Wade made in England"

	Name	Description
1	Santa on Roof with Sack and Tree	White; red and white suit; green gloves; brown boots
2	Santa Skating with	White; red and white suit; blue gloves;
3	Santa Walking	White; red and white suit; green gloves; black boots
4	Santa with Sack and List	White; red and white suit; green gloves; brown boots
5	Snowman Flying	White; black hat; red and green scarf
6	Snowman Laughing	White; black hat; red and green scarf

	Name	U.S. $	Can. $	U.K. £
1	Santa on Roof	5.00	7.00	4.00
2	Santa Skating	5.00	7.00	4.00
3	Santa Walking	5.00	7.00	4.00
4	Santa with Sack/List	5.00	7.00	4.00
5	Snowman Flying	5.00	7.00	4.00
6	Snowman Laughing	5.00	7.00	4.00

Tree Decoration Discs

Plain white ceramic discs, tap tops and lamp pulls were decorated with Christmas transfers and coloured ribbon, converting them into tree decorations.

Size:	63mm (diameter)
Colour:	1 Presents and garland transfer
	2 Windows and garland transfer
Issued:	1997
Issue Price:	£1.00
Backstamp:	Printed "Wade made in England"

	Colourway	U.S. $	Can. $	U.K. £
1	Presents/garland	5.00	7.00	4.00
2	Windows/garland	5.00	7.00	4.00

Tree Decoration Discs

Tree Decoration Lamp Pulls

Size:	1	40mm (1, 2, 3, 4, 6)
	2	38mm (5)
Colour:	See below	
Issued:	1997	
Issue Price:	£1.50	
Backstamp:	None	
Price:	See below	

	Name	Description
1	Children	White pull; multi-coloured print
2	Holly	White; green holly; red berries
3	Pine Tree	White pull; multi-coloured print
4	Present	White: multi-coloured print
5	Santa, large beard	White pull; multi-coloured print
6	Santa, small beard	White; red suit; green glove

	Name	U.S. $	Can. $	U.K. £
1	Children	5.00	7.00	4.00
2	Holly	5.00	7.00	4.00
3	Pine Tree	5.00	7.00	4.00
4	Present	5.00	7.00	4.00
5	Santa, large	5.00	7.00	4.00
6	Santa, small	5.00	7.00	4.00

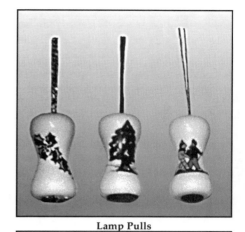

Lamp Pulls

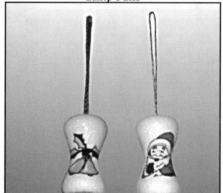

Tree Decoration Tap Caps

Size:	33mm (diameter)
Colour:	See Below
Issued:	1997
Issue Price:	£1.50
Backstamp:	None
Price:	See below

	Name	Description
1	Bells and Holly	White; green holly; red berries yellow bells
2	Christmas Crackers	White pull; multi-coloured print Decorations
3	Santa, large beard	White; red suit; green gloves
4	Santa, small beard	White; red suit; green gloves

	Name	U.S. $	Can. $	U.K. £
1	Bells and Holly	5.00	7.00	4.00
2	Christmas Crackers	5.00	7.00	4.00
3	Santa, large	5.00	7.00	4.00
4	Santa, small	5.00	7.00	4.00

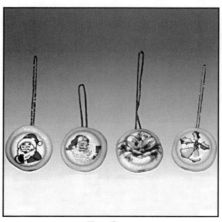

Tap Caps

ONE-OF-A-KIND

These models were auctioned at the 1997 Christmas Extravaganza in December.

Christmas Puppy

This was the 1995 membership model.

Size:	57mm
Colour:	Dark brown matt finish
Issued:	1997
Backstamp:	Red "Wade"

Cornish Tin Mine Pixie

Size:	110mm
Colour:	Black hat and shoes; green coat; brown trousers; gold hammer; silver buckle
Issued:	1997
Backstamp:	Unknown
Series:	Myths and Legends (yet to be released at time of auction)

Smudger

This was the 1997 membership model.

Size:	70mm
Colour:	Matt black; glossy eyes and nose
Issued:	1997
Backstamp:	Red "Wade"

Note: Since these are unique, or one-of-a-kind pieces, the price must be determined between the buyer and seller.

TRENTHAM GARDENS FAIR - MARCH 1998

GENERAL ISSUE

The City Gent Catkins

Some models appear to have a matt finish on their face. Commissioned by UK Fairs Ltd. and Wade Ceramics.

Size:	115mm
Colour:	Brown body; green eyes and base; light grey coat; dark grey pants; black shoes and cane
Issued:	1998 in a limited edition of 1,500
Issue Price:	£25.00
Series:	Catkins (first in series)
Backstamp:	Printed "The City Gent Catkins ® 1 of 1,500 Exclusive Limited Edition For The Trentham Gardens Wade Fair 1998 © UK Fairs LTD & Wade Ceramics LTD"

Description	U.S. $	Can. $	U.K. £
The City Gent	65.00	90.00	45.00

Out and About The Travelling Badger

This model was available at all Wade Events throughout 1998, and was introduced at this fair.

Size:	90mm
Colour:	Black and white badger; blue hat and coat; brown suitcase; green base
Issued:	1998
Issue Price:	£15.00
Backstamp:	Printed circular "The Official International Wade Collectors Club Travelling Badger Wade on Tour 1998"

Description	U.S. $	Can. $	U.K. £
Traveling Badger	35.00	45.00	20.00

ONE-OF-A-KIND

Pantomime Horse

This model was the Tombola prize at Trentham Gardens.

Size:	90mm
Colour:	Yellow; black stripes; green patch
Issued:	1998
Backstamp:	Unknown

Photograph not available at press time

Note: Since this is a unique, or one-of-a-kind piece, the price must be determined between the buyer and seller.

TRENTHAM GARDENS FAIR - 1999

Gypsy Catkins

Size:	140mm
Colour:	Brown cat; white shirt; blue trousers; maroon waistcoat; black scarf and shoes; blue base
Issued:	1999 in a limited edition of 1,000
Issue Price:	£20.00
Series:	Catkins (third model in series)
Backstamp:	Printed "Gypsy Catkins 1 of 1,000 Exclusive Limited Edition for the Trentham Wade Fair 1999 UKWCO3 ©UK Fairs & Wade® Ceramics Ltd"

Description	U.S. $	Can. $	U.K. £
Gypsy Catkins	55.00	70.00	35.00

Penguins

Wade produced these two *Penguins* using the original Jessie Van Hallen moulds (which she produced after her retirement from the Wade Pottery).

Size:	1 80mm
	2 60mm
Colour:	1 Black and white; yellow beak and ring around neck
	2 Black and white; yellow beak and ring around neck
Issued:	1999 in a limited edition of 750 (set of 2)
Issue Price:	£35.00/set
Backstamp:	Printed "Wade Made in England"

Description	U.S. $	Can. $	U.K. £
Penguins - Set (2) (Boxed)	90.00	120.00	50.00

Puppy Love "Sidney"

Size:	50mm
Colour:	Tan and white; brown nose; blue cushion
Issued:	1999 in a limited edition of 500
Issue Price:	£20.00
Series:	Puppy Love (first in series)
Backstamp:	Black paw print with black and red lettering "Puppy L♥ve By Wade Puppy L♥ve Limited Edition 500 1999 Sidney"

Description	U.S. $	Can. $	U.K. £
Sidney	45.00	60.00	30.00

THE TEDDY BEAR SHOW - 1998

Wade Ceramics attended the Teddy Scene Event at Alexandra Palace held on October 31st - November 1st, 1998.

Library Bear

Size:	165mm
Colour:	Amber; black hat with yellow band; gold bow tie; black and gold book base
Issued:	1998 in a limited edition of 500
Issue Price:	£30.00
Backstamp:	Gold printed "The Library Bear Limited edition of 500 Wade England"

Description	U.S. $	Can. $	U.K. £
Library Bear	65.00	90.00	45.00

U.S. WADE COLLECTORS SHOWS

The four U.S. Wade Collectors Shows (Seattle, Oconomowoc, Buffalo and San Antonio) were all held in conjuction with The Jim Beam Bottles and Specialty Clubs.

FIRST U.S. WADE COLLECTORS SHOW, SEATTLE, WASHINGTON - 1996

Westie the West Highland Terrier

Size:	75 x 78mm
Colour:	White; black eyes; pink tongue
Issued:	1996 in a limited edition of 3,000
Issue Price:	$20.00 US
Backstamp:	Printed black and red "The Official International Wade Collectors Club," and black "Seattle 1996"

Description	U.S. $	Can. $	U.K. £
Westie	45.00	60.00	40.00

SECOND U.S. WADE COLLECTORS SHOW, OCONOMOWOC, WISCONSIN - 1997

Madison Mouse

Size:	95 x 60mm
Colour:	Beige; pink ears and tongue; yellow cheese
Issued:	1997 in a limited edition
Issue Price:	$30.00 US
Backstamp:	Black and red circular "The Official International Wade Collectors Club Wisconsin 1997"

Description	U.S. $	Can. $	U.K. £
Madison Mouse	38.00	50.00	25.00

ONE-OF-A-KIND
Daddy Bear

This one-of-a-kind issue was the prize draw for Wisconsin; other one-of-a-kind *Daddy Bears* were won at Trentham Gardens and Arundel.

Size:	105mm
Colour:	Black hair, glasses, moustache and suit; red waistcoat; yellow buttons, spoon and plate
Issued:	1997
Backstamp:	Unknown

Note: Since this is a unique, or one-of-a-kind piece, the price must be determined between the buyer and seller.

THIRD COLLECTORS SHOW, BUFFALO, NEW YORK - 1998

Arthur Hare Key Ring

This piece was commissioned by C & S Collectables and Wade Watch Ltd, and was given as a promotional item.

Size:	35mm (diameter)
Colour:	White; multi-coloured transfer; blue and red lettering
Issued:	1998
Backstamp:	None

Description	U.S. $	Can. $	U.K. £
Arthur Hare Key Ring	8.00	10.00	6.00

New York Tourist

Size:	110mm
Colour:	Black cap and trousers; blue t-shirt; brown shoes; green base
Issued:	1998
Issue Price:	$24.00 US
Backstamp:	Printed "Buffalo Fair Special 1998" with The Official International Wade Collectors Club logo

Description	U.S. $	Can. $	U.K. £
New York Tourist	45.00	60.00	30.00

Teddy Bear Plaque

This piece was produced in four different colourways for the Ripley Castle, Arundel, Buffalo and Christmas Extravaganza shows.

Size:	195mm
Colour:	Chocolate brown bear and plaque; dark brown paw pads; gold lettering
Issued:	1998 in a limited edition of 1,500
Issue Price:	$40.00 US
Backstamp:	Gold printed "Wade England Buffalo 1998"

Description	U.S. $	Can. $	U.K. £
Teddy Bear Plaque	50.00	65.00	32.00

Betty Boop Beach Belle

Bunny Mug (Ringtons)

Chuckles the Clown

ONE-OF-A-KIND

The following one-of-a-kind models were the prizes in the Bran Tub Lucky Dip and in the one-of-a-kind auction at Buffalo.

Size: See below
Colour: See below
Issued: 1998
Backstamp:
    A. Printed "© 1998 King Features Syndicate, INC. Fleischer Studios, INC. TM Hearst Corporation Betty Boop Beach Belle by Wade England 2000 Limited edition C&S with Certificate of Authenticity" (1)
    B. Printed "Genuine Wade Porcelain" (2)
    C. Red printed "Wade" (7a, 7b)

Name	Description	Size
1 Betty Boop Beach Belle with Bikini (C&S)	Black hat; black bikini with yellow spots; pink towel	147
2 Bunny Mug (Ringtons)	Cream bunny; blue eyes; pink nose and mouth; brown edging to ears and red edging on clothes	105
3 Camping Bear (Teddy Bears Picnic)	Light brown bear; yellow pack; light green jacket; dark green trousers; pale blue boots; grey base	115
4a Chuckles the Clown (Toy Box)	Back hat with pink flower; red nose and coat with pink flower; dark blue bow tie white shirt with blue buttons; yellow trousers with black patch; black shoes; grey chair	115
4b Chuckles the Clown	Black hat, coat and shoes; white nose, shirt and buttons; yellow trousers; dark blue bow tie; brown chair	115
5 Emily the Doll (Toy Box)	Yellow hat; brown hair; white dress with yellow bands and dark blue edging; black shoes	85
6 Glove Former, large	White; multi-coloured hand painted art deco design	430
7a Glove Former, miniature	White; hand painted yellow butterfly; orange flower; green stem and leaves	110
7b Glove Former miniature	White; hand painted large yellow and orange flowers; green leaves	110
8 Puck (Myths and Legends)	White horns and hooves; brown hair and tree stump with dark green top; flesh coloured body; gold flute; blue-grey legs	114
9 St. George (Myths and Legends)	Brown hair, cloak and base; gold armour and lance; blue-grey dragon	110

Note: Since these are unique, or one-of-a-kind pieces, the price must be determined between the buyer and seller.

Oscar The Christmas Teddy Bear

Size:	110mm
Colour:	Honey brown; green hat; black eyes and nose; brown sack; blue soldier
Issued:	1998 in a limited edition of 75
Issue Price:	$35.00 US
Backstamp:	Printed "Oscar Special Colourway Buffalo 1998 The Official International Wade Collectors Club" with O.I.W.C.C. logo

Description	U.S. $	Can. $	U.K. £
Oscar the Christmas Teddy Bear	300.00	400.00	200.00

FOURTH U.S. WADE COLLECTORS SHOW, SAN ANTONIO, TEXAS - 1999

GENERAL ISSUE

Prairie Dog

Unsold models were offered at the Arundel Swap Meet held in August 1999.

Size:	120mm
Colour:	Brown; white muzzle and chest; black eyes and nose; yellow rose; ochre base
Issued:	1999 in a limited edition of 500
Issue Price:	$20.00 US
Backstamp:	Printed "The Prairie Dog" with O.I.W.C.C. logo

Description	U.S. $	Can. $	U.K. £
Prairie Dog	25.00	35.00	30.00

Puppy Love "Shelby"

Size:	50mm
Colour:	White; brown patches; green base
Issued:	1999 in a limited edition of 500
Issue Price:	$20.00 US
Series:	Puppy Love (third in series)
Backstamp:	Black paw print with black and red lettering "Puppy L♥ve by Wade Puppy L♥ve Limited Edition 500 1999 Shelby"

Description	U.S. $	Can. $	U.K. £
Shelby	45.00	60.00	30.00

Rufus on Tour

This model was produced in four new colourways for the San Antonio show and were sold together.

Size: 65 x 84mm
Colour:
1 Tan; black ears; copper base
2 Grey; black ears; gold base
3 Beige; black ears; pearlized beige base
4 Honey; black ears; platinum base
Issued: 1999 in a limited edition of 100 (per colour)
Issue Price: $200.00/set (US)
Backstamp: Printed "Genuine Wade Porcelain limited edition of 100"

Colourway	U.S. $	Can. $	U.K. £
1 Tan	90.00	110.00	55.00
2 Grey	90.00	110.00	55.00
3 Beige	90.00	110.00	55.00
4 Honey	90.00	110.00	55.00

ONE-OF-A-KIND

These models were prizes in the Wade Bran Tub, which cost $1.00 per draw at the San Antonio show.

Cornish Tin Mine Pixie

Size: 110mm
Colour: Black hat, coat, trousers and shoes; yellow hair, hammer and socks; silver buckles
Issued: 1999
Backstamp: Unknown

Daddy Bear

Size: 105mm
Colour: Pale blue jacket; white bow tie; yellow trousers
Issued: 1999
Backstamp: Unknown

Note: Since these are unique, or one-of-a-kind pieces, the price must be determined between the buyer and seller.

Two models in a one-of-a-kind colourways were the special prizes in a draw held at the Wade Hospitality Night in San Antonio.

Amelia Teddy Bear

Size:	90mm
Colour:	Black with multi-coloured flowers; gold eyes and nose
Issued:	1999
Backstamp:	Printed "Wade England"

Arundel Bunny

Size:	55 x 110mm
Colour:	Platinum ears and tail; multi-coloured floral body
Issued:	1999
Backstamp:	Embossed "Wade England"

Note: Since these are unique, or one-of-a-kind pieces, the price must be determined between the buyer and seller.

ROSEMONT TRADE SHOW, ROSEMONT, ILLINOIS - 1999

Puppy Love "Henry"

Size:	85mm
Colour:	White and grey
Issued:	1999 in a limited edition of 500
Issue Price:	$20.00 US
Series:	Puppy Love (second in series)
Backstamp:	Black paw print with black and red lettering "Puppy L♥ve By Wade Puppy L♥ve Limited Edition 500 1999 Henry"

Description	U.S. $	Can. $	U.K. £
Henry	45.00	60.00	30.00

MINI WADE FAIR, YORK, PENNSYLVANIA - 1999

Jenny the Black Poodle

Commissioned by Patti Keenan of Keenan Collectables for her "Mini Wade Fair" August 1999.

Size: 40 x 45mm
Colour: Black
Issued: 1999
Issue Price: Originally given free with admission, extra *Poodles* were sold for $5.00 US
Backstamp: Embossed "Wade England"

Description	U.S. $	Can. $	U.K. £
Jenny	30.00	40.00	20.00

EVENT FIGURES

RIPLEY VILLAGE FETE AND TEDDY BEARS' PICNIC

The Wade Village fete and Teddy Bears' Picnic was held on Sunday June 7th, 1998 at The Castle Flatts, Ripley Castle, Warwickshire.

Admiral San and Alex the Aviator

Artistic Edward and Beatrice Ballerina

Locomotive Joe and Musical Marco

Bear Ambitions

Re-issued in a new colourway for the Teddy Bears' Picnic.

Size:	1 50mm (1, 4, 5)
	2 45mm (2, 6)
	3 40mm (3)
Colour:	Green
Issued:	1998 in a limited edition of 2,000
Issue Price:	£18.00/set
Backstamp:	**A.** Embossed "Wade England" (3)
	B. Embossed "Wade Eng" (1, 2, 4, 5, 6)
Price:	See below

	Name	U.S. $	Can. $	U.K. £
1	Admiral Sam	5.00	8.00	4.00
2	Alex the Aviator	5.00	8.00	4.00
3	Artistic Edward	5.00	8.00	4.00
4	Beatrice Ballerina	5.00	8.00	4.00
5	Locomotive Joe	5.00	8.00	4.00
6	Musical Marco	5.00	8.00	4.00

Note: For *Bear Ambitions* in different colourways, please see Tom Smith Crackers and Olympia Incentive Exhibition 1998.

Camping Bear

Size:	115mm
Colour:	Light brown bear; dark green jacket; grey trousers and pack; black boots; pale blue base
Issued:	1998 in a limited edition of 2,000
Issue Price:	£15.00
Backstamp:	Printed "Camping Bear 1998 The Official International Wade Collectors Club" with O.I.W.C.C. logo

Description	U.S. $	Can. $	U.K. £
Camping Bear	35.00	45.00	22.00

Teddy Bear Plaque

This piece was produced in four different colourways for the Ripley Castle, Arundel, Buffalo and Christmas Extravaganza shows.

Size:	195mm
Colour:	Honey bear; white plaque; brown paw pads; blue lettering
Issued:	1998 in a limited edition of 1,500
Issue Price:	£20.00
Backstamp:	Gold printed "Wade England Ripley 1998"

Description	U.S. $	Can. $	U.K. £
Teddy Bear Plaque	45.00	60.00	30.00

OLYMPIA INCENTIVE EXHIBITION - 1998

Admiral Sam

This 1997 *Bear Ambitions* model was re-issued at this Trade Exhibition, and was handed out at random to visitors of the Wade Stand. Surplus models were placed in the Bran Tub at the San Antonio show.

Size: 45mm
Colour: Pale blue
Issued: 1998 in a limited edition of 200
Backstamp: Embossed "Wade Eng" on back rim

Description	U.S. $	Can. $	U.K. £
Admiral Sam	50.00	80.00	40.00

Note: For *Bear Ambitions* in different colourways, please see Tom Smith Crackers, Ripley Village Fete and Teddy Bears' Picnic.

ARUNDEL CHRISTMAS BONANZA - 1999

Oops! The Bear
Version Two

The second model of *Oops!* has a sad face and a bandaged left leg.

Size: 95mm
Colour: Amber bear; creamy pink bandage on leg; brown crutch
Issued: 1999 in a limited edition of 300
Backstamp: "Oops! The Bear Ltd Edition of 300 Wade England"

Description	U.S. $	Can. $	U.K. £
Oops! The Bear (Version Two)	38.00	50.00	25.00

THE OFFICIAL INTERNATIONAL WADE COLLECTORS CLUB COMPLIMENTARY FIGURES

THE OFFICIAL INTERNATIONAL WADE COLLECTORS CLUB MEMBERSHIP FIGURES

Membership figures were given free of charge to new and renewing members.

FIRST MEMBERSHIP FIGURE - 1994-1995

The Works Cat Burslem (also known as Factory Cat)

Size: 75 x 75mm
Colour: White with black patches
Issued: 1994
Backstamp: **A.** Large embossed "Wade"
B. Unmarked

Description	U.S. $	Can. $	U.K. £
The Works Cat Burslem	175.00	230.00	100.00

SECOND MEMBERSHIP FIGURE - 1995-1996

The Christmas Puppy

Size: 57mm
Colour: Amber
Issued: 1995
Backstamp: Embossed "Wade"

Description	U.S. $	Can. $	U.K. £
The Christmas Puppy	80.00	105.00	50.00

THIRD MEMBERSHIP FIGURE - 1996-1997

Smudger

This was the first year that members received an enamel Wade Official International Collectors Club badge with their membership.

Size: 1 Smudger - 70mm
2 Badge - 29mm
Colour: 1 Black; grey detailing; brown eyes
2 Brass and enamel; black, gold and red design and lettering
Issued: 1996
Backstamp: Circular white printed "The Official International Collectors Club" red "Wade" between two lines and white "Membership Special 1996-1997"

Description	U.S. $	Can. $	U.K. £
1 Smudger	45.00	60.00	30.00
2 Badge	15.00	20.00	10.00

FOURTH MEMBERSHIP FIGURE - 1997-1998

The Wade Baby

Size: 1   Wade Baby - 83mm
           2   Badge - 25mm (diameter)
Colour: 1   Brown hair and teddy bear; white vest and pants;
             green shoes; blue base
           2   Gold, red and black enamel; gold lettering
Issued: 1997
Backstamp: Printed circular "The Official International Wade Collectors
                Club Membership Piece 19997/1998"

Description	U.S. $	Can. $	U.K. £
1 Wade Baby	45.00	60.00	28.00
2 Badge	15.00	20.00	10.00

FIFTH MEMBERSHIP FIGURE - 1999

Alice in Wonderland

In late 1998, the O.I.W.C.C. changed their membership renewal system
so that all memberships ended and started January 1st - December 31st.
Alice in Wonderland is the first in a series of six models that members had the
opportunity to purchase.

Size: 1   Alice - 120mm   2   Badge - 25mm (diameter)
Colour: 1   Yellow hair; blue dress; white pinafore; black shoes;
           2   Gold, red and black enamel; gold lettering
Issued: 1998-1999
Backstamp: Printed "Alice in Wonderland Collection Alice 1999
                Membership Piece made in England ©MacMPub 1999"
                with O.I.W.C.C. logo

Description	U.S. $	Can. $	U.K. £
1 Alice	45.00	60.00	30.00
2 Badge	15.00	20.00	10.00

SIXTH MEMBERSHIP FIGURE - 2000

Toad of Toad Hall

Part of the *Wind in the Willows* story, members had the opportunity to
purchase the other three models of this set throughout the year.

Size: 1   Toad - 105mm
           2   Badge - 25mm
Colour: 1   Dark green; brown coat/hat; white collar; yellow/black
             checked waistcoat; grey base
           2   Gold/yellow; brass/enamel; gold lettering
Issued: 2000
Backstamp: Printed "The Wind in the Willows Toad ©EHS"

Description	U.S. $	Can. $	U.K. £
1 Toad	46.00	45.00	22.50
2 Badge	8.00	10.00	5.00

CHESHIRE CAT
1999

THE OFFICIAL INTERNATIONAL WADE COLLECTORS CLUB MEMBERSHIP EXCLUSIVES

MEMBERSHIP EXCLUSIVES

Snowman

This model was produced in November 1994.

Size: 125mm
Colour: Off-white; black hat; dark blue scarf
Issued: 1994 in a limited edition of 1,000
Backstamp: Black transfer "Wade England"

Description	U.S. $	Can. $	U.K. £
Snowman	130.00	175.00	75.00

Snow Woman

Produced for Christmas 1995.

Size: 127mm
Colour: Off-white; dark blue scarf; black purse and umbrella
Issued: 1995 in a limited edition of 1,500
Backstamp: Black transfer "Christmas 1995 Wade Made in England" with two lines

Description	U.S. $	Can. $	U.K. £
Snow Woman	100.00	130.00	65.00

Snow Children

Produced for Christmas 1996, the model was limited to one per member.

Size: 120mm
Colour: Boy: white; dark blue hat and scarf
Girl: pale blue hat and scarf; brown sleigh
Issued: 1996 in a limited edition of 2,500
Issue Price: £15.00
Backstamp: Black printed "Christmas 1996 Wade Made in England" with two black lines

Description	U.S. $	Can. $	U.K. £
Snow Children	85.00	100.00	45.00

Big Bad Wolf and the Three Little Pigs

Wade produced four models in 1995 based on the fairy tale, *The Three Little Pigs*. The first two figures produced, "The Straw House Pig" and "The Wood House Pig," were issued in a limited edition of 1,250 each. Due to high demand, the production of the next two models was increased to 1,500 each.

Big Bad Wolf

Size:	See below
Colour:	See below
Issued:	1 Big Band Wolf - 1995 in a limited edition of 1,500
	2 Brick House Pig - 1995 in a limited edition of 1,500
	3 Straw House Pig - 1995 in a limited edition of 1,250
	4 Wood House Pig - 1995 in a limited edition of 1,250
Issue Price:	£15.00/each
Backstamp:	Red print "Wade England" with two lines and black print "The Offical Wade International Collectors Club (name of model) 1995"
Price:	See below

	Name	Description	Size
1	Big Bad Wolf	Mottled grey; white patch on throat; red tongue; black nose, eyes and claws	101
2	Brick House Pig	Pinky beige; red-brown trousers; grey brick wall	130
3	Straw House Pig	Pinky beige; dark blue dungarees; yellow straw	123
4	Wood House Pig	Pinky beige; brown cap; dark green dungarees; brown wood	117

Brick House Pig

	Name	U.S. $	Can. $	U.K. £
1	Big Bad Wolf	75.00	100.00	45.00
2	Brick House Pig	75.00	100.00	45.00
3	Straw House Pig	90.00	120.00	60.00
4	Wood House Pig	90.00	120.00	60.00

Straw House Pig and Wood House Pig

Mummy Bear and Daddy Bear

Baby Bear and Goldilocks

Goldilocks and the Three Bears
Style Two

The *Daddy Bear*, in one-of-a-kind form, was given as prizes at the Trentham Gardens and Wisconsin Wade Fairs.

Size:	See below
Colour:	See below
Issued:	1996 in a limited edition of 2,750
Issue Price:	£15.00/each
Backstamp:	Circular black and red printed "Official International Wade Collectors Club" Black printed "(name) 1996"
Price:	See below

Name		Description	Size
1	Mummy Bear	Light brown; white cap, apron; dark blue dress; brown bowl	102
2	Daddy Bear	Light brown; dark blue suit; red bowtie; brown spoon and bowl	105
3	Goldilocks	Light brown chair; yellow hair; pink dress; white socks, porridge, brown spoon and bowl	85
4	Baby Bear	Light brown; dark blue dungarees; white shirt with yellow stripes; white hankie; brown spoon	80

Name		U.S. $	Can. $	U.K. £
1	Mummy Bear	68.00	90.00	35.00
2	Daddy Bear	68.00	90.00	35.00
3	Goldilocks	68.00	90.00	35.00
4	Baby Bear	68.00	90.00	35.00

Enrol a Friend White Seal Pup

Previously used in the *English Whimsies* and the Tom Smith *Snowlife* series, both the Wade Club member and the new member who enroled in the International Collectors Club in 1996-1997 received a *Seal Pup* model.

Size:	17 x 30mm
Colour:	White seal; blue base
Issued:	1996-1997
Backstsamp:	Embossed "Wade England"

Description	U.S. $	Can. $	U.K. £
White Seal Pup	15.00	25.00	10.00

Pantomime Series

This series was available to club members only, and limited to one per member.

Size:	See below
Colour:	See below
Issued:	1997 in a limited edition of 4,000
Issue Price:	£15.00/each
Backstamp:	Circular black and red printed "(Name) The Official International Wade Collectors Club 1997"
Price:	See below

Pantomine Horse and Mother Goose

	Name	Description	Size
1	Pantomime Horse	White; black mane, hooves, tail, spots; brown patch	90
2	Mother Goose	White; pale blue bonnet, ribbon, bloomers black eyes, shoes; dull yellow beak; red and white striped socks	110
3	Dick Whittington's Cat	Grey cat; brown stick and lunch bag; light blue trousers; black boots; beige milestone	110
4	Pantomime Dame	Light blue hair; red cheeks; sea green dress; white bow; black shoes; red and white bloomers	110

	Name	U.S. $	Can. $	U.K. £
1	Pantomime Horse	40.00	55.00	25.00
2	Mother Goose	40.00	55.00	25.00
3	Dick Whittington's Cat	45.00	60.00	30.00
4	Pantomime Dame	40.00	50.00	25.00

Dick Whittington's Cat and Pantomine

Oscar the Christmas Teddy Bear

Produced for the Wade Christmas Extravaganza held at Trentham Gardens, Stoke-on-Trent, in November 1997, unsold models were available from the O.I.W.C.C. throughout 1998.

Size:	110mm
Colour:	Honey brown; red hat; brown paw patches and sack; red, yellow and brown toys
Issued:	1997-1998 in a limited edition of 2,500
Backstamp:	Printed circular "The Official International Wade Collectors Club Christmas Teddy 1997" with O.I.W.C.C. logo

Description	U.S. $	Can. $	U.K. £
Oscar the Christmas Teddy Bear	40.00	50.00	25.00

230

Sir Lancelot and King Arthur

The Lady of the Lake

Queen Guinivere and The Wizard Merlin

The Camelot Collection

This new series of slip cast models based on the legend of King Arthur was introduced at the Wade/Jim Beam fair held in Wisconsin in July 1997. Two hundred of each had a C & S backstamp added to the regular backstamp.

Size:	See below
Colour:	See below
Issued:	1997-1999 in a limited edition of 2,000
Issue Price:	£20.00/each
Backstamp:	**A.** Black printed "Camelot Collection" logo and (name of model) "The Camelot Collection Wade"
	B. Black printed "C&S" logo, "Camelot Collection" logo and (name of model) "The Camelot Collection Wade"
Price:	See below

	Name	Description	Size
1	King Arthur	Light brown; brown cloak; dull yellow crown, cloak chain, cross belt; dull yellow sword with black pummel and hilt	108
2	Queen Guinivere	Light brown; brown dress; dark green collar, cuffs; dull yellow belt	108
3	Sir Lancelot	Light brown; brown cloak	108
4	The Wizard Merlin	Light brown; blue-grey hooded cloak; brown staff	108
5	The Lady of the Lake	Light brown; brown cloak; dull yellow sword; dark blue/green base	83

	Name	U.S. $	Can. $	U.K. £
1	King Arthur	45.00	60.00	20.00
2	Queen Guinivere	45.00	60.00	20.00
3	Sir Lancelot	45.00	60.00	20.00
4	The Wizard Merlin	45.00	60.00	20.00
5	The Lady of the Lake	45.00	60.00	20.00

Toy Box Series

This series was created by Sue Ames, winner of a competition run by The Wade Collectors Club. The *Toy Soldier* (first in the series) was released at the Trentham Gardens Wade Fair in March 1998.

Size: See below
Colour: See below
Issued: 1998 in a limited edition of 3,000
Issue Price: £20.00/each or £75.00/set
Backstamp: Printed "The Official Wade Collectors Club 1998" with O.I.W.C.C. logo and name of model
Price: See below

Toy Soldier and Amelia Teddy Bear

Name		Description	Size
1	Toy Soldier	Pale blue helmet/pants; white plume/band on helmet; yellow jacket; black and gold epaulettes and buttons; black cuffs and boots; white base	110
2	Amelia Teddy Bear	Brown bear; dark brown paw pads; blue dress; white trim with yellow ducklings	90
3	Chuckles the Clown	Black hat, bow tie, patch and shoes; yellow hair; red coat; white shirt and trousers; light brown chair	115
4	Emily the Doll	Blue bonnet/dress; yellow hair; maroon ribbon, bow and stripes; black shoes	85

Name		U.S. $	Can. $	U.K. £
1	Toy Soldier	45.00	60.00	30.00
2	Amelia Teddy Bear	45.00	60.00	30.00
3	Chuckles the Clown	45.00	60.00	30.00
4	Emily the Doll	45.00	60.00	30.00

Chuckles the Clown and Emily the Doll

Annabel Waiting for Christmas

Size: 110mm
Colour: Brown bear; red bow; blue dress; white collar and cuffs; green tree with gold balls; yellow cracker
Issued: 1998 in a limited edition of 2,000
Issue Price: £20.00
Backstamp: Printed "Christmas 1998" with O.I.W.C.C. logo

Description	U.S. $	Can. $	U.K. £
Annabel Waiting for Christmas	40.00	50.00	25.00

Cornish Tin Mine Pixie and Green Man

King Canute and Mermaid

Puck and St. George

British Myths and Legends Series

This series released in 1998-1999 depicts characters from British Folklore. The sixth model, *King Canute,* was sent free of charge (upon application) to club members who had previously purchased a *Myths and Legends* set.

Size:	See below
Colour:	See below
Issued:	1998-1999 in a limited edition of 2,000
Issue Price:	£115.00/set
Backstamp:	Printed "British Myths and Legends Wade" with name of model
Price:	See below

	Name	Description	Size
1	Cornish Tin Mine Pixie	Brown hat/suit/shoes; honey brown pixie; gold hammer head; greenish blue rock	108
2	Green Man	Greenish white figure; green hair and loin cloth; brown tree truck	114
3	Mermaid	Brown hair; honey brown body; greenish blue tail; brown and silver mirror; green rock	120
4	Puck	Brown hair/legs; amber horns/body; gold flute; grey hooves; dark brown tree trunk	114
5	St. George	Dark brown hair; brown cloak; grey armour and rock; gold lance; brown and beige dragon	101
6	King Canute	Amber figure; silver crown; dark brown cloak; black straps on legs; olive chair; brown base with sea green waves	120

	Name	U.S. $	Can. $	U.K. £
1	Cornisn Tin Mine Pixie	42.00	60.00	25.00
2	Green Man	42.00	60.00	25.00
3	Mermaid	42.00	60.00	25.00
4	Puck	42.00	60.00	25.00
5	St. George	42.00	60.00	25.00
6	King Canute	42.00	60.00	25.00

Alice in Wonderland Series

The membership model for 1999 was *Alice in Wonderland,* the first in a series (see Membership Models). Members had the opportunity to purchase the other models in the series at quarterly intervals throughout the 1999 membership year (the Queen of Hearts was made available to members who purchased all four *Alice* models by February 14th, 2000).

Size:	See below
Colour:	See below
Issued:	1999 in a limited edition of 2,000
Issue Price:	£28.50/each
Backstamp:	Printed "Alice in Wonderland Collection made in England ©MacMPub 1999" with O.I.W.C.C. logo and name of model

Cheshire Cat

Name		Description	Size
1	Mad Hatter	Grey top hat; white collar; yellow/red spotted bow tie; purple coat; red and blue striped trouseres; brown chair and shoes; silver teapot	110
2	White Rabbit	White; olive green coat; yellow and red striped waistcoat; gold watch and buttons; grey rock base	113
3	Dormouse	Amber dormouse; white chest; brown nose; platinum lustre teapot	90
4	Cheshire Cat	Brown; pink inside ears; green eyes; grey base	60
5	Queen of Hearts	Yellow crown; black head scarf; red dress; gold heart and decoration	130

Name		U.S. $	Can. $	U.K. £
1	Mad Hatter	45.00	58.00	29.00
2	White Rabbit	45.00	58.00	29.00
3	Dormouse	45.00	58.00	29.00
4	Cheshire Cat	45.00	58.00	29.00
5	Queen of Hearts		Unknown	

Mad Hatter and White Rabbit

Dormouse

Blue Angelfish

The *Blue Angelfish* (a re-coloured model originally from the 1978 *English Whimsies* set) was sent to the first 10,000 members of The Official International Wade Collectors Club that renewed or joined the club during late 1998 to 1999.

Size: 35 x 30mm
Colour: Dark blue
Issued: 1998-1999
Backstamp: Embossed "Wade England"

Description	U.S. $	Can. $	U.K. £
Blue Angelfish	15.00	20.00	5.00

Photograph not available
at press time

Santa

The Wade limited edition Christmas piece for 1999 was a miniature Santa Claus with a sack of toys.

Size: 75mm
Colour: Red and white suit; brown sack; orange and blue toys
Issued: 1999 in a limited edition of 1,500
Issue Price: £15.00
Backstamp: Unknown

Description	U.S. $	Can. $	U.K. £
Santa	27.00	30.00	15.00

The Wind in the Willows Series

The first model in this series "Toad of Toad Hall", was the membership model for 2000. Members could then purchase the other models in this series at intervals during the year. The next model, "Mole" was produced in a limited edition of 2,000 and limited to one per member.

Size: Unknown
Colour: Unknown
Issued: 1 Mole - 2000 in a limited edition of 2,000
2 Ratty - Unknown
3 Badger - Unknown
Issue Price: 1 £22.50 2 Unknown 3 Unknown
Backstamp: Unknown

Name	U.S. $	Can. $	U.K. £
1 Mole	46.00	45.00	22.50
2 Ratty		Unknown	
3 Badger		Unknown	

Photograph not available
at press time

MAD HATTER AND WHITE RABBIT
1999

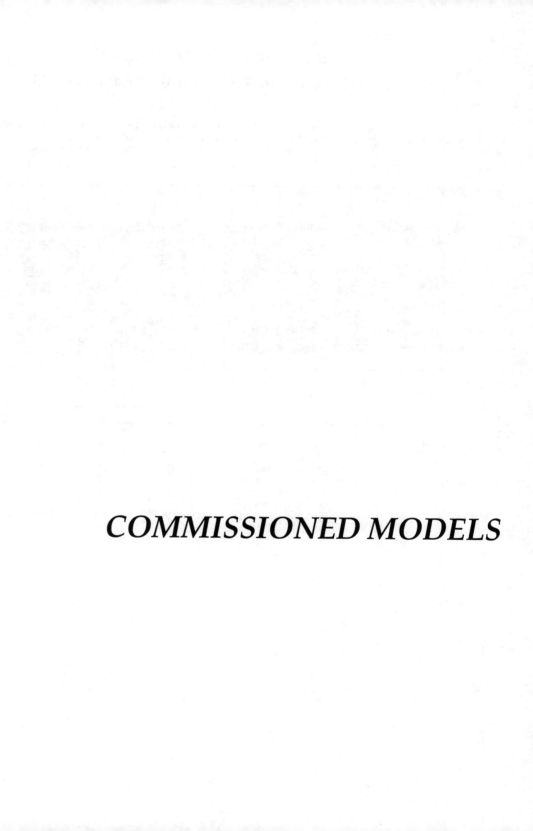

COMMISSIONED MODELS

BALDING AND MANSELL

FLINTSTONES CHRISTMAS CRACKER PREMIUMS

1965

The four prehistoric Comic Animals (based on the television series *The Flintstones*) were only used in Balding & Mansell's Christmas Crackers. The "Bluebird," "Crocodile," "Hedgehog" and "Terrapin" were re-issued in 1967 and were included in the Red Rose Tea of Canada promotion. For other Christmas cracker models, see Great Universal Stores and Tom Smith and Company.

A box of *Flintstones Christmas Crackers* containing these models was auctioned in 1997 for £35.00.

Backstamp: **A.** Embossed "Wade England" in recessed base
B. Embossed "Wade England" on rim

No.	Name	Description	Size	U.S. $	Can. $	U.K. £
1	Bluebird	Beige and blue	15 x 35	10.00	8.00	4.00
2	Bronti	Brown; beige face, feet, base; blue ears	20 x 35	15.00	20.00	6.00
3	Crocodile	Brownish Green	14 x 40	10.00	8.00	5.00
4	Dino	Beige; green eyes; black-brown base	35 x 35	15.00	20.00	8.00
5	Hedgehog	Dark red brown; honey face; black nose	23 x 40	9.00	7.00	3.00
6	Rhinno	Beige; blue eyes, ears	20 x 40	15.00	20.00	7.00
7	Terrapin	Beige; brown markings	10 x 40	8.00	6.00	4.00
8	Tigger	Yellow brown; black stripes, nose; brown feet	38 x 28	25.00	30.00	10.00

BJ PROMOTIONS
DENNIS THE MENACE AND GNASHER
1999

Commissioned in a limited edition of 1,500 models by BJ Promotions, *Dennis The Menace* is a character from the British children's comic *The Beano*. Other models planned for the series are Dennis's faithful dog *Gnasher*, *Minnie the Minx* and *Roger the Dodger*.

With the first one thousand of the *Dennis the Menace* models sold, purchasers received a Beano Collection keyring which was produced in a limited edition of 1,000. *Gnasher* was introduced in late October 1999. The original cost of *Dennis* and *Gnasher* was £39.95

NOTE: There is no backstamp on the keyring.

Dennis the Menace and Beano Keyring

Gnasher

Backstamp: **A.** Circular printed "© D.C.Thomson & Co. Ltd, 1999 Wade England Limited Edition Of 1,500"
B. Circular printed "© D.C.Thomson & Co. Ltd, 1999 Wade England Limited Edition Of 1,000"

No.	Name	Description	Size	U.S. $	Can. $	U.K. £
1	Beano Collection Keyring	White; black panel; black, white and yellow/orange lettering	35 (diam.)	10.00	15.00	8.00
2	Dennis the Menace	Black hair/shorts; red/black striped jumper; red socks; grey shoes; khaki brown base	130	60.00	80.00	39.95
3	Gnasher	Pink face/arms /legs; black fur; green base	90	60.00	80.00	39.95

BLYTH CERAMICS
SID THE SEXIST AND SAN THE FAT SLAG
June 1998

Produced for a Northumberland company Blyth Ceramics, *Sid the Sexist* is the first in a series of characters from the British comic *Viz*. *San the Fat Slag* was the second model in the *Viz Collection*. Both models were produced in a limited edition of 1,000 and were issued with a Certificate of Authenticity. Original cost direct from Blyth Ceramics was £36.00.

Backstamp: Printed "Wade Viz 1998 © John Brown Publishing House Viz © Blyth Ceramics Limited Edition of 1000 with Certificate of Authenticity" with name of model

No.	Name	Description	Size	U.S. $	Can. $	U.K. £
1	Sid the Sexist	Black hair/trousers; dark red shirt; grey bottle in hand; black/white trainers; brown fence; grey base	127	55.00	70.00	36.00
2	San the Fat Slag	Brown hair; red tank top; black slacks; white slippers; off-white base	127	55.00	70.00	36.00

BRIGHTON CORPORATION
BRIGHTON PAVILION

1988

The *Brighton Pavilion* set consists of a circular pavilion and two oblong pavilions. The famous British landmark, a Turkish-style domed palace built by King George IV as a summer residence in the seaside town of Brighton, is now a museum owned by the Brighton Corporation.

Backstamp: Unmarked

No.	Name	Description	Size	U.S. $	Can. $	U.K. £
1	Circular Pavilion	Blue/black/yellow doors, windows	75 x 53	28.00	35.00	15.00
2	Oblong Pavilion	Blue/black/yellow doors, windows	50 x 53	28.00	35.00	15.00

BROOKE BOND OXO LTD., ENGLAND

1969-1970

After the success of the *Miniature Animals* promotion by its sister company in Canada (Red Rose Tea), Brooke Bond Oxo Ltd. of London (England) offered nine figures from the same set in its 1969 promotion of Brooke Bond Teabags. One model was included in the 72-teabag box and two models in the 144-teabag box.

The first models were so popular that a further six models from Red Rose Tea were added to the series in late 1969 and early 1970, for a total of 15 models. All these figures are in the same colours as the original Red Rose Tea Canada issue. Wade later used some of them in its *English Whimsies* series. They are listed in alphabetical order.

Backstamp: Embossed "Wade England"

No.	Name	Description	Size	U.S. $	Can. $	U.K. £
1	Bear Cub	Grey; beige face	30 x 40	7.00	5.00	2.00
2	Beaver	Grey-brown; honey brown face	35 x 45	6.00	6.00	2.00
3	Bison, Small	Honey brown body; dark brown head, mane	30 x 40	7.00	5.00	4.00
4	Bushbaby	Brown; blue ears; black eyes, nose	30 x 30	6.00	4.00	2.00
5	Butterfly	Green/brown; green tips; raised circles	10 x 45	10.00	8.00	5.00
6	Corgi	Honey brown; black nose	30 x 35	9.00	7.00	2.00
7	Duck	Blue/brown; yellow beak	30 x 40	9.00	7.00	2.00
8	Fantail Goldfish	Green/yellow; blue rock	30 x 35	10.00	8.00	5.00
9	Fox	Dark brown; fawn face, chest	30 x 30	9.00	7.00	2.00
10	Frog	Green & yellow	15 x 30	8.00	5.00	3.00
11	Otter	Beige; blue base	30 x 35	7.00	5.00	2.00
12	Owl	Dark brown; light brown chest, face	35 x 20	8.00	6.00	2.00
13	Seal on Rock	Light brown; blue rock	35 x 35	10.00	8.00	5.00
14	Setter	Light brown; grey-green base	35 x 50	7.00	5.00	2.00
15	Trout	Brown; red tail; grey-green base	30 x 30	8.00	6.00	3.00

C&S COLLECTABLES DIRECT
ARTHUR HARE SERIES
1993, 1996, 1997

C&S Collectables commissioned "Arthur Hare" and "Holly Hedgehog" in late 1993 and "Felicity Squirrel" in March 1996. A limited edition of 2,000 each of the blue-grey "Arthur Hare" and "Holly Hedgehog," modelled by Ken Holmes, were produced, along with 200 of the fawn "Arthur Hare." They are the first of a series of comic animals based on the characters from a British storybook, *The Adventures of Arthur Hare and the Silent Butterfly.*

"Felicity Squirrel," modelled by Robert Feather and the third in the series, was produced in a limited edition of 1,250 in grey glaze and 250 in a dark red glaze. Collectors Corner of Colorado, U.S.A. had their name included in the backstamp of six of the dark red models and on 250 of the grey models "Edward Fox," introduced in 1997, is the fourth model in the series and was modelled by Robert Feather. The "Arthur Hare" character is a trademark of C&S Collectables Direct.

Backstamp:
- **A.** Black transfer "Arthur Hare © C&S Collectables Wade England" (1a, 1b)
- **B.** Black transfer "Holly Hedgehog © C&S Collectables Wade England" (2)
- **C.** Black transfer "Felicity Squirrel 1250 Limited Edition © C&S Collectables 1995 Arthur Hare Productions Wade England" between two lines (3b)
- **D.** Printed "Felicity Squirrel 250 Limited Edition Collectors Corner © 1995 Arthur Hare Productions Wade" with two lines
- **E.** Printed in red "Genuine Wade" (3a)
- **F.** Black printed "Edward Fox 1000 Limited Edition © C&S Collectables 1997 Arthur Hare Productions Wade" (4)

No.	Name	Description	Size	U.S. $	Can. $	U.K. £
1a	Arthur Hare	Blue-grey/white; red tongue	130 x 100	55.00	75.00	35.00
1b	Arthur Hare	Fawn/white; red tongue	130 x 100	110.00	150.00	75.00
2	Holly Hedgehog	Beige; brown prickles; grey ball	95 x 70	50.00	75.00	35.00
3a	Felicity Squirrel	Dark red; pink cheeks/ears; white tail tip	105 x 68	85.00	110.00	55.00
3b	Felicity Squirrel	Grey; pink cheeks, inside ears; white tail tip	105 x 68	55.00	60.00	30.00
4	Edward Fox	Light orange; pink ears; black eyes/nose/mouth; white muzzle/tail tip/feet	115	50.00	70.00	35.00

ANDY CAPP AND FLO

1994-1995

Produced in early 1994 for C&S Collectables, *Andy Capp* depicts the cartoon character created by Reg Smythe in 1958 for the *British Daily Mirror*. The second model *Flo*, Andy's long-suffering wife, was issued in 1995. In styles 1b and 2b, the models have a cigarette hand-painted on the face. Only 100 each of these cigarette models were produced.

Backstamp: **A.** Black transfer "1994 © Mirror Group Newspapers Ltd C&S Collectables Wade England" (1a, 1b)
　　　　　　B. Black transfer "1994 © Mirror Group Newspapers Ltd C&S Collectables Wade England Flo 1995" (2a, 2b)

No.	Name	Description	Size	U.S. $	Can. $	U.K. £
1a	Andy Capp	Green cap, scarf; black suit; white hexagonal base	75 x 36	45.00	60.00	35.00
1b	Andy Capp, Cigarette	Green cap, scarf; black suit; white hexagonal base	75 x 36	75.00	100.00	50.00
2a	Flo	Yellow hair; green blouse, shoes; black skirt, bucket; white apron, base	75 x 36	45.00	60.00	35.00
2b	Flo, Cigarette	Yellow hair; green blouse, shoes; black skirt; white apron, bucket, base	75 x 36	75.00	100.00	50.00

MUGS (WADE FAIR SPECIALS)

1994-1996

Four mugs were produced for C&S Collectables between September 1994 and September 1996. Each mug was produced in a limited edition: "Arthur Hare" - 280, "Holly Hedgehog" and "Felicity Squirrel" - 400 of each, and The International Wade Collectors Club mug - 250. Although commissioned by C&S Collectables from Wade, plain white mugs were bought in from a local pottery (John Tams Ltd) and were decorated in the Wade pottery.

NOTE: The first mug with Backstamp A has a different handle and base than the next three, which are from the same mould.

Backstamp: **A.** Embossed "Made In England"
B. Embossed "Tams Made in England"
C. None

No.	Name	Description	Size	U.S. $	Can. $	U.K. £
1	1994 1st UK Wade Fair Birmingham Arthur Hare	White mug; blue Arthur Hare print; black/red lettering	90	20.00	28.00	8.00
2a	1995 2nd UK Wade Fair Birmingham Holly Hedgehog	White mug; brown Holly Hedgehog print; black/red lettering	90	20.00	28.00	8.00
2b	1996 3rd UK Wade Fair Birmingham Felicity Squirrel	White mug; grey Felicity Squirrel print; black/red lettering	90	20.00	28.00	8.00
2c	1996 4th UK Wade Fair Dunstable O.I.W.C.C. Logo	White mug; black and red O.I.W.C.C. logo print/lettering	90	20.00	28.00	8.00

WHIMBLES

Whimbles (a registered trademark of C&S Collectables) were first produced for the U.K. Wade Show held at Birmingham on June 11th, 1995. The first *Whimble* was of "Holly Hedgehog."

New *Whimbles* were introduced at the U.S.A. Wade Show held in Seattle, Washington, July 12-13th, 1996. The "International Wade Collectors Club logo Whimble" (a globe with WADE across it) and the house shaped "Whimble of Spooners" (the collectors shop run by C&S Collectables in Arundel,) were produced in limited editions of 1,000.

The "Seattle Space Needle," "Three Bears" and "Puss in Boots" *Whimbles* were produced in association with Collectors Corner, (Wade Watch) of Arvada, U.S.A. in a limited edition of 500. One hundred of the "Seattle Space Needle" *Whimbles* with only the Needle print and the Wade backstamp were produced for sale at the Seattle Space Needle complex. All additional Whimbles were produced in limited editions of 500.

ROUND WHIMBLES

1995-1997

Backstamp: Red transfer printed "Whimbles by Wade" with two lines

No.	Name	Description	Size	U.S. $	Can. $	U.K. £
1a	Holly Hedgehog	White; gold band; black lettering, print	27	8.00	10.00	4.00
1b	Felicity Squirrel	White; gold band; black lettering, print	27	8.00	10.00	4.00
1c	O.I.W.C.C. Logo	White; gold band; black/red lettering	27	8.00	10.00	4.00
1d	Seattle Space Needle	White; gold band; blue lettering, print	27	15.00	20.00	5.00
1e	Betty Boop	White; gold band; black lettering; black/red print	27	25.00	25.00	12.00
1f	Arthur Hare	White; gold band; red lettering; blue print	27	8.00	10.00	4.00
1g	Whimbles by Wade	White; gold band; red lettering	27	8.00	10.00	4.00
1h	The Three Bears	White; gold band; black lettering; brown print	27	8.00	10.00	4.00
1i	Arundel Castle	White; gold band; black lettering; multi-coloured print of castle	27	8.00	10.00	4.00
1j	Puss in Boots	White; gold band/lettering; print of cat	27	8.00	10.00	4.00
1k	Edward Fox	White; gold band; red lettering; brown print	27	8.00	10.00	4.00
1l	Wisconsin Mouse	White; gold band; black lettering; white mouse; fawn cheese	27	8.00	10.00	4.00

HOUSE-SHAPED WHIMBLE

1996

Backstamp: Red transfer printed "Whimbles by Wade" with two lines

No.	Name	Description	Size	U.S. $	Can. $	U.K. £
2	Spooners	White; black/red lettering; black hare; red door print	27	8.00	10.00	4.00

BOXED SETS OF WHIMBLES

1996-1997

In September 1996 the first of specially boxed and numbered *Whimbles* were sold at the U.K. Wade Show held at Dunstable, Bedfordshire. The sets were issued in limited editions of 25 and sold for £15 for the boxed set of four and £25.00 for the boxed set of six. The sets consist of previously issued *Whimbles* with the current new design added.

Backstamp: Red transfer printed "Whimbles by Wade" with two lines

No.	Name	Description	U.S. $	Can. $	U.K. £
1	Dunstable	Whimbles; Betty Boop; Arthur Hare; Spooners; Wade Club Logo; Seattle Space Needle	65.00	85.00	45.00
2	Trentham Gardens	Wade Club Logo; Arthur Hare; Spooners; Edward Fox; Puss in Boots; The Three Bears	55.00	75.00	40.00
3	Wisconsin	Wisconsin Mouse; Seattle Space Needle; Arthur Hare; Edward Fox	40.00	55.00	30.00

BETTY BOOP

1996-1997

Originally created in 1930 by animator Grim Natwick and made famous by film producer Max Fleisher in 1931, *Betty Boop* was a popular North American cartoon character who was usually accompanied by her dog "Pudgy." King Features produced a comic strip cartoon of her in the mid-late 1930s, and her cartoons appeared on North American television in the late 1950s and again in the early 1970s.

BETTY BOOP

1996

The first model in a series of *Betty Boop's* commissioned by C&S Collectables is wearing a red dress. She was produced in a limited edition of 1,500 and sold for £35.00 direct from C&S Collectables. A limited edition of 500 *Betty Boop's* in a blue dress were produced for the July 1997, Wisconsin, U.S.A. Jim Beam/Wade Show. Those models not sold at the Wisconsin show in July were sold at the August 1997, Arundel Swap Meet.

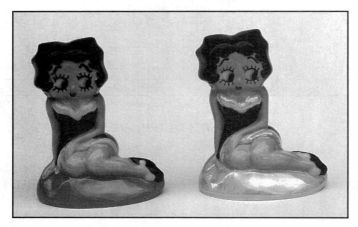

Backstamps: **A.** Black printed circular "© 1996 King Features Syndicate, Inc. Fleisher Studios, Inc. 2000 Limited Edition (C&S) Betty Boop by Wade England" (1a)
B. Black printed circular "© 1996 King Features Syndicate, Inc. Fleisher Studios, Inc. 2000 Limited Edition (C&S) Betty Boop by Wade England and black printed Wisconsin 1997" (1b)

No.	Description	Size	U.S. $	Can. $	U.K. £
1a	Black hair/eyes/shoes; red dress; white collar/hem; green base	95	90.00	120.00	60.00
1b	Black hair/eyes/shoes; blue dress; pearlised collar/hem/base	95	100.00	130.00	65.00

BETTY BOOP CHRISTMAS SURPRISE

1997

A special Christmas edition of *Betty Boop* sitting on a pile of presents was issued in a limited edition of 1,750 with a pearlised base and 250 with a gold base. The gold based *Betty Boop Christmas Surprise* models were sold a year later at the *Collect It!* fair held on December 5th 1998 at the Royal Showground in Warwickshire, UK. The original cost was £39.95.

Backstamp: Black printed circular "© 1996 King Features Syndicate, Inc. Fleisher Studios, Inc. ™ Hearst Corporation. 2000 Limited Edition (C&S) With Certificate of Authenticity Betty Boop Christmas Surprise by Wade England"

No.	Description	Size	U.S. $	Can. $	U.K. £
1a	Red hat and dress; white trim; black hair and shoes; dark green sack; white teddy and parcels; gold base	132	140.00	200.00	90.00
1b	Red hat and dress; white trim; black hair and shoes; brown sack; white teddy and parcels; pearl base	132	140.00	200.00	90.00

BETTY BOOP WALL PLAQUE

1997

The *Betty Boop* with white dress wall plaque was produced in a limited edition of 1,250. The model was based on a famous photo of Marilyn Monroe standing on a subway grill with her dress blowing upward. For *Betty Boop* with red dress, please see *Collect It!* Magazine (see page 272).

Backstamp: Black printed circular "© 1996 King Features Syndicate, Inc. Fleisher Studios, Inc. ™ Hearst Corporation. 1250 Limited Edition (C&S) With Certificate of Authenticity Betty Boop Classic by Wade England"

No.	Description	Size	U.S. $	Can. $	U.K. £
1	Pearlised moon; white dress; gold earrings and bracelets; red garter; white and black dog	Unknown	75.00	100.00	50.00

ARTHUR HARE

THE VILLAGE PEOPLE COLLECTION

1997-1999

A new series of *Arthur Hare* models dressed in character clothes and modelled by freelance artist Andy Moss was introduced in December 1997. The first in the series was "Santhare Paws." Other models produced during 1998-1999 were "Shareriff," a cowboy hare, "Big Chief Bravehare," a North American Indian hare, and "P.C. Gotchare," a British policeman. Each model was issued in a limited edition of 500.

The Arthur Hare "Jesthares" in two different colourways were issued as Fair Specials: the platinum version was introduced at the Brunel University Uxbridge, Wade, Beswick and Doulton show held on 15th November 1998, and the gold version was introduced at the Alton Towers Staffordshire, Christmas Extravaganza on 22nd November 1998. Both were produced in a limited edition of 350. The last in the Arthur Hare Village People was produced for the combined Wade and I.A.J.B.B.S.C. show held in San Antonio, Texas on July 11th 1999. The model, which was of Arthur Hare dressed as an "Harestronaut" (Astronaut), was issued in 1999 in a limited edition of 500. The cost direct from C&S Collectables was £30.00

Big Chief Bravehare, Shareiff, Santhare Paws, PC Gotchare

Gold Jesthare, Harestronaut

Backstamp: A. Printed black and red circular "© 1997 C&S Collectables Limited Edition With Certificate of Authenticity Modelled by Andy Moss Special Limited Edition (C&S) Arthur Hare™ Santhare Paws by Wade England"
   B. Printed "With Certificate of Authenticity © 1998 C&S Wade England Arthur Hare The Jesthare 350 Special Edition C&S"
   C. Printed "With Certificate of Authenticity. 500 Limited Edition. Harestronaut by Wade England © 1999 C&S"

No.	Name	Description	Size	U.S. $	Can. $	U.K. £
1	Santhare Paws	Grey hare; red and white Santa coat; brown sack; black belt; pearlised base	124	80.00	110.00	55.00
2	Shareriff	Grey hare; brown hat; red shirt; yellow sheriffs badge; blue trousers	110	65.00	90.00	45.00
3	Big Chief Bravehare	Green feathered war bonnet; red shirt; yellow trousers	115	55.00	80.00	40.00
4	PC Gotchare	Dark blue helmet and jacket; yellow helmet badge brown truncheon	115	75.00	100.00	50.00
5a	Platinum Jesthare	Grey hare; dark blue; orange/yellow jester suit; platinum bells and base	115	150.00	200.00	100.00
5b	Gold Jesthare	Grey hare; dark blue; orange/yellow jester suit; gold bells and base	115	120.00	160.00	85.00
6	Harestronaut	Grey hare; light grey suit with gold decoration and USA flag; silver helmet; black boots; silver base	115	65.00	90.00	45.00

BETTY BOOP BEACH BELLE

1998

In mid-1998 C&S introduced a new *Betty Boop* figurine *Betty Boop Beach Belle*. The new model wearing a swimsuit and was produced in a limited edition of 2,000 at the original cost of £41.95. For model wearing bikini please see Wade Buffalo, USA Show, see page 212.

Backstamp: Circular printed "©1998 King Features Syndicate Inc Fleisher Studios Inc TM Hearst Corporation 2000 Limited Edition (C&S) With Certificate of Authenticity Betty Boop Beach Belle by Wade England"

No.	Description	Size	U.S. $	Can. $	U.K. £
1	Blue hat; dark blue band; black hair, eyes; black yellow spotted swimsuit; pink towel; khaki base	145	135.00	180.00	90.00

MR. MAGOO

1998

A new Walt Disney feature film released in 1998 inspired C&S Collectables to commission a *Mr. Magoo* model in a limited edition of 1,000. Forty sample models of *Mr. Magoo* were produced with a gold base; C&S Collectables later sold these. The original cost of Mr Magoo was £37.00.

Backstamp: Printed "Mr Magoo Wade England ©1998 UPA Pictures, Inc. With Certificate of Authenticity 1,000 Limited Edition C&S"

No.	Name	Description	Size	U.S. $	Can. $	U.K. £
1a	Mr. Magoo	Brown hat with black band; black collar/shoes; dark green coat; brown walking stick; white base	105	85.00	100.00	45.00
1b	Mr. Magoo	Brown hat with black band; black collar/shoes; dark green coat; brown walking stick; gold base	105	250.00	320.00	190.00

ARTHUR HARE

THE COLLECTHARE COLLECTION

1998-1999

C&S introducted three new versions of the *Collecthare* in 1998-1999. At the Wade Christmas Bonanza 1998, a version of Arthur Hare wearing a red shirt and reading a book entitled "Christmas Bonanza" was introduced. It was produced in a limited edition of 400.

In early 1999, a new version of the *Collecthare* wearing a yellow tee shirt and carrying a "Wade's World" magazine was made available direct to mail order customers. At the UK Wade Collectors Fair held at Trentham Gardens in April 1999, a *Collecthare* with a purple top and carrying a "Jolly Potter" magazine was introduced. Both of these models were produced in a limited edition of 500, and their original cost direct from C&S was £39.95/each.

Backstamp: **A.** Printed "With Certificate of Authenticity. 500 Limited Edition. Arthur Hare the Collecthare by Wade England © 1998 C&S"

B. Printed "With Certificate of Authenticity. 500 Limited Edition. Arthur Hare the Collecthare by Wade England © 1999 C&S"

No.	Name	Description	Size	U.S. $	Can. $	U.K. £
1	Christmas Bonanza Collecthare 1998	Grey hare; red shirt; black trousers; blue Christmas Bonanza magazine; pearl base	120	65.00	90.00	45.00
2a	Jolly Potter Collecthare 1999	Grey hare; purple vest; black shorts; green satchel; orange strap; Jolly Potter magazine; gold base	120	65.00	90.00	45.00
2b	Wades World Collecthare 1999	Grey hare; yellow vest; black shorts; green satchel; orange strap; Wades World magazine; brown base	120	80.00	110.00	55.00

ARTHUR HARE

THE TRAVELHARE COLLECTION

1998-1999

A model of *Arthur Hare* in vest and shorts and with his left hand holding a sign post on which is printed "The Arthur Travelhare Collection by Wade" was produced in limited editions with colour changes of the vest for each Wade event it was issued for. The Arthur Hare Character is a trademark of C&S Collectables Direct.

All the Travelhares carry the same backstamp.

Backstamp: Gold Circular printed "© 1998 C&S Collectables Fair Special Uxbridge, Trentham Gardens, Buffalo, Arundel Swapmeet, Dunstable. Modelled by Andy Moss Special Limited Edition C&S Arthur Hare with Certificate of Authenticity by Wade England"

Arundel, Britanniahare Travelhare

July 1998

A limited edition of 500 *Travelhares* with white vest and a Union Jack flag on a gold base were produced for the Arundel, West Sussex, Swap Meet. One hundred models were held back and sold at the combined Wade/I.A.J.B.B.S.C. 1998 Show held in Buffalo USA. The cost direct from C&S was £35.00. At an Auction held at Arundel during the swap meet a boxed set of seven *Travelhares* were sold for £1,400.

Backstamp: See above

No.	Name	Description	Size	U.S. $	Can. $	U.K. £
1a	Britanniahare Arundel	Grey hare; white vest with red, white and blue Union Jack flag; black pants; gold base; black and red lettering	115	135.00	180.00	90.00

Buffalo, Travelhare

July 1998

A limited edition of 250 *Travelhares*, with a Stars & Stripes flag on his white vest and with a gold base. The *Travelhare* shipment did not arrive and C&S took orders for the models which, were then mailed to the purchasers. The cost direct from C&S was $60.00 US.

Backstamp: See above

No.	Name	Description	Size	U.S. $	Can. $	U.K. £
1b	Buffalo Travelhare	Grey hare; white vest with U.S.A. flag; black pants; gold base; black and red lettering	115	180.00	240.00	125.00

Dunstable, Travelhare

October 1998

A limited edition of 350 *Travelhares,* with a pearl lustre vest, were produced for the Dunstable, Bedfordshire, Wade Fair. The pearl lustre vest model with a gold base was originally intended as the show model for the 1998 Arundel Swap meet but the colour of the Swapmeet model was changed. Only twenty sample models with a gold base are known to exist.

Backstamp: See above

No.	Name	Description	Size	U.S. $	Can. $	U.K. £
1c	Dunstable Travelhare	Grey hare; pearl lustre vest; black pants; dark green base; black and red lettering	115	140.00	200.00	95.00
1d	Dunstable Travelhare	Grey hare; pearl lustre vest; black pants; gold base; black & red lettering	115	400.00	500.00	250.00

Newark, Collect It! Travelhare

August 1998

A limited edition of 400 *Travelhares,* with *Collect It! The Magazine for Collectors* printed on his white vest, and with a gold base, was produced for the Newark, Nottinghamshire *Collect It! Show.* This model has the same backstamp as all the *Travelhares,* Newark Collect It! is not included in the list of Fair venues. The cost direct from C&S was £40.00.

Backstamp: See above

No.	Name	Description	Size	U.S. $	Can. $	U.K. £
1e	Collect It! Travelhare	Grey hare; white vest; black pants; gold base; black and red lettering Collect It! The Magazine for Collectors	115	180.00	240.00	125.00

Special Edition Travelhare

1998

A limited edition of 250 *Travelhares,* with a gold vest was specially produced for those collectors who had purchased the Arthur Hare "PC Gotchare," "Shareiff" and "Bravehare" series. Cost direct from C&S was £35.00.

Backstamp: Unknown

No.	Name	Description	Size	U.S. $	Can. $	U.K. £
1g	Gold Special Edition Travelhare	Grey hare; gold vest; black pants; black base; black and red lettering	115	275.00	325.00	165.00

Trentham Gardens, Staffordshire, UK Travelhare

March 1998

A limited edition of 250 *Travelhares* with red vest. The cost direct from C&S was £35.00

Backstamp: See above

No.	Name	Description	Size	U.S. $	Can. $	U.K. £
1f	Red Trentham 1998 Travelhare	Grey hare; red vest; black pants; dark green base; black and red lettering	115	195 .00	260.00	135.00

Uxbridge, Travelhare

May 1998

Because of the high demand for the 250 limited edition yellow vest *Travelhares* at the Uxbridge show, C&S promised to mail to people who paid in advance a purple vest *Travelhare* which was originally intended for the Dunstable Show to be held in October. The purple vest *Travelhares* were mailed five days after the Uxbridge show. The cost direct from C&S was £35.00

Backstamp: See above

No.	Name	Description	Size	U.S. $	Can. $	U.K. £
1h	Yellow Uxbridge Travelhare	Grey hare; yellow vest; black pants; green base; black and red lettering	115	210.00	270.00	135.00
1i	Purple Uxbridge Travelhare	Grey hare; purple vest; black pants; green base; black and red lettering	115	165.00	220.00	110.00

ARTHUR HARE TEENIES

December 1999

The *Arthur Hare Teenies* were on sale at the Wade Christmas Bonanza held on December 4th at the Official Wade Collectors Centre in Arundel, West Sussex. The new *Arthur Hare Teenies* are miniature, two-colour versions of "PC Gotchare," the "Jesthare" and the "Harestronaut." The Teenies were produced in a limited edition of 300. The cost direct from C&S was £20.00 for the set of three.

Backstamp: Embossed "Wade" on back rim

No.	Name	Description	Size	U.S. $	Can. $	U.K. £
1	Teenie Harestronaut	Grey hare; black boots	40			
2	Teenie Jesthare	Grey hare; red costume	40			
3	Teenie PC Gotchare	Grey hare; dark blue uniform	40			
—	3 pce set	Boxed	—	35.00	50.00	25.00

BETTY BOOP SOUTHERN BELLE

1999

Introduced at the 3rd Wade Arundel Swapmeet (held in Arundel, West Sussex on August 1999). *Betty Boop Southern Belle* was produced with two different coloured hats and ribbons (the white hat with pink ribbon model [limited edition 500] and the blue hat with gold ribbon model [limited edition 100]). The blue hat models were packed and sold at random on the day of the meet. The original cost on the day was £35.00.

Backstamp: Printed "With Certificate of Authenticity © 1999 King Features Syndicate, Inc. Fleisher Studios, Inc. TM Hearst Corporation. Special Edition C&S Betty Boop Southern Belle Frankly, My Dear I Dont Give A Boop! Miniature Movie Queens #1 by Wade England"

No.	Name	Description	Size	U.S. $	Can. $	U.K. £
1a	Betty Boop Southern Belle	Blue hat; gold ribbon; white dress; pink flowers	80	175.00	230.00	115.00
1b	Betty Boop Southern Belle	White hat/dress; pink ribbon/flowers	80	120.00	150.00	70.00

BETTY BOOP HALLOWEEN TRICK OR TREAT

October 1999

The C&S model of *Betty Boop* in a Halloween witch costume was produced in a limited edition of 1,000. This is the first model of Betty Boop dressed in a Halloween costume. Original cost direct from C&S was £42.00.

Backstamp: Printed circular "© 1999 King Features Syndicate, Inc. Fleisher Studios, Inc. TM Hearst Corporation/Fleisher Studies Inc. 1000 Limited Edition C&S With Certificate of Authenticity Betty Boop Halloween Trick or Treat by Wade England"

No.	Name	Description	Size	U.S. $	Can. $	U.K. £
1	Betty Boop Halloween	Betty: black hat, dress, gloves and shoes; Cat: brown, black cloak; orange goody bags; white ghost; grey base	155	65.00	90.00	45.00

GARFIELD

1999

Garfield, the loveable cartoon cat, was produced in a special limited edition of 500.

Backstamp: Printed "With Certificate of Authenticity C&S 500 Special Edition Wade England"

No.	Name	Description	Size	U.S. $	Can. $	U.K. £
1	Garfield	Orange; black markings; pink nose; yellow cheeks	70	68.00	90.00	45.00

ORINOCO WOMBLE

1999

Orinoco is a well-known character from the British television cartoon series *The Wombles*. Seven hundred and fifty models of *Orinoco* with a green base were produced, as were 250 models of a gold-based Orinoco. The original cost direct from C&S was £39.95.

Backstamp: Printed "With Certificate of Authenticity 1,000 limited edition C&S The Wombles Orinoco by Wade England. 1,000 Limited Edition, © Elisabeth Berrisford / FilmFair Ltd 1999"

No.	Name	Description	Size	U.S. $	Can. $	U.K. £
1a	Orinoco	Red hat/scarf; yellow face/hands; grey hair and body; gold base	110	80.00	110.00	55.00
1b	Orinoco	Red hat/scarf; yellow face/hands; grey hair and body; green base	110	65.00	90.00	45.00

POCKET PAL "TANGO"

1999

Produced exclusively for C&S Collectables in a special limited edition of 1,000, the Wade Pocket Pal Cat Slinky was recoloured and re-named "Tango." The original cost from C&S was £6.50.

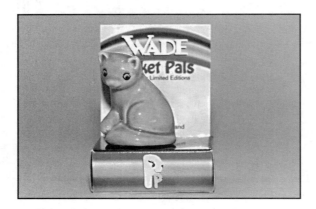

Backstamp: Gold Transfer "Wade Pp" in shield

No.	Name	Description	Size	U.S.$	Can.$	U.K.£
1	Cat Tango	Apricot; blue eyes	45 x 35	12.00	16.00	8.00

SNOOPY & WOODSTOCK

1999

Snoopy & Woodstock, a pair of the *Charlie Brown* cartoon characters, were produced in a limited edition of 1,000 of each. The original cost direct from C&S was £38.00 for the pair.

Backstamp: Printed "C&S © UFS Inc, Wade England"

No.	Name	Description	Size	U.S. $	Can. $	U.K. £
1	Snoopy	White; black markings; red collar	65	55.00	70.00	35.00
2	Woodstock	Yellow; black eyes and mouth	58	55.00	70.00	35.00

BETTY BOOP LIBERTY

February 2000

The first *Betty Boop* of the Millennium was of Betty as the Statue of Liberty. The model was produced in a limited edition of 1,000 and the original price was £42.00.

Backstamp: Printed circular "© 2000 King Features Syndicate, Inc./Fleisher Studios, Inc. TM Hearst Holdings, Inc/Fleisher Studies Inc. 1000 Limited Edition C&S With Certificate of Authenticity Betty Boop Liberty by Wade England"

No.	Name	Description	Size	U.S. $	Can. $	U.K. £
1	Betty Boop Liberty	Yellow flame; platinum torch, crown and book; dark blue dress	158	60.00	85.00	42.00

CAMTRAK
CHILDHOOD FAVOURITES SERIES
1995-1997

DOUGAL
1995

Dougal, a cartoon dog from the British childrens television series, *The Magic Roundabout,* was the first model of this series, produced for Camtrak of Nottingham, England. It was issued in a limited edition of 2,000 figures. The first 220 models were fired twice, leaving the model with a dark mushroom-coloured face, and is known as the brown-faced Dougal. The other 1,780 models were fired once only and have a lighter, pale ivory face. The original price, direct from Camtrak, was £27.50.

Backstamp: Transfer print "Camtrak's Childhood Favourites No.1 Dougal by Wade © Serge Danot/AB Productions SA 1995 Licensed by Link Licensing Ltd."

No.	Name	Description	Size	U.S. $	Can. $	U.K. £
1a	Dougal	Dark straw-coloured body; mushroom face	84 x 155	75.00	100.00	45.00
1b	Dougal	Dark straw-coloured body; pale ivory face	84 x 155	60.00	80.00	30.00

RUPERT BEAR

1996

Rupert Bear was created by Mary Tourtel and was featured in a British daily newspaper as well as children's books from the 1950s to the present. Rupert was the second in the *Childhood Favourites* series. He was produced in a limited edition of 1,000 (900 green-based models and 100 models with a gold base). The original price was £30.00.

Backstamp: Printed "Camtrak's Childhood Favourites by Wade No 2 Rupert © 1996 Express Newspapers plc Licensed by A.H.E/Nelvana"

No.	Description	Size	U.S. $	Can. $	U.K. £
1a	White head; black eyes, nose; yellow/black checked scarf and trousers; red jacket; gold base	130	275.00	370.00	185.00
1b	White head; black eyes, nose; yellow/black checked scarf and trousers; red jacket; green base	130	95.00	130.00	65.00

CHILDHOOD FAVOURITES DISPLAY PLAQUE

1997

The display plaque is in the shape of a 1950s television set.

Backstamp: Printed "Camtrak's Childhood Favourites A Series Display Plaque 1997 by Wade"

No.	Name	Description	Size	U.S. $	Can. $	U.K. £
1	Plaque	Brown/white; black and red lettering "Camtrak's Childhood Favourites by Wade"	70	45.00	60.00	30.00

DRACULA

1997

Wade produced *Dracula* in conjunction with *Nexus* a subsidiary name used by Camtrak, as *Dracula* was deemed too much of a contrast to Camtrak's cute *Childhood Favourites* series. The model, which stands on a wooden plinth, was sold in a special window shaped gift box. The production was limited to 2,500 models: Wade marketed 1,250 models in a matt glaze and Nexus (Camtrak) marketed 1,250 models in a high gloss glaze. The original cost was £85.00 for club members and £90.00 for non-members.

Backstamp: Unknown

No.	Description	Size	U.S. $	Can. $	U.K. £
1a	Black hair, cloak; red lining (gloss)	254	150.00	180.00	90.00
1b	Black hair, cloak; red lining (matt)	254	150.00	180.00	90.00

PADDINGTON BEAR

1997

Paddington Bear, created by Michael Bond, made his debut in 1958. He was the third model in the *Childhood Favourites* series commissioned by Camtrak. The original price was £33.00.

Backstamp: Printed "Camtrak's Childhood Favourites No 3 Paddington © Paddington and Company LTD 1997 Licensed by Copyrights Wade Made in England"

No.	Description	Size	U.S. $	Can. $	U.K. £
1a	Red hat/boots; royal blue coat; white label; brown suitcase; gold base	90	225.00	300.00	150.00
1b	Red hat/boots; royal blue coat; white label; brown suitcase; grey base	90	70.00	95.00	48.00

RUPERT AND THE SNOWMAN

1997

Rupert and the Snowman was the fourth model in Camtrak's *Childhood Favourites* series and was also the first in an intended series of *Seasonal* models. There were 1,900 models produced with a dark blue Snowman's scarf. One hundred of those models were produced with small gold buttons on Rupert's coat. A special limited edition of 110 models were produced with a pale blue Snowman's scarf for the City of London Police Fund (CLP).

Backstamp: **A.** Printed "Camtrak's Childhood Favourites by Wade No.4 Rupert and the Snowman. Rupert Characters and ©Express Newspapers Plc 1997 Licenced by Nelvana Marketing Inc. UK representative Abbey Home Entertainment"

B. Printed "Camtrak's Childhood Favourites by Wade No.4 Rupert and the Snowman. Rupert Characters and ©Express Newspapers Plc 1997 Licenced by Nelvana Marketing Inc. UK representative Abbey Home Entertainment Limited Edition of 110 Exclusive to the CLP Fund" with print of policeman and child

No.	Description	Size	U.S. $	Can. $	U.K. £
1a	Rupert: yellow/black check scarf, trousers; red coat; black gloves/buttons; Snowman: white; black eyes/buttons; dark blue scarf	120 x 110	90.00	140.00	65.00
1b	Rupert: yellow/black check scarf, trousers; red coat; black gloves; gold buttons; Snowman: white; black eyes/buttons; dark blue scarf	120 x 110	150.00	200.00	100.00
1c	Rupert: yellow/black check scarf, trousers; red coat; black gloves/buttons; Snowman: white; black eyes/buttons; pale blue scarf	120 x 110	200.00	270.00	135.00

SOOTY AND SWEEP 50TH ANNIVERSARY

1998

Sooty, a teddy bear, and *Sweep,* a puppy with long ears, were glove puppets operated by Harry Corbett and were featured on a BBC children's television program from 1950 to the 1980s. *Sooty* was produced in May 1998 and *Sweep* was issued in December 1998 as a companion piece. Produced in a limited edition of 2,000 each, *Sooty* and *Sweep* are the fifth and sixth figures in Camtrack's *Childhood Favourites* series. The original cost from Camtrack was £38.50.

Backstamp: A. Printed "Childhood Favourites by Wade No5 Sooty - Sooty ™ and © Sooty international Limited 1998 Licenced by Chatsworth enterprises Ltd 50 Golden Years" with "50 Golden Years Sooty" logo
B. Printed "Childhood Favourites by Wade No6 Sweep Sooty ™ and © Sooty international Limited 1998 Licenced by Chatsworth enterprises Ltd 50 Golden Years" with "50 Golden Years Sooty" logo

No.	Name	Description	Size	U.S. $	Can. $	U.K. £
1	Sooty	Amber bear; black ears/eyes/nose; blue dungarees; grey base	132	100.00	130.00	65.00
2	Sweep	Grey puppy/base; black ears/eyes; red nose/ collar/braces/trousers	136	100.00	130.00	65.00

PADDINGTON'S SNOWY DAY 40TH ANNIVERSARY

1999

The 40th anniversary of Paddington Bear's arrival from Peru was marked by a limited edition piece of 2,000 entitled *Paddington's Snowy Day*. This model is the second of the *Seasonal Specials* and is the seventh figure in Camtrak's *Childhood Favourites* series. Although similar to the 1997 *Paddington Bear,* this model has the left arm out and a rounded base. The original cost was £38.50.

Backstamp: Printed "Camtrak Childhood Favourites by Wade No7 Paddingtons Snowy Day. ©Paddington and Company. Ltd 1999 Licenced by Copyrights"

No.	Name	Description	Size	U.S. $	Can. $	U.K. £
1	Paddington's Snowy Day	Black hat; red coat; brown suitcase and boots; pearlised base; black lettering on suitcase 1958-1998	100		Unknown	

TINY CLANGER

1999

Tiny Clanger one of the "Clanger's," a family of long-nosed moon creatures that appeared in a BBC children's television program. He is the eighth model in Camtrak's *Childhood Favourites* Series.

Backstamp: Unknown

No.	Name	Description	Size	U.S. $	Can. $	U.K. £
1	Tiny Clanger	Pink; brown hair; red jacket; black shoes; grey base	110		Unknown	

CARRYER CRAFT OF CALIFORNIA
PAINTED LADIES
1984-1986

The beautiful Victorian houses of San Francisco survived the 1906 earthquake, but by the 1960s they had deteriorated badly. A few owners then decided to repaint their homes in the flamboyant colours of the original era, and the Painted Ladies were reborn. A Cable Car with different decals has been found: on one side of the car is a "Dewar's" decal and on the other "White Label" (the normal decals are "Fisherman's Wharf"). No information has been found to explain the change.

George Wade & Son Ltd. was commissioned by Carryer Craft of California (Iris Carryer was the elder daughter of Sir George Wade) to reproduce the Painted Ladies in porcelain. Because this short-lived series was made for export to the United States, only very limited quantities were released onto the British market.

All models are marked with "Wade England" in black on their side walls. The boxed set comprises six models, but the "Pink Lady," "Brown Lady," "White Lady" and the "Cable Car" are the most difficult to find. The original price was £10 for a box of eight models.

Backstamp: Black transfer "Wade Porcelain England SF/[number of model]"

No.	Name	Description	Size	U.S. $	Can. $	U.K. £
SF/1	Pink Lady	Pink; black roof	55 x 25	65.00	85.00	40.00
SF/2	White Lady	White; grey roof	55 x 25	65.00	85.00	40.00
SF/3	Brown Lady	Brown; beige roof	65 x 30	65.00	85.00	40.00
SF/4a	Yellow Lady	Yellow; grey roof; black apex	63 x 30	60.00	80.00	35.00
SF/4b	Yellow Lady	Yellow; grey roof; blue apex	63 x 30	60.00	80.00	35.00
SF/5	Blue Lady	Blue; grey roof	70 x 38	60.00	80.00	35.00
SF/6a	Cable Car	Blue/green; red front; Fisherman's Wharf	20 x 38	90.00	120.00	55.00
6b	Cable Car	Blue/green; yellow front; Dewar's White Label	20 x 38	90.00	120.00	55.00

CERAMECCA
I'M ON MY WAY

A model of a mouse with a suitcase and named *I'm On My Way*, was commissioned by Ceramecca and is the first in an intended series entitled *Wish You Were Here*. The model was produced in a limited edition of 750, and was introduced at the 1999 Trentham Gardens Wade Show. The original price was £29.00.

Backstamp: Printed "Wish You Were Here Collection I'm On My Way Ceramecca Limited Ed 750 With Certificate Wade England"

No.	Name	Description	Size	U.S. $	Can. $	U.K. £
1	I'm On My Way	Light brown mouse; green shirt; blue collar and trousers; brown suitcase; grey base	130	45.00	60.00	30.00

CIBA GEIGY
SLOW FE AND SLOW K
1969

In 1969, George Wade was commissioned by the British drug company Ciba Geigy to produce models of tortoises with the words *Slow Fe* and *Slow K* on their backs. These models were never issued as a retail line, but were presented to general practitioners by Ciba Geigy sales representatives as a promotional novelty to assist in marketing their iron and potassium preparations, Slow Fe (slow-release iron) and Slow K (slow-release potassium).

Approximately ten thousand of these models were produced. Wade retooled the "Medium (Mother)" tortoise from the *Tortoise Family* by embossing either the name Slow Fe or Slow K in the top shell.

Backstamp: Embossed "Wade Porcelain Made in England"

No.	Name	Description	Size	U.S. $	Can. $	U.K. £
1	Slow Fe	Brown; blue markings	35 x 75	100.00	125.00	50.00
2	Slow K	Brown; blue markings	35 x 75	100.00	125.00	50.00

COLLECT IT! MAGAZINE

1998 - 1999

BETTY BOOP WALL PLAQUE

1998

A model of the C&S Collectables *Betty Boop Wall Plaque* wearing a red glazed dress was produced in a limited edition of 1,250, and was a special offer in the May 1998 edition of *Collect It!* Magazine, selling out in four days. The original cost was £41.95.

Backstamp: Unknown

No.	Name	Description	Size	U.S. $	Can. $	U.K. £
1	Betty Boop Wall Plaque	Black hair; red dress; black and white dog; grey base	225	150.00	200.00	120.00

COLLECT IT! POCKET PALS "HOPPER" THE FROG AND "WOOFIT" THE DOG

November 1999

A special colourway Pocket Pal Frog named *Hopper* was given free with the November 1999 issue of *Collect It!* Magazine. The frog was attached to the front cover of the magazine and was only available through Smith's the British Bookstore to subscribers of *Collect it!* In the same issue was an offer for a special colourway of the Wade Pocket Pal dog named *Woofit*. The original cost of *Woofit* was £5.95.

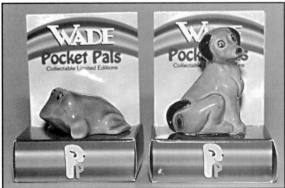

Backstamp: Gold transfer print "Wade Pp" in shield

No.	Name	Description	Size	U.S. $	Can. $	U.K. £
1	Frog Hopper	Green; blue eyes; pink mouth	25 x 45	12.00	18.00	9.00
2	Dog Woofit	Honey; dark brown ears and tail; brown eyes	55 x 35	12.00	18.00	9.00

COLLECT IT! FAIRIES

1998-1999

For the *Collect It!* fair held during the weekend of August 8th and 9th 1998 at the Showgrounds in Newark, Nottinghamshire, England, a special show model of a fairy named *Collectania* was commissioned by *Collect It!* in a limited edition of 2,500. Two more Fairy models, *Collectus* and *Collecteenie* were produced for the *Collect It!* Magazine and were offered in October 1998, and January 1999, respectively. The models came with a Certificate of Authenticity; the original cost was £39.95 each.

Backstamp: A. Black Printed "Collectania Made Exclusively for Collect it! By Wade Limited edition of 2,500"
B. Black Printed "Collectus Made Exclusively for Collect it! By Wade Limited edition of 2,500"
C. Black Printed "Collecteenie Made Exclusively for Collect it! By Wade Limited edition of 1,500"

No.	Name	Description	Size	U.S. $	Can. $	U.K. £
1	Collectania	Yellow hair; pearl wings; purple dress; red flowers; brown stump; green base with flowers	110	95.00	130.00	65.00
2	Collectus	Yellow hair; pearl wings; white shirt; purple pants; brown shoes/stump; red/white spotted toadstools; green base	105	95.00	130.00	65.00
3	Collecteenie	Blue toy sack; red suit; pearl wings	65	80.00	100.00	45.00

THE COLLECTOR
IN THE FOREST DEEP SERIES
1997-1999

This new series commissioned by *The Collector*, of Church Street, London is of British animals "Oswald Owl," "Morris Mole" and "Santa Hedgehog." The models were first seen at the October 1997 Dunstable Wade show. "Oswald" and "Morris" were issued in limited editions of 1,000 and "Santa" was issued in a limited edition of 2,000. "Bertram the Badger" and "Tailwarmer Squirrel" followed in March 1998. The last two models in the series were "Gentleman Rabbit" and "Huntsman Fox" produced in 1999, in a limited edition of 1,000 each. The original cost of the models was £39.00.

Backstamp: A. Printed "In The Forest Deep Series [name of model] for The Collector London Limited Edition of 1000 Wade"
B. Printed "In The Forest Deep Series Santa Hedgehog for The Collector London Limited Edition of 2000 Wade"

No.	Name	Description	Size	U.S. $	Can. $	U.K. £
1	Oswald Owl	Black mortar hat; dark brown back/brows/wings, log; light brown body; olive green base	113	75.00	100.00	50.00
2	Morris Mole	Grey body; buff chin/front/earthworms; brown mole hill; green base	105	75.00	100.00	50.00
3	Santa Hedgehog	Red and white Santa suit; black eyes/nose/belt, boots; light brown spines/face/paws; brown tree stump; buff toy sack; white snow base	132	75.00	100.00	50.00
4	Bertram Badger	Black and white badger; black coat/shoes; blue-grey shirt/trousers; brown hot water bottle/base	135	68.00	90.00	45.00
5	Tailwarmer Squirrel	Brown squirrel; blue/green striped tailwarmer; cream and brown acorns; brown base	110	68.00	90.00	45.00
6	Gentleman Rabbit	Beige rabbit; light grey hat/suit; white/black spotted cravat; brown walking stick; green base	115	60.00	80.00	40.00
7	Huntsman Fox	Red brown fox; black hat/bow tie/boots; white shirt and pants; red waistcoat; dark grey base	115	60.00	80.00	40.00

COTSWOLD COLLECTABLES
TUFTY AND HIS FURRYFOLK FRIENDS
1998-1999

Commissioned by Stuart Mitchell & Caroline Murray of *Cotswold Collectables,* the model is of "Tufty the Red Squirrel" a character created by Elsie Mills MBE in her storybooks of *Tufty and his Furryfolk Friends.* Tufty was produced in a limited edition of 1,500 the original cost was £39.95.

NOTE : A Belisha beacon is a bright yellow lighted globe on top of a black and white striped pole mounted at British Zebra Crossings (road crossings). In October 1999 a limited edition of 150 Tufty models with a gold base were introduced at the *Collect It!* Fair held in Wembley, UK. The cost of the gold-based Tufty was £37.00

Backstamp: Circular printed "©Tufty and his Furryfolk Friends by Cotswold Collectables 1998 Wade 'Tufty' ©RoSPA Enterprises Ltd. Limited Edition 1,500"

No.	Name	Description	Size	U.S. $	Can. $	U.K. £
1a	Tufty	Brown squirrel; dark blue jacket and shoes; yellow buttons and trousers; white/black striped Belisha Beacon with yellow top and grey base	140	60.00	80.00	40.00
1b	Tufty	Brown squirrel; dark blue jacket and shoes; yellow buttons and trousers; white/black striped Belisha Beacon with yellow top and gold base	140	55.00	75.00	37.00

E. AND A. CRUMPTON
THE LONG ARM OF THE LAW
1993-1995

The Long Arm Of The Law set was commissioned and designed by Elaine and Adrian Crumpton and modeled by Ken Holmes, in a limited edition of 2,000 each. "The Burglar" was issued in June 1993, the "Policeman" followed in October, the "Barrister" in August 1994 and the "Prisoner" in June 1995. The prisoner was produced with black hair and brown hair. The first 400 Policeman models have impressed faces, due to production problems; the next 1,600 have hand-painted faces. A mislaid Policeman mould resulted in the unauthorized production of a black-suited earthenware version which has an embossed Wade Backstamp but was not produced by Wade Ceramics.

Painted Face (left), Impressed Face (right)

Backstamp: **A.** Large embossed "Wade" (1)
B. Embossed "Wade" (2a, 2b, 4a, 4b)
C. Red transfer "Wade Made in England" (3)

No.	Name	Description	Size	U.S. $	Can. $	U.K. £
1	The Burglar	Black/white top; black cap, mask, shoes	85	65.00	90.00	45.00
2a	Policeman	Impressed face; dark blue uniform	90	80.00	105.00	75.00
2b	Policeman	Painted face; dark blue uniform	90	55.00	75.00	45.00
3	Barrister	Black gown, shoes; grey trousers	80	60.00	80.00	45.00
4a	Prisoner	Black hair, ball, chain; white suit with black arrows; grey shoes	70	60.00	80.00	45.00
4b	Prisoner	Brown hair; black ball, chain; white suit with black arrows; brown shoes	70	90.00	120.00	45.00
4c	Prisoner	Brown hair; black ball, chain; white suit with black arrows; grey shoes	70	90.00	120.00	45.00

FRISCO COFFEE
ENGLISH WHIMSIES
1973-1974

During 1973-1974 Frisco coffee (a division of Liptons Tea) of Cape Town South Africa distributed *Whimsie* Models wrapped in cellophane packets in their boxes of Frisco Coffee. Seven models have been reported, but it is believed there may have been more. The models are the same colours as the original *English Whimsies* and are listed in alphabetical order.

Photograph not available
at press time

Backstamp: Embossed "Wade England" on rim

No.	Name	Description	Size	U.S. $	Can.$	U.K.£
1	Bear Cub	Grey; beige face	30 x 40	7.00	4.00	2.00
2	Bushbaby	Brown; blue ears	30 x 30	6.00	4.00	2.00
3	Duck	Blue/brown; yellow beak	30 x 40	9.00	6.00	3.00
4	Fawn	Brown; blue ears	30 x 30	7.00	4.00	3.00
5	Kitten	Dark/light brown; pink wool	30 x 30	6.00	6.00	3.00
6	Owl	Dark/light brown	35 x 20	8.00	6.00	4.00
7	Rabbit	Beige open ears	30 x 30	8.00	6.00	3.00

G&G COLLECTABLES
SCOOBY-DOO
1994

Scooby-Doo was commissioned by G&G Collectables for a limited edition of 2,000 numbered models.

Backstamp: Black transfer "© H/B Inc Scooby-Doo Limited Edition of 2,000 Wade England G & G Collectables"

No.	Description	Size	U.S. $	Can. $	U.K. £
1	Brown; black spots; blue collar; gold medallion	115 x 85	105.00	140.00	70.00

SCRAPPY DOO
1995

This model was issued in a limited edition of 2,000. The original price was £29.95.

Backstamp: Transfer print "© H/B Inc Scrappy Doo Limited Edition of 2,000 Wade England G&G Collectables"

No.	Description	Size	U.S. $	Can. $	U.K. £
1	Brown; black nose, eyes; blue collar; yellow medallion; green base	Unknown	575.00	110.00	55.00

MR. JINKS, PIXIE & DIXIE
1997

Mr. Jinks, a Hanna-Barbera cartoon character of the late 1950s-1960s, was commissioned by G&G Collectables and first seen at the October 1997 Dunstable Wade Show. *Pixie* and *Dixie* a pair of cartoon mice, were produced in a limited edition of 1,500 models of each. The original cost was £75.00 for the pair.

Backstamp A: Printed "Wade England Mr. Jinks © 1997 H.B. Prod Inc G&G Collectables"
B: Printed "Wade England © 1997 H.B. Prod Inc Worldwide edition of 1,500 G&G Collectables" with name of model

No.	Name	Description	Size	U.S. $	Can. $	U.K. £
1	Mr. Jinks	Orange cat; black eyes/nose; blue bow tie; yellow cheese; white base	152	75.00	100.00	50.00
2	Pixie	Grey mouse; black eyes/nose/whiskers; red waistcoat; red tomato; cream burger; yellow cheese	115	60.00	80.00	40.00
3	Dixie	Grey mouse; black eyes/nose/whiskers; blue bow tie; red cherry; green/chocolate cupcake	115	60.00	80.00	40.00

SANTA CLAUS
1997

This model of *Santa Claus* in a chimney was commissioned by G&G Collectables in a limited edition of 1,000 and was modelled by Nigel Weaver. The cost direct from G&G Collectables was £36.00.

Backstamp: Unknown

No.	Name	Description	Size	U.S. $	Can. $	U.K. £
1	Santa Claus	Red and white hat and jacket; black belt and gloves; grey chimney; white snow	133	55.00	75.00	36.00

YOGI BEAR AND BOO BOO

1997

Yogi Bear was produced in a limited edition of 1,500 in early 1997 for G&G Collectables. *Boo Boo*, the second model in the series, was available in late 1997. The original cost of both models was £34.00.

Backstamp: **A.** Printed Black printed "Wade England Yogi Bear" "©1997 H.B.Prod Inc Worldwide Edition of 1500 G&G Collectables"
B. Printed Black printed "Wade England Boo Boo" "©1997 H.B.Prod Inc Worldwide Edition of 1500 G&G Collectables"

No.	Name	Description	Size	U.S. $	Can. $	U.K. £
1	Yogi Bear	Dark brown bear; green hat, tie; white collar; dark blue waistcoat; brown picnic basket, tree stump	130	75.00	100.00	50.00
2	Boo Boo	Brown bear; black eyes, nose, bow tie/waistcoat; white honey pot; light brown tree stump	114	65.00	90.00	45.00

HUCKLEBERRY HOUND

1998

Huckleberry Hound was produced in a limited edition of 1,500 models. The original cost for Huckleberry Hound was £38.00.

Backstamp: Unknown

No.	Name	Description	Size	U.S. $	Can. $	U.K. £
1	Huckleberry Hound	Blue hound; black ears, eyes, nose; yellow hat; black drum base with gold lines	135	60.00	80.00	40.00

LITTLE RED RIDING HOOD AND THE BIG BAD WOLF

1998-1999

The Big Bad Wolf was the first model in the *Once Upon A Time* series produced in 1998. *Little Red Riding Hood,* the second model in the series, followed in 1999. Both models were produced in a limited edition of 1,000. The original cost of both was £30.00.

Backstamp: Printed "Limited Edition 1,000 © G&G Collectables &Wade" with name of model

No.	Name	Description	Size	U.S. $	Can. $	U.K. £
1	Big Bad Wolf	Brown wolf; blue cape; white nightdress	92	50.00	70.00	35.00
2	Red Riding Hood	Brown hair/basket; red cloak; blue dress; green base	100	50.00	70.00	35.00

PEGGY GAMBLE (Formerly Gamble and Styles)
MR. PUNCH AND JUDY
1996 - 1999

A model of *Mr. Punch* sitting on a white drum was commissioned by Peggy Gamble and Sue Styles in a limited edition of 2,000. One thousand, eight hundred are dressed in burgundy and two hundred are in green. The model was sold at the 3rd Wade Collectors Fair, held in Birmingham, England, in 1996, for a cost of £45.00. Each figure is numbered and issued with a matching, numbered card signed by Gamble and Styles.

The beautifully modelled figure of *Judy* was the second in a limited edition series commissioned by Peggy Gamble and Sue Styles. *Judy*, seated and holding a baby on her lap, was issued in a limited edition of 1,800 models. The original issue price was £42.00. The signature of modeler Ken Holmes is included in the backstamp.

The Gamble and Styles partnership was discontinued in late 1997. Peggy Gamble commissioned the *Toby* the dog model which was issued in 1998. One thousand, five hundred models were produced with a red hat and two hundred models with a green hat. Toby was signed by modeler Ken Holmes. *Judy's Ghost* was produced in 1999. Eight hundred models have a gold base and 200 have a green base. *Judy's Ghost* was signed by modeler Simon Millard. Each model comes with a Certificate of Authenticity. The original cost of *Mr. Punch & Judy* was £41.00 each, and *Toby* and *Judy's Ghost* was £35.00

Mr. Punch   Toby   Judy

Judy's ghost

Backstamp: A. Black transfer outline of a corgi, "P&S" stamped on the body, "Wade" between two black lines and the issue number (1)
B. Black transfer outline of a Corgi, "P&S" stamped on the body, "Modelled by K Holmes Wade" and the issue number (2)
C. Black transfer outline of a Corgi, "PG" stamped on the body, "Modelled by Simon Millard Wade"

No.	Name	Description	Size	U.S. $	Can. $	U.K. £
1a	Mr. Punch	Burgundy hat/suit; white ruff; yellow hat tassel, socks; black stick/shoes; white drum	165	95.00	125.00	45.00
1b	Mr. Punch	Green hat/suit; white ruff; yellow hat tassel, socks; black stick/shoes; white drum	165	220.00	290.00	145.00
2a	Judy	White mop cap/collar/cuffs; black string bow; pale blue dress; baby in white cap and gown	150	95.00	125.00	45.00
2b	Judy	White mop cap/collar/cuffs; black string bow; green dress; baby in white cap and gown	150	220.00	290.00	145.00
3a	Toby	Brown dog; red hat; yellow pom pom; white ruff; white and blue base	122	55.00	75.00	37.00
3a	Toby	Brown dog; green hat; yellow pom pom; white ruff; white and blue base	122	125.00	170.00	85.00
4a	Judy's Ghost	Pearlised ghost; grey tombstone; black lettering RIP JUDY; gold base	143	65.00	90.00	45.00
4b	Judy's Ghost	Pearlised ghost; grey tombstone; black lettering RIP JUDY; green base	143	95.00	130.00	65.00

GENERAL FOODS

CIRCA 1990

A planned promotion for General Foods of England that included miscellaneous animals of two or three colours and *Miniature Nursery Rhymes* characters in one-colour glazes was cancelled before it began. A number of models that had been intended for the promotion were released onto the market for a short time in late 1990.

MISCELLANEOUS ANIMALS

1990

TS: Tom Smith   EW: *English Whimsies*   WL: *Whimsie-land* series

Photograph not available
at press time

Backstamp: Embossed "Wade England"

No.	Name	Description	Size	U.S. $	Can. $	U.K. £
1	Badger (TS British Wildlife)	Light grey/white; green base	25 x 40	10.00	12.00	4.00
2	Chimpanzee (EW)	Olive/green-brown	35 x 35	12.00	15.00	6.00
3	Owl (WL)	White; orange beak; green base	35 x 25	10.00	15.00	7.00
4	Panda (WL)	Black/white	37 x 20	20.00	30.00	8.00
5	Penguin (TS 1987)	Black/white; orange beak	45 x 17	10.00	12.00	4.00
6	Rabbit (EW)	White; pinky beige; pink nose	30 x 30	8.00	6.00	2.00
7	Zebra (EW)	Black; green grass	40 x 35	9.00	11.00	4.00

MINIATURE NURSERY RHYMES

1990

These models are all in one colour.

Photograph not available
at press time

Backstamp: Embossed "Wade England"

No.	Name	Description	Size	U.S. $	Can. $	U.K. £
1	Jack	Beige	35 x 35	6.00	8.00	4.00
2	Jill	Beige	35 x 35	6.00	8.00	4.00
3	Little Bo-Peep	Green	45 x 25	10.00	12.00	6.00
4	Little Jack Horner	Beige	40 x 20	6.00	8.00	4.00
5	Mother Goose	Beige	40 x 32	6.00	8.00	4.00
6	Old King Cole	Light blue	40 x 35	15.00	20.00	10.00
7	Old Woman Who Lived in a Shoe	Beige	40 x 40	6.00	8.00	4.00
8	Pied Piper	Green	50 x 30	10.00	12.00	6.00
9	Red Riding Hood	Pink	45 x 20	10.00	12.00	6.00
10	Tom the Piper's Son	Blue	40 x 35	15.00	20.00	10.00
11	Wee Willie Winkie	Blue	45 x 25	15.00	20.00	10.00

GOLD STAR GIFTHOUSE
NURSERY FAVOURITES
1990-1991

Only five of the original 20 *Nursery Favourites* models were reissued for the Gold Star Gifthouse, a California Wade dealer. The last two models are the hardest to find of the original *Nursery Favourites*.

Backstamp: A. Embossed "Wade England 1990" (1, 2, 3)
           B. Embossed "Wade England 1991" and ink stamp "GSG" (4)
           C. Embossed "Wade England 1991" (5)

No.	Name	Description	Size	U.S. $	Can. $	U.K. £
1	Mary Mary	Brighter than original; blue dress; yellow hair; pink shoes; green base	75 x 45	35.00	45.00	20.00
2	Polly Put the Kettle On	Same colours as original; brown; pink cap, kettle	75 x 35	35.00	45.00	20.00
3	Tom Tom the Piper's Son	Brighter than original; blue-grey kilt; yellow/honey jacket	65 x 55	35.00	45.00	20.00
4	Old Woman in a Shoe	Blue bonnet, dress; beige dog/door	60 x 55	50.00	60.00	35.00
5	Goosey Goosey Gander	Same as original; beige; pink beak	66 x 55	90.00	120.00	60.00

GRANADA TELEVISION
CORONATION STREET HOUSES
1988-1989

The *Coronation Street Houses* set was commissioned by Granada Television as a promotional item for its long-running television series, *Coronation Street*, and sold at the studio gift shop and by mail order. Only three models of the set were produced, although others were planned. The figures are very similar to the *Whimsey-on-Why* houses. They were sold on cards with details of the series printed on the back.

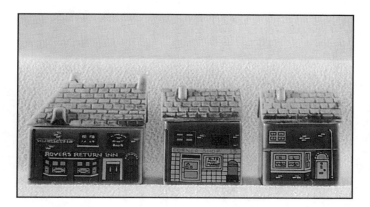

Backstamp: Embossed "Wade England"

No.	Name	Description	Size	U.S. $	Can. $	U.K. £
1	The Rovers Return	Brown; grey roof	45 x 48	20.00	30.00	15.00
2	No.9 The Duckworths	Yellow/grey windows, door	45 x 33	20.00	30.00	15.00
3	Alf's Corner Shop	Brown; grey roof	45 x 33	20.00	30.00	15.00

GREAT UNIVERSAL STORES

For a number of years, Tom Smith and Company marketed a line of Christmas crackers through Great Universal Stores (G.U.S.).

SET ONE: SNOW LIFE

1993-1994

The Tom Smith *Snow Animals* series was reissued for G.U.S., with the addition of the Tom Smith *Survival Animals* "Whale" in grey and the Red Rose *Miniature Nurseries* "Goosey Goosey Gander," coloured white and renamed the "Snow Goose." The "Reindeer" model can be found with or without a gap between the legs.

Although there are ten models in this set, the box only contains eight crackers. This can cause problems for collectors wishing to complete a set and will cause a future rise in price for some figures.

Backstamp: Embossed "Wade England"

No.	Name	Description	Size	U.S.$	Can.$	U.K.£
1	Fox (WL)	Red-brown	35 x 36	15.00	20.00	3.00
2	Penguin (EW)	Blue-grey	49 x 21	15.00	20.00	3.00
3	Polar Bear (EW)	White	27 x 45	10.00	12.00	4.00
4	Reindeer (TS)	Beige	34 x 35	15.00	20.00	3.00
5	Seal Pup (EW)	Blue-grey	26 x 39	15.00	20.00	3.00
6	Snow Goose (RR)	White	33 x 37	12.00	15.00	3.00
7	Snowshoe Hare (TS)	White	45 x 33	15.00	20.00	3.00
8	Snowy Owl (WL)	White	35 x 25	15.00	20.00	3.00
9	Walrus (EW)	Beige	34 x 36	12.00	15.00	3.00
10	Whale (Baleen TS)	Grey	22 x 52	15.00	20.00	3.00

Note: The following initials indicate the origin of the models:
TS: Tom Smith
WL: *Whimsie-land* Series
EW: *English Whimsies*
RR: Red Rose *Miniature Nurseries*

SET TWO: ENDANGERED SPECIES

1994

Backstamp: Embossed "Wade England"

No.	Name	Description	Size	U.S.$	Can.$	U.K.£
1	Cockatoo (TS)	Green	41 x 47	8.00	10.00	4.00
2	Fox (WL)	Light brown	35 x 36	8.00	10.00	10.00
3	Gorilla (EW)	Brown	37 x 28	4.00	6.00	3.00
4	Koala Bear (EW)	Beige	35 x 29	6.00	9.00	4.00
5	Leopard (EW)	Honey brown	20 x 47	6.00	8.00	4.00
6	Orang-Outan (EW)	Brown	30 x 34	5.00	7.00	4.00
7	Polar Bear (EW)	White	27 x 45	10.00	12.00	4.00
8	Rhino (EW)	Grey	25 x 43	8.00	6.00	4.00
9	Tiger (EW)	Honey brown	37 x 30	15.00	20.00	5.00
10	Whale (Baleen TS)	Grey	22 x 52	8.00	10.00	4.00

Note: The following initials indicate the origin of the models:
EW: *English Whimsies*
WL: *Whimsie-land* Series
TS: Tom Smith

SET THREE: TALES FROM THE NURSERY

1994-1995

Also reissued for G.U.S. was the Tom Smith *Tales from the Nurseries* set. There are slight colour variations from the previous set in "Hickory Dickory Dock," "Little Bo-Peep," "Humpty Dumpty," "Queen of Hearts," "Little Jack Horner" and "Ride a Cock Horse." The remaining models are the same colour as before.

Backstamp: Embossed "Wade England"

No.	Name	Description	Size	U.S.$	Can.$	U.K.£
1	Cat and the Fiddle (RR)	Grey	47 x 31	8.00	10.00	3.00
2	Dr. Foster (RR)	Dark brown	45 x 30	8.00	10.00	3.00
3	Hickory Dickory Dock (RR)	Beige	45 x 20	8.00	10.00	3.00
4	Humpty Dumpty (RR)	Blue-grey	35 x 23	8.00	10.00	3.00
5	Little Bo-Peep (RR)	Purple	45 x 25	8.00	10.00	3.00
6	Little Boy Blue (TS)	Blue	41 x 25	10.00	12.00	4.00
7	Little Jack Horner (RR)	Honey	38 x 20	8.00	10.00	3.00
8	Queen of Hearts (RR)	Apricot	43 x 25	8.00	10.00	4.00
9	Ride a Cock Horse (TS)	Green	36 x 41	10.00	12.00	4.00
10	Tom Tom the Piper's Son (RR)	Honey	40 x 34	8.00	10.00	3.00

Note: The following initials indicate the origin of the models:
RR: Red Rose
TS: Tom Smith

SET FOUR: MISCELLANEOUS MODELS

Backstamp: Unknown

No.	Name	Description	Size	U.S.$	Can.$	U.K.£
1	Beaver (EW)	Dark brown	35 x 45	8.00	6.00	2.00
2	Camel (EW)	Beige	35 x 55	9.00	11.00	4.00
3	Circus lion (TS)	Honey	40 x 22	5.00	12.00	4.00
4	Giraffe (EW)	Beige	35 x 35	7.00	5.00	2.00
5	Langur Type 2 (EW)	Dark brown	35 x 30	5.00	7.00	4.00
6	Pine marten (EW)	Honey	34 x 34	6.00	5.00	2.00
7	Pony (TS)	Beige	25 x 30	10.00	12.00	4.00
8	Puppy (TS)	Honey	25 x 30	10.00	12.00	4.00
9	Raccoon (EW)	Light brown	25 x 35	15.00	12.00	4.00
10	Zebra (EW)	Grey	40 x 35	9.00	11.00	4.00

Note: The following initials indicate the origin of the models:
EW: *English Whimsies*
TS: Tom Smith

HARRODS OF KNIGHTSBRIDGE
DOORMAN EGG CUP, MONEY BOX, CRUET AND COOKIE JAR
1991-1996

These models were produced for Harrods of Knightsbridge. The egg cups, issued in 1991, are in the shape of a Harrods doorman and were sold in the store at Easter, packaged with miniature chocolate eggs, and at Christmas, filled with sweets or sugared almonds. The moneybox, issued in 1993, is the same shape as the eggcups, only larger. Its original selling price at Harrods was £16.95. The cookie jar was released in 1996 and features a younger looking doorman.

Cookie Jar

Backstamp: Black transfer "Harrods Knightsbridge"

No.	Name	Description	Size	U.S. $	Can. $	U.K. £
1	Cookie Jar	Green cap, coat; gold buttons, trim	185	60.00	80.00	35.00
2	Egg Cup	Green cap, coat; gold buttons, trim	103 x 48	35.00	45.00	30.00
3	Money Box	Green cap, coat; gold buttons, trim	175 x 125	45.00	60.00	50.00
4	Pepper Cruet Saluting	Green cap, coat; gold buttons, trim	105	30.00	45.00	25.00
5	Salt Cruet Holding Package	Green cap, coat; gold buttons, trim	105	30.00	45.00	25.00

K.P. FOODS LTD.

K.P. FRIARS

1983

The *K.P. Friars* set was commissioned by K.P. Foods Ltd. to promote the sales of its potato crisps (chips). The first model, the "Father Abbot," was free with a given number of tokens from the packets. The remaining five models could be obtained with tokens, plus a small charge.

The "Father Abbot" came either in a cardboard box with a friar's design on it or in a small box with a cellophane front. The rest of the figures were issued together as a set of five, in a box with a folding cardboard lid or one with a cellophane sleeve. Although K.P. Friars was first issued as a set of five and in late 1983, as a set of six, with the inclusion of the "Father Abbot," for some reason the last three models — "Brother Crispin," "Brother Angelo" and "Brother Francis" — are the hardest to find, so have higher collector's prices. Each model stands on a square base, with the name of the friar embossed on the front.

NOTE: The origin of the two models with grey robes is unknown.

Backstamp: Embossed "Wade"

No.	Name	Description	Size	U.S. $	Can. $	U.K. £
1	Father Abbot	Beige head, base; brown robes	45 x 18	18.00	25.00	10.00
2a	Brother Peter	Beige head, base; brown robes	40 x 18	15.00	20.00	10.00
2b	Brother Peter	Honey head, base; grey robes	40 x 18	15.00	20.00	10.00
3	Brother Benjamin	Beige head, base; brown robes	40 x 18	15.00	20.00	10.00
4	Brother Crispin	Beige head, base; brown robes	40 x 20	45.00	60.00	20.00
5	Brother Angelo	Beige head, base; brown robes	48 x 20	45.00	60.00	20.00
6a	Brother Francis	Beige head, base; brown robes	42 x 20	45.00	60.00	20.00
6b	Brother Francis	Honey head, base; grey robes	42 x 20	45.00	60.00	20.00

PATTY KEENAN
CHRISTMAS ORNAMENTS
1994-1997

Commissioned by Patty Keenan of Pennsylvania, U.S.A., the first model in the *Christmas Ornaments* series was "Santa's Sleigh," produced in November 1994 in a limited edition of 2,000. The second model, a "Rocking Horse" was produced for Christmas 1995, and was also produced in a limited edition of 2,000. In 1996, the "Rocking Horse" ornament was re-issued in a limited edition of 600 in new colours.

The Christmas 1997 ornament was a model of a train with multi-coloured prints of Santa Claus, reindeer and holly leaves. Both Wade Ceramics and Keenan Antiques sold "Santa's Train," but only 500 models have a Keenan Antiques Backstamp that reads "Keenan Antiques Wade England Christmas No 4." The original cost from Wade Ceramics for the "Santa Train" was £10.50 and from Keenan Antiques $16.95 (U.S.).

Backstamp: A. Red ink stamped "Wade made in England"
　　　　　　 B. Printed "Wade Ceramics"
　　　　　　 C. Printed "Keenan Antiques Wade England Christmas No 4" (on 500 Santa's Train models)

No.	Name	Description	Size	U.S. $	Can. $	U.K. £
1	Santa's Sleigh	White Reindeer and sleigh; Santa in red coat	40	25.00	40.00	20.00
2a	Rocking Horse	Grey; dark grey mane, tail and rockers	38	25.00	40.00	20.00
2b	Rocking Horse	Honey; dark brown mane, tail and rockers	38	25.00	40.00	20.00
3	Santa's Train	Grey; multi coloured prints; black No 25	35	24.00	32.00	15.00

MINIATURE TANKARD
1996

Patty Keenan commissioned a Miniature Tankard with a print of a Rocking Horse Ornament on the front for the first Wade Show held in Seattle July 1996. The miniature tankards were produced in a limited edition of 500.

Backstamp: Red printed "Wade Made in England"

No.	Name	Description	Size	U.S. $	Can. $	U.K. £
1	Miniature Tankard	White; gold rim; grey Rocking Horse print	31	10.00	14.00	5.00

KEY KOLLECTABLES
THE STRAW FAMILY

1999

A new series produced in early 1999 was *The Straw Family* of Millfield Farm. The first models in the series were "Pa" and "Ma Straw": both models were issued in a limited edition of 2,000. "Teen Straw" was produced in late 1999 at a cost of £27.00.

Backstamp: Printed "Key Kollectables - Limited Edition of 2,000 with Certificate of Authenticity - Wade England" with name of model

No.	Name	Description	Size	U.S. $	Can. $	U.K. £
1	Pa Straw	Black hat; yellow straw; red jacket with black collar; grey waistcoat and trousers; green base	140	45.00	60.00	30.00
2	Ma Straw	Brown hat; yellow straw; red ribbon; blue dress; white apron green base; yellow basket; green base	134	40.00	55.00	27.00
3	Teen Straw	Black baseball cap; yellow straw; green jacket; red scarf; green base	120	40.00	55.00	27.00

KING AQUARIUMS LTD.
AQUARIUM SET
1976-1980

The *Aquarium Set* was produced for King Aquariums Ltd., a British company that supplied aquarium products to pet stores, and were not on sale in gift stores. The "Bridge" is marked with "Wade England" embossed at the base of each span, whereas the other figures are marked on the back rims.

Backstamp: Embossed "Wade England"

No.	Name	Description	Size	U.S. $	Can. $	U.K. £
1	Bridge	Beige; light brown bases	45 x 80	120.00	160.00	65.00
2	Diver	Honey brown; brown base	70 x 28	25.00	35.00	15.00
3a	Lighthouse	Beige/honey brown; grey-green base	75 x 45	50.00	70.00	35.00
3b	Lighthouse	Honey brown; grey-green base	75 x 45	50.00	70.00	35.00
4	Mermaid	Beige; yellow hair; grey-green base	60 x 58	50.00	68.00	45.00
5	Seahorse	Blue/beige pattern	70 x 30	185.00	250.00	120.00
6	Water Snail/Whelk	Honey brown; green-grey shell	30 x 35	100.00	125.00	50.00

LEVER REXONA
NURSERY RHYME MODELS
Early 1970s

Lever Rexona, makers of Signal 2 toothpaste, offered 24 miniature *Nursery Rhyme* models as a promotion, one model per box. The same models were used in the 1972-1979 Canadian Red Rose Tea promotion.

Backstamp: Unknown

No.	Name	Description	Size	U.S. $	Can. $	U.K. £
1	Baa Baa Black Sheep	Black	25 x 30	15.00	12.00	15.00
2	Cat and the Fiddle	Beige cat; yellow fiddle	45 x 25	35.00	15.00	10.00
3	Dr. Foster	Light brown; yellow tie; blue puddle	45 x 25	10.00	6.00	10.00
4	Gingerbread Man	Red-brown; grey-green base	40 x 28	45.00	35.00	25.00
5	Goosey Gander	Honey head, neck; dark brown wings; pink beak	30 x 35	8.00	6.00	4.00
6	Hickory Dickory Dock	Red-brown/honey clock; brown mouse	45 x 20	6.00	4.00	5.00
7	House that Jack Built	Honey; red-brown roof	35 x 35	12.00	8.00	15.00
8	Humpty Dumpty	Honey; pink cheeks; blue bowtie; brown wall	45 x 35	7.00	5.00	5.00
9	Jack	Light brown; blue shirt, bucket	35 x 35	10.00	6.00	9.00
10	Jill	Yellow hair; beige dress; blue bucket	35 x 35	10.00	6.00	9.00
11	Little Bo Peep	Light brown; blue apron; green base	45 x 25	5.00	4.00	6.00
12	Little Boy Blue	Blue hat, coat; honey trousers	43 x 25	15.00	12.00	6.00
13	Little Jack Horner	Beige; blue plum; pink cushion	40 x 20	6.00	4.00	6.00
14	Little Miss Muffett	Honey/grey dress; red-brown spider	45 x 20	10.00	6.00	10.00
15	Mother Goose	Blue hat, bodice; honey dress, goose	40 x 32	10.00	8.00	15.00
16	Old King Cole (Gap)	Beige; blue hat, hem; pink sleeves	40 x 35	7.00	4.00	6.00
17	Old Woman Who Lived in a Shoe	Red-brown roof; honey woman	40 x 40	8.00	4.00	6.00
18	Pied Piper	Light brown coat; green bush	50 x 30	10.00	8.00	6.00
19	Puss in Boots	Brown; blue boots; green base	45 x 20	10.00	8.00	15.00
20	Queen of Hearts	Pink hat; beige dress; two red hearts	45 x 25	15.00	8.00	10.00
21	Red Riding Hood	Beige dress; red/pink hood, cape; green base	45 x 20	6.00	5.00	6.00
22	Three Bears	Dark brown; honey base	35 x 38	35.00	20.00	20.00
23	Tom Tom the Piper's Son	Honey; blue hat, kilt; brown jacket	40 x 35	15.00	8.00	8.00
24	Wee Willie Winkie	Yellow hair, candle; beige nightshirt	45 x 25	10.00	7.00	6.00

MEMORY JARS
YEAR OF THE RABBIT
1999

Memory Jars commissioned a new colourway of the *English Whimsie Rabbit* to mark the last year of the Millennium (the Chinese Year of the Rabbit). Four hundred and fifty rabbits are in a blue glaze and fifty in an all-over gold glaze. Obtainable with the purchase of a limited edition Memory Jar, they were made available June 1999.

Backstamp: Embossed "Wade England" on rim

No.	Name	Description	Size	U.S.$	Can.$	U.K.£
1a	Rabbit	Blue	30 x 30	Unknown		
1b	Rabbit	Gold	30 x 30	Unknown		

OUT OF THE BLUE CERAMICS (COLLECTABLES MAGAZINE)

TINY TREASURES

1999

Tiny Treasures of *Collectables* magazine commissioned a set of slipcast (hollow) figurines from Wade Ceramics in April 1999. The set consists of four models: "Batman" and "Alfred" (Batman's Butler) "Supergirl" and "Lois Lane" (Superman's Reporter Girlfriend).

"Batman" and "Alfred" were produced in a limited edition of 1,939 models "Supergirl" and "Lois Lane" were produced in a limited edition of 1,938 models. The original cost of the models direct from *Collectables Magazine* was £5.90 each.

Backstamp: Red printed "Wade Made in England" on the back of the model base and Black printed "DC Comics 1999 Wade" with name of model on the bottom of the model base. Some models also have the initials of the painter on the base.

No.	Name	Description	Size	U.S.$	Can.$	U.K.£
1	Alfred	Beige figure; white shirt; black suit	58	9.00	12.00	6.00
2	Batman	Amber figure; black cloak/mask/boots /gloves; yellow belt	58	9.00	12.00	6.00
3	Lois Lane	Amber figure; brown hair/skirt; maroon jacket	55	9.00	12.00	6.00
4	Supergirl	Amber figure; yellow hair; red cloak; blue two-piece suit	55	9.00	12.00	6.00

PEX NYLONS
FAIRY AND CANDLE HOLDER
Circa 1952

One of the first promotional models produced by Wade was made at the Wade (Ulster) Pottery in the early 1950s for Pex Nylons. It was a model of a fairy sitting in a pink water lily, and was also produced as a candleholder, although only a very limited number of the candleholders exist. The models were issued with Wade labels; however, they are often seen unmarked because the labels have fallen off.

In the late 1950s, the surplus fairy models were sent to the George Wade Pottery, with the intention of using them in a water babies series. Because of high production costs, however, the series was never issued.

Backstamp: A. Unmarked (1-2)
B. Black and gold label "Made in Ireland by Wade Co. Armagh" (1-2)

No.	Name	Description	Size	U.S.$	Can.$	U.K.£
1a	Fairy	Blue wings; blue/pink/yellow flowers	55 x 35	450.00	600.00	225.00
1b	Fairy	Pink wings; blue/pink/yellow flowers	55 x 35	340.00	450.00	210.00
1c	Fairy	Yellow wings; blue/pink/yellow flowers	55 x 35	450.00	600.00	225.00
2	Fairy Candle Holder	Pink; green	25 x 75	900.00	1,300.00	650.00

POS-NER ASSOCIATES
SHERWOOD FOREST
1989-1999

Each model in the *Sherwood Forest* set was limited to a production run of 5,000. Three coloured versions of "Friar Tuck" with greenish-blue robes were produced in a limited edition of 500 in 1999.

Backstamp A. Embossed "Mianco 89 Wade England"
B. Embossed "Mianco 90 Wade England"
C. Embossed "Wade Mianco 94"

No.	Name	Description	Size	U.S. $	Can. $	U.K. £
1	Robin Hood	Green/honey brown	70 x 30	30.00	40.00	18.00
2	Maid Marian	Grey-blue/brown	65 x 25	30.00	40.00	18.00
3a	Friar Tuck	Red-brown/honey brown	45 x 30	30.00	40.00	18.00
3b	Friar Tuck	Red-brown hair; amber face/hands/feet; greenish blue robe	45 x 30	40.00	60.00	30.00

WHIMBLE FRIAR TUCK
1997

This *Whimble* was commissioned by Pos-ner Associates through C&S Collectables and has a print of "Friar Tuck" on the front.

Backstamp: Red printed "Whimbles by Wade" with two lines

No.	Name	Description	Size	U.S. $	Can. $	U.K. £
1	Friar Tuck	White; gold band; black lettering; beige print	27	4.00	6.00	3.00

ARTHUR PRICE OF ENGLAND
THE WONDERFUL WORLD OF ANIMALS SERIES
Late 1970s-Early 1980s

Arthur Price of England, a Silver Plated Ware manufacturer, commissioned an unknown quantity of Wade English *Whimsie* models to compliment his boxed sets of children's nursery ware of a spoon, fork and a napkin ring.

"English Silver Plated Ware and English Porcelain" is printed on the lid of the box. The title on the box reads "The Wonderful World of Animals" with "Pets and Companions" as a sub-heading; other sets known are "On the Farm" and "Jungle Babies." In the boxed set in the photo can be seen the "Donkey" and the "Cat" from the *English Whimsies Set No 8* which was produced in 1977: therefore a date of late 1970s-early 1980s has been estimated for this series. As the models are indistinguishable from *English Whimsies* a value has been given for a boxed set only. Models are listed in alphabetical order for ease of reference.

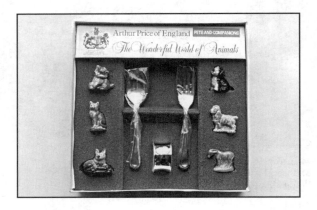

Backstamp: Embossed "Wade England" on back of model rim

Jungle Babies

No.	Name	Description	Size	U.S. $	Can. $	U.K. £
1	Bushbaby	Brown; blue ears	30 x 30			
2	Chimp	Dark brown; light brown face, patches	35 x 35			
3	Fawn	Brown; blue ears	30 x 30			
4	Koala	Yellow brown; black nose; green base	35 x 25			
5	Langur	Light brown; dark brown stump	35 x 30			
6	Pine Martin	Honey brown	30 x 30			
—	Boxed Set		—	60.00	80.00	25.00

On the Farm

No.	Name	Description	Size	U.S. $	Can. $	U.K. £
1	Collie	Golden brown; green base	35 x 35			
2	Cow	Honey brown	35 x 35			
3	Horse	Dark grey; green base	45 x 35			
4	Lamb	Fawn brown; green base	35 x 25			
5	Pig	Beige; green base	25 x 35			
6	Ram	White; grey face; green base	30 x 30			
—	Boxed Set		—	60.00	80.00	25.00

Pets and Companions

No.	Name	Description	Size	U.S. $	Can. $	U.K. £
1	Alsatian	Grey; tan face	30 x 40			
2	Cat	Light brown / ginger; green base	40 x 17			
3	Donkey	Light brown; green base	30 x 30			
4	Kitten	Dark & light brown; pink ball of wool	30 x 30			
5	Mongrel	Dark & light brown	35 x 35			
6	Spaniel	Honey brown	35 x 35			
—	Boxed Set		—	60.00	80.00	25.00

R.H.M. FOODS OF ENGLAND
BISTO KIDS
1977

The *Bisto Kids* salt and pepper cruets were marked "Wade Staffordshire" on their bases, because even though they were made in the Wade Ireland Pottery, they were intended for the British market. They were produced in November and December 1977 for Rank, Hovis & McDougall Foods Co. (R.H.M.) of England and were based on a pair of well-known characters in advertisements for Bisto Gravy Powder on British television. To receive the *Bisto Kids*, one had to mail in two tokens from the packet tops, plus a cheque for £1.95.

Backstamp: Brown transfer "Copyright RHM Foods Ltd. & Applied Creativity, Wade Staffordshire"

No.	Name	Description	Size	U.S. $	Can. $	U.K. £
1	Bisto Boy	Red hat; blue braces, trousers; grey jacket	110 x 58	200.00	260.00	90.00
2	Bisto Girl	Yellow hair, blouse; brown hat	115 x 48	200.00	260.00	90.00
—	Set (2)		—	400.00	500.00	170.00

RED ROSE TEA (CANADA) LTD.
MINIATURE ANIMALS

FIRST ISSUE
1967-1973

In early 1967, when the sales of Red Rose Tea were in decline and the company was falling behind its competitors, it decided to start a promotional campaign to win back customers. In its campaign Wade miniature animals were used as free premiums in packages of Red Rose Tea Bags.

The first 12 promotional models were released in early 1967 and used in a trial run in Quebec, Canada, to test the public's reaction. The idea proved so successful that the series was quickly increased to 32 models in autumn 1967. The models were then offered nationally, region by region across Canada. Their popularity was so great that the promotional area and period (originally intended for two to three years) was extended to cover all of Canada for six years (from 1967 to 1973).

The models marked with "Wade England" in a recessed base were the first of this series to be produced. When the dies on six of these — the "Bear Cub," "Beaver," "Bushbaby," "Kitten," "Owl" and "Squirrel" — were retooled in 1967, the marks were placed on the back rim of the models.

The "Bison" and "Hippo" are found in two sizes because, when the original dies broke, the new dies produced smaller models. In fact, there can be slight size variations in all the models listed below.

A second "Rabbit" was made with open ears because the closed ears on the first version were too difficult to fettle. The first issue "Trout" was unmarked, and the back of the base differs slightly from the second issue, which is marked "Wade England" on the back rim.

This first issue was later produced as English Whimsies, except for the "Fantail Goldfish," "Butterfly," "Frog," "Poodle," "Crocodile," "Terrapin," "Seal on Rock" and "Rabbit" with closed ears. The "Butterfly," "Frog" and "Fantail Goldfish" were also used for a Brooke Bond Tea, UK (Sister Company to Red Rose Tea) promotion and the "Crocodile" and "Terrapin" were previously used in the Balding and Mansell Flintstones Christmas Cracker set.

The following list is in alphabetical order.

Backstamp: **A.** Embossed "Wade England" on rim (1, 2a, 3a, 4a, 4b, 6a, 8, 9, 11, 12, 13, 14, 16, 18a, 18b, 19a, 19b, 20, 21, 22, 23a, 24, 25a, 25b, 26, 27, 28, 29a, 31a, 32)
              B. Embossed "Wade England" in recessed base (2b, 3b, 5, 6b, 7a, 7b, 10a, 10b, 15a, 15b, 17a, 17b, 19b, 23b, 29b, 30a, 30b, 30c)
              C. Embossed "Wade England" on disk (10a)
              D. Unmarked (31b)

No.	Name	Description	Size	U.S. $	Can. $	U.K. £
1	Alsatian	Grey; tan face	30 x 40	9.00	7.00	3.00
2a	Bear Cub	Grey; beige face	30 x 40	7.00	5.00	2.00
2b	Bear Cub	Grey; beige face	30 x 40	20.00	15.00	5.00
3a	Beaver	Grey-brown; honey brown face	35 x 45	8.00	6.00	2.00
3b	Beaver	Grey-brown; honey brown face	35 x 45	20.00	15.00	5.00
4a	Bison, Large	Honey brown body; dark brown head, mane	32 x 45	14.00	10.00	4.00
4b	Bison, Small	Honey brown body; dark brown head, mane	28 x 40	7.00	5.00	4.00
5	Bluebird	Beige body, tail; blue wings, head	15 x 35	10.00	8.00	4.00
6a	Bushbaby	Brown; blue ears; black eyes, nose	30 x 30	6.00	4.00	2.00
6b	Bushbaby	Brown; blue ears; black eyes, nose	30 x 30	7.00	5.00	3.00
7a	Butterfly	Olive/brown; green tips; raised circles	10 x 45	10.00	8.00	5.00
7b	Butterfly	Honey brown	10 x 45	10.00	8.00	5.00
8	Chimpanzee	Dark brown; light brown face, patches	35 x 35	7.00	5.00	2.00

No.	Name	Description	Size	U.S. $	Can. $	U.K. £
9	Corgi	Honey brown; black nose	30 x 35	9.00	7.00	2.00
10a	Crocodile	Brownish green	14 x 40	10.00	8.00	5.00
10b	Crocodile	Brownish green	14 x 40	10.00	8.00	5.00
11	Duck	Blue/brown; yellow beak	30 x 40	9.00	7.00	3.00
12	Fantail Goldfish	Green/yellow; blue rock	30 x 35	10.00	8.00	5.00
13	Fawn	Brown; blue ears; black nose	30 x 30	7.00	5.00	3.00
14	Fox	Dark brown; fawn face, chest	30 x 30	9.00	7.00	3.00
15a	Frog	Green	15 x 30	7.00	5.00	3.00
15b	Frog	Yellow	15 x 30	7.00	5.00	3.00
16	Giraffe	Beige	35 x 35	7.00	5.00	3.00

No.	Name	Description	Size	U.S. $	Can. $	U.K. £
17a	Hedgehog	Light brown; honey face; black nose	23 x 40	9.00	7.00	3.00
17b	Hedgehog	Dark red brown; honey face; black nose	23 x 40	9.00	7.00	3.00
18a	Hippo, Large	Honey brown	25 x 45	16.00	12.00	4.00
18b	Hippo, Small	Honey brown	20 x 40	6.00	4.00	2.00
19a	Kitten	Dark/light brown; pink wool	30 x 30	8.00	6.00	3.00
19b	Kitten	Dark/light brown; red wool	30 x 30	10.00	8.00	4.00
20	Lion	Light brown; dark brown head, mane	35 x 45	8.00	6.00	2.00
21	Mongrel	Dark brown back; light brown front	35 x 35	7.00	5.00	2.00
22	Otter	Beige; blue base	30 x 35	7.00	5.00	2.00
23a	Owl	Dark/light brown	35 x 20	8.00	6.00	4.00
23b	Owl	Dark/light brown	35 x 20	20.00	12.00	5.00
24	Poodle	White	40 x 45	10.00	7.00	4.00

No.	Name	Description	Size	U.S. $	Can. $	U.K. £
25a	Rabbit	Beige; closed ears	30 x 30	22.00	12.00	7.00
25b	Rabbit	Beige; ears open	30 x 30	8.00	6.00	3.00
26	Seal on Rock	Brown; blue rock	35 x 35	8.00	4.00	5.00
27	Setter	Brown; grey-green base	35 x 50	7.00	5.00	2.00
28	Spaniel	Honey brown; green nose	35 x 35	8.00	5.00	2.00
29a	Squirrel	Grey; brown head, legs; yellow acorn	35 x 30	7.00	5.00	2.00
29b	Squirrel	Grey; brown head, legs; yellow acorn	35 x 30	12.00	9.00	5.00
30a	Terrapin	Beige; brown markings	10 x 40	8.00	6.00	4.00
30b	Terrapin	Beige; grey markings	10 x 40	8.00	6.00	4.00
30c	Terrapin	Beige; purple-blue markings	10 x 40	8.00	6.00	4.00
31a	Trout	Brown; red tail; grey-green base	30 x 30	8.00	6.00	3.00
31b	Trout	Brown; red tail; grey-green base	30 x 30	8.00	6.00	3.00
32	Wild Boar	Brown; green on base	30 x 40	15.00	12.00	4.00

MINIATURE NURSERIES

SECOND ISSUE

1972-1979

A series of 24 miniature nursery rhyme characters was given away free in the second Red Rose Tea promotion. For the first two years, these models were only distributed in selected areas; it was not until 1973 that they were distributed throughout Canada.

When a new die replaces a worn one, variations in models sometimes occur, as in "The Queen of Hearts" and "Old King Cole." Models with colour variations may indicate a painters whim or that a particular glaze was temporarily out of stock. All the models are marked "Wade England" around the rim of the base.

Because over 20 million of these models are reported to have been made; only the undamaged models are worth keeping. Thin, more breakable models in mint condition are worth more than the solid, heavier models, which stand up to, rough handling better. Lever Rexona of New Zealand used the same 24 models in an early 1970s promotion for Signal Toothpaste. Five of the models were released in England as a boxed set.

Backstamp: Embossed "Wade England"

No.	Name	Description	Size	U.S. $	Can. $	U.K. £
1	Baa Baa Black Sheep	Black all over	25 x 30	15.00	12.00	15.00
2	Cat and the Fiddle	Beige front; grey back; yellow fiddle	45 x 25	28.00	15.00	20.00
3a	Dr. Foster	Light brown all over	45 x 25	12.00	6.00	15.00
3b	Dr. Foster	Light brown; blue puddle	45 x 25	12.00	6.00	15.00
3c	Dr. Foster	Light brown; yellow tie; blue puddle	45 x 25	12.00	6.00	15.00
3d	Dr. Foster	Brown; grey puddle	45 x 25	12.00	6.00	15.00
4	Gingerbread Man	Red-brown; grey-green base	40 x 28	45.00	35.00	30.00
5	Goosey Goosey Gander	Honey brown head; pink beak	30 x 35	8.00	6.00	4.00
6	Hickory Dickory Dock	Red-brown/honey brown	45 x 20	6.00	4.00	6.00
7	House that Jack Built	Honey brown; red-brown roof	35 x 35	12.00	8.00	15.00
8a	Humpty Dumpty	Honey brown; blue tie; brown wall	45 x 35	7.00	5.00	5.00
8b	Humpty Dumpty	Honey brown; brown wall	45 x 35	7.00	5.00	5.00
9a	Jack	Brown; blue shirt; brown bucket	35 x 35	10.00	6.00	9.00

Backstamp: Embossed "Wade England"

No.	Name	Description	Size	U.S. $	Can. $	U.K. £
9b	Jack	Brown; blue shirt; blue bucket	35 x 35	10.00	6.00	9.00
10	Jill	Yellow hair; beige dress; blue bucket	35 x 35	10.00	6.00	9.00
11	Little Bo-Peep	Brown; blue apron; green base	45 x 25	5.00	4.00	6.00
12	Little Boy Blue	Blue hat, coat; brown trousers	43 x 25	15.00	12.00	6.00
13	Little Jack Horner	Beige; pink cushion; blue plum	40 x 20	6.00	4.00	6.00
14	Little Miss Muffett	Honey/grey dress; red-brown spider	45 x 20	10.00	6.00	10.00
15	Little Red Riding Hood	Beige dress; red cape; green base	45 x 20	6.00	5.00	6.00
16a	Mother Goose	Brown hat; honey brown dress	40 x 32	10.00	8.00	15.00
16b	Mother Goose	Blue hat; honey brown dress	40 x 32	10.00	8.00	15.00
17a	Old King Cole Type 1	Gap; brown body, shoes, pot; blue hat, cloak	40 x 35	7.00	4.00	6.00

Backstamp: Embossed "Wade England"

No.	Name	Description	Size	U.S. $	Can. $	U.K. £
17b	Old King Cole Type 1	Gap; brown body, pot blue hat, cloak, shoes	40 x 35	7.00	4.00	6.00
17c	Old King Cole Type 2	No gap; brown body shoes, pot blue hat	40 x 35	7.00	4.00	6.00
17d	Old King Cole Type 2	No gap; brown body;blue hat, cloak, shoes, pot	40 x 35	7.00	4.00	6.00
18a	Old Woman Who Lived in a Shoe	Honey brown; red-brown roof	40 x 40	8.00	4.00	6.00
18b	Old Woman Who Lived in a Shoe	Honey brown	35 x 40	7.00	4.00	5.00
19a	Pied Piper	Light brown coat; green bush	50 x 30	10.00	8.00	6.00
19b	Pied Piper	Pink/brown coat; green bush	50 x 30	10.00	8.00	6.00
20	Puss in Boots	Brown; blue boots; green base	45 x 20	12.00	8.00	15.00
21a	Queen of Hearts	2 small hearts; beige dress; pink hat	45 x 25	15.00	8.00	10.00
21b	Queen of Hearts	2 large hearts; beige dress; pink hat	45 x 25	15.00	8.00	10.00
21c	Queen of Hearts	8 small hearts; beige dress; pink hat	45 x 25	40.00	30.00	20.00
22a	The Three Bears	Dark brown, honey brown base	35 x 38	22.00	18.00	30.00
22b	The Three Bears	Light brown, honey brown base	35 x 38	35.00	20.00	30.00
23a	Tom Tom the Piper's Son	Honey brown; blue tam, kilt	40 x 35	15.00	8.00	8.00
23b	Tom Tom the Piper's Son	Honey brown; brown tam, kilt	40 x 35	15.00	8.00	8.00
23c	Tom Tom the Piper's Son	Honey brown; grey tam, kilt	40 x 35	15.00	8.00	8.00
24	Wee Willie Winkie	Yellow hair; beige nightshirt	45 x 25	10.00	7.00	6.00

WHOPPAS

THIRD ISSUE

1981

In 1981 the English series of *Whoppas* came to an end, and the surplus stock was used for Red Rose Tea Canada premiums. To obtain a model, Canadian collectors had to mail in the tab from a box of Red Rose Tea, plus $1.00 for postage. All are marked "Wade England" around the rim of the base. Numbers 1 through 5 are from Wade's *Whoppas*, set 1; 6 to 10 are from *Whoppas*, set 2; 11 to 15 are from *Whoppas*, set 3.

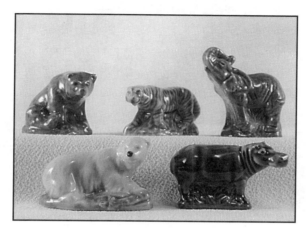

Backstamp: Embossed "Wade England"

SET 1

No.	Name	Description	Size	U.S. $	Can. $	U.K. £
1	Brown Bear	Red-brown; brown base	35 x 45	20.00	28.00	7.00
2	Elephant	Grey	55 x 50	25.00	35.00	7.00
3	Hippo	Grey; green base	35 x 50	25.00	35.00	8.00
4	Polar Bear	White; grey-blue base	35 x 55	25.00	35.00	7.00
5	Tiger	Yellow/brown; green base	30 x 60	20.00	28.00	7.00

SET 2

No.	Name	Description	Size	U.S. $	Can. $	U.K. £
6	Bison	Brown; green base	40 x 50	25.00	35.00	7.00
7	Bobcat	Light brown; dark brown spots; green base	55 x 50	30.00	40.00	10.00
8	Chipmunk	Brown; dark brown base	55 x 40	30.00	40.00	10.00
9	Raccoon	Brown; black stripes, eye patches; green base	40 x 50	30.00	40.00	10.00
10	Wolf	Grey; green base	60 x 45	30.00	40.00	10.00

SET 3

No.	Name	Description	Size	U.S. $	Can. $	U.K.
11	Badger	Brown; cream stripe; green base	35 x 45	35.00	45.00	20.00
12	Hedgehog	Brown; green base	30 x 50	35.00	45.00	20.00
13	Fox	Red-brown; green base	30 x 60	35.00	45.00	20.00
14	Otter	Brown; blue base	30 x 55	35.00	45.00	20.00
15	Stoat	Brown; green base	35 x 55	35.00	45.00	20.00

MINIATURE ANIMALS
FOURTH ISSUE
1982-1984

Six animal models from the first Red Rose Tea Canada Promotion were re-issued some with slight colour variations and 17 models from the 1971-1984 English *Whimsies* series were added to make this fourth promotion of 23 animals. New dies resulted in three sizes of pig.

Backstamp: Embossed "Wade England"

No.	Name	Description	Size	U.S. $	Can. $	U.K. £
1	Angel Fish	Grey; dark grey stripes; blue base	35 x 30	15.00	12.00	5.00
2	Beaver	Brown; honey brown face	35 x 45	8.00	6.00	2.00
3	Bushbaby	Beige	30 x 30	5.00	7.00	5.00
4	Camel	Dark grey	35 x 35	9.00	11.00	4.00
5	Collie	Honey brown/green	35 x 35	10.00	8.00	4.00
6	Corgi	Honey brown; black nose	30 x 35	9.00	7.00	2.00
7	Cow	Light orange	35 x 35	12.00	12.00	4.00
8	Fox	Dark brown	30 x 30	9.00	7.00	2.00

No.	Name	Description	Size	U.S. $	Can. $	U.K. £
9	Giraffe	Beige	35 x 35	7.00	5.00	2.00
10	Gorilla	Dark grey; green	35 x 25	8.00	8.00	4.00
11	Horse	Black	35 x 35	15.00	12.00	4.00
12	Lamb	White	30 x 25	8.00	10.00	4.00
13	Languar	Beige; brown stsump	35 x 30	5.00	7.00	4.00
14	Leopard	Yellow-brown	17 x 45	6.00	8.00	4.00
15	Orang-Utan	Dark brown	30 x 30	5.00	7.00	5.00

Backstamp: Embossed "Wade England"

No.	Name	Description	Size	U.S. $	Can. $	U.K. £
16	Pelican	Brown/yellow; green base	45 x 40	20.00	25.00	6.00
17a	Pig, large	Beige	27 x 44	25.00	20.00	10.00
17b	Pig, medium	Beige	25 x 40	25.00	20.00	10.00
17c	Pig, small	Beige	25 x 35	25.00	20.00	10.00
18	Pine Marten	Yellow/brown	30 x 30	6.00	5.00	2.00
19a	Rabbit ears open	Beige	30 x 30	8.00	6.00	2.00
19b	Rabbit ears closed	Beige	30 x 30	22.00	12.00	7.00
20	Rhino	Dark grey	17 x 45	8.00	6.00	4.00
21	Seahorse	Yellow/brown; blue base	50 x 17	20.00	25.00	7.00
22a	Turtle	Dark grey	15 x 50	10.00	8.00	6.00
22b	Turtle	Greenish grey	15 x 50	10.00	8.00	6.00
23	Zebra	Beige	40 x 35	9.00	11.00	4.00

Note: The above pricing tables are listed in photograph order from bottom left to upper right.

RED ROSE TEA U.S.A. LTD. (REDCO FOODS LTD.)

The Canadian Red Rose Tea promotion was so successful that it was extended to the United States in 1983. Red Rose estimates that over two hundred million Wade models have been distributed in packets of Red Rose Tea in the U.S.A. and in Canada during its promotions.

In many states figurine promotions overlap, with some model series still being offered in one area whilst a new series is offered in another.

MINIATURE ANIMALS

FIRST ISSUE

1983-1985

In this first American series, two of the models, the "Hare" and "Squirrel," were not original *English Whimsies*, but models from the 1980-1981 Tom Smith *British Wildlife* set. All figures are in all-over, one-colour glazes, and they may vary slightly from the measurements indicated below. They are listed in alphabetical order.

Backstamp: Embossed "Wade England"

No.	Name	Description	Size	U.S. $	Can. $	U.K. £
1	Bear Cub (RR/EW)	Beige	30 x 40	5.00	7.00	5.00
2	Bison (RR/EW)	Dark brown	30 x 40	6.00	8.00	4.00
3	Bluebird (RR/EW)	Beige	15 x 35	6.00	8.00	6.00
4	Bushbaby (RR/EW)	Beige	30 x 30	5.00	7.00	5.00
5	Chimpanzee (RR/EW)	Honey brown	35 x 35	5.00	7.00	5.00
6	Elephant (EW)	Blue; no eyes	35 x 45	12.00	15.00	10.00
7	Hare (TS)	Dark brown	50 x 30	6.00	12.00	6.00
8	Hippo (RR/EW)	Honey brown	23 x 35	12.00	12.00	4.00
9	Lion (RR/EW)	Honey brown	35 x 45	5.00	8.00	4.00
10	Otter (RR/EW)	Beige	30 x 35	6.00	5.00	2.00
11	Owl (RR/EW)	Dark brown	35 x 20	6.00	5.00	10.00
12	Seal (RR/TS)	Blue	35 x 35	8.00	12.00	6.00
13a	Squirrel (TS)	Dark blue	40 x 40	6.00	12.00	12.00
13b	Squirrel (TS)	Grey-blue	40 x 40	6.00	12.00	12.00
14	Turtle (EW)	Light grey	15 x 50	10.00	8.00	6.00
15	Wild Boar (RR/EW)	Beige	30 x 40	8.00	10.00	4.00

Note: EW: *English Whimsies*
RR: Red Rose Tea
TS: Tom Smith *British Wildlife* set

SECOND ISSUE

1985-1990

All the models in this series are in all-over, one-colour glazes. Some of these figures are in the same colours used in the 1982-1984 Canada Red Rose Tea promotion.

Backstamp: Embossed "Wade England"

No.	Name	Description	Size	U.S. $	Can. $	U.K.£
1	Beaver (EW/RRC)	Light brown	35 x 45	6.00	10.00	6.00
2	Camel (EW/RRC)	Beige	35 x 35	9.00	11.00	4.00
3	Giraffe (EW/RRC)	Beige	35 x 35	7.00	5.00	2.00
4	Gorilla (EW/RRC)	Dark brown	35 x 25	4.00	6.00	3.00
5	Kangaroo (EW)	Honey brown	45 x 25	10.00	15.00	5.00
6a	Koala Bear (EW)	Beige	35 x 25	6.00	9.00	4.00
6b	Koala Bear (EW)	Brown	35 x 25	6.00	9.00	4.00
7	Langur (EW/RRC)	Dark brown	35 x 30	6.00	8.00	5.00
8	Leopard (EW/RRC)	Yellow brown	17 x 45	6.00	8.00	4.00
9	Orang-Outan (EW/RRC)	Dark brown	30 x 30	5.00	7.00	5.00
10	Pine Marten (EW/RRC)	Honey brown	30 x 30	6.00	5.00	2.00
11	Polar Bear (EW/TS)	White	30 x 30	10.00	12.00	4.00
12	Raccoon (EW)	Dark brown	25 x 35	4.00	6.00	5.00
13	Rhino (EW/RRC)	Blue-grey	17 x 45	8.00	6.00	4.00
14	Tiger (EW)	Honey brown	35 x 25	15.00	20.00	5.00
15	Zebra (EW/RRC)	Grey	40 x 35	5.00	8.00	8.00

Note: EW: *English Whimsies*
RRC: Red Rose Tea Canada
TS: Tom Smith

THIRD ISSUE

1990-1995

The 15 models offered in the 1985-1990 Red Rose Tea promotion were increased to 20 in late 1990, with the addition of five Tom Smith 1988-1989 models (indicated below by TS). By late 1993 in New York State, Philadelphia, Florida and in Portland, Maine, the models were no longer included free in boxes of teabags, but could be obtained by sending in the UPC code and a small shipping and handling charge. In other areas of the U.S., the 20 animal figurines were available until mid 1995.

Backstamp: Embossed "Wade England"

No.	Name	Description	Size	U.S. $	Can. $	U.K. £
1	Cock-a-teel (TS)	Green	35 x 30	8.00	10.00	3.00
2	Kitten (TS)	Grey	25 x 33	6.00	8.00	5.00
3	Pony (TS)	Beige	25 x 30	10.00	12.00	4.00
4	Rabbit (TS)	Dark brown	30 x 25	8.00	10.00	4.00
5	Spaniel Puppy (TS)	Honey brown	25 x 30	10.00	12.00	4.00

FOURTH ISSUE

1992

Due to increasing demand, Red Rose U.S.A. offered these models as a mail-in offer with their packages of decaffeinated tea in early 1992. This series includes the same models as offered in the second issue in different colourways with the addition of the third issue models in the same colourways.

This series was limited to mail order because packaging methods for decaffeinated tea did not allow for the inclusion of the model in the tea packet. For each model a special card was required from the tea packet, plus a postage charge of $1.00 for one to three models, $2.00 for four to nine models and $3.00 for ten to 15 models.

All these figures are in all-over, one-colour glazes, unless otherwise stated.

Backstamp: Embossed "Wade England"

No.	Name	Description	Size	U.S. $	Can. $	U.K. £
1	Beaver (EW/RRC/RRU)	Dark brown	35 x 45	3.00	3.00	3.00
2	Camel (EW/RRC)	Dark grey	35 x 35	9.00	11.00	4.00
3	Cock-a-teel (TS)	Green	35 x 30	8.00	10.00	3.00
5	Giraffe (EW/RRC)	Beige	35 x 35	7.00	5.00	2.00
5	Gorilla (EW/RRC)	Black	35 x 25	20.00	26.00	14.00
6	Kangaroo (EW/RRU)	Honey brown	45 x 25	10.00	15.00	5.00
7	Kitten (TS)	Grey	25 x 33	6.00	8.00	5.00
8	Koala Bear (EW/RRU)	Dark grey; beige stump	35 x 25	15.00	25.00	6.00
9	Langur (EW/RRC)	Light brown; brown stump	35 x 30	5.00	7.00	4.00
10	Leopard (EW/RRC/RRU)	Mottled olive brown	17 x 45	6.00	8.00	5.00
11	Orang-Utan (EW/RRC)	Brown	30 x 30	5.00	7.00	5.00
12	Pine Marten (EW/RRC)	Yellow-brown	30 x 30	6.00	5.00	2.00
13	Polar Bear (EW/TS/RRU)	White	30 x 30	10.00	12.00	4.00
14	Pony (TS)	Beige	25 x 30	10.00	12.00	4.00
15	Rabbit (TS)	Dark brown	30 x 25	10.00	12.00	6.00
16	Raccoon (EW/RRU)	Brown	25 x 35	4.00	6.00	5.00
17	Rhino (EW/RRC/RRU)	Blue-grey/light grey	17 x 45	8.00	6.00	4.00
18	Spaniel Puppy (TS)	Honey	25 x 30	10.00	12.00	4.00
19	Tiger (EW/RRU)	Mottled olive brown	35 x 25	15.00	20.00	6.00
20	Zebra (EW/RRC/RRU)	Light grey	40 x 35	5.00	8.00	8.00

Note: For an illustration of model numbers 3, 7, 14, 15 and 18 please see previous page.
The following initials indicate the origin of the models:
EW: *English Whimsies*
RRC: Red Rose Tea Canada
RRU: Red Rose Tea U.S.A.
TS: Tom Smith

CIRCUS ANIMALS

1993-1999

In late 1993, Red Rose offered a reissue of the most popular of the Tom Smith cracker models, *The Circus* set, originally issued in England from 1978 to 1979 (indicated by the initials TS). The original moulds were used, and with only a slight variation in colour from the older models. Two variations have been found in the *Circus* Tiger due a new mould being made: the mouth of the second variation appears to be more open and there is more detailing in the fur of the throat and chest which gives it the appearance of a beard.

Left: Tom Smith *Circus* Elephant (blue
Right: Red Rose (U.S.A.) Elephant (pale blue)

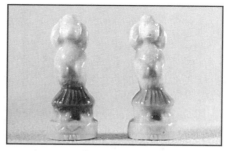

Left: Tom Smith *Circus* Poodle (dark blue)
Right: Red Rose (U.S.A.) Poodle (light blue)

FIFTH ISSUE

1993-1998

Backstamp: A. Embossed "Wade England" on back rim of base
B. Embossed "Wade Eng" on back rim of base

No.	Name	Description	Size	U.S. $	Can. $	U.K. £
1	Brown Bear (TS)	Dark brown	35 x 30	5.00	12.00	6.00
2	Chimpanzee Boy (TS)	Brown	40 x 20	5.00	12.00	8.00
3	Chimpanzee Girl (TS)	Brown	40 x 20	5.00	12.00	8.00
4	Elephant, Sitting (TS)	Pale blue	30 x 30	5.00	12.00	6.00
5	Elephant, Standing (TS)	Pale blue	30 x 25	5.00	12.00	6.00
6	Pony (TS)	Beige	45 x 22	5.00	12.00	6.00
7	Lion (TS)	Honey brown	40 x 22	5.00	12.00	6.00
8	Poodle (TS)	White; blue skirt	35 x 30	5.00	12.00	6.00
9	Sea Lion (TS)	Light grey	40 x 30	5.00	12.00	8.00
10a	Tiger Type 1	Honey brown	43 x 20	3.00	8.00	4.00
10b	Tiger Type 2	Honey brown; with beard	43 x 20	4.00	10.00	5.00

SIXTH ISSUE

1996-1998

Five new *Circus* models were produced for Redco Foods (Red Rose Tea U.S.A.) and were available in all U.S.A. states where Red Rose Tea is sold from July of 1996. The five new models were added to the *Circus* set which was first introduced in 1993, making a total of 15 models for this series. A brown glazed version of the "Human Cannon-ball" has been reported the reason for the colour variation is unknown. Red Rose advertising proclaims that over two hundred million Wade Whimsicals have been distributed between 1983-1996.

Backstamp: Embossed "Wade England"

No.	Name	Description	Size	U.S. $	Can. $	U.K. £
11	Clown Custard Pie	Pale blue	40	5.00	12.00	5.00
12	Clown Water Bucket	Light green	44	5.00	12.00	5.00
13a	Human Cannonball	Light grey	30	5.00	12.00	5.00
13b	Human Cannonball	Brown	30	7.00	15.00	8.00
14	Ringmaster	Light grey	44	5.00	12.00	5.00
15	Strongman	Honey brown	40	5.00	12.00	5.00

ENDANGERED NORTH AMERICAN ANIMALS

SEVENTH ISSUE

1998-present

In late 1998, Red Rose Tea U.S.A. started to phase out the *Circus* models in preparation for their new *Endangered North American Animals* which was a set of 10 models included in Red Rose Tea boxes from December 1998. Also in the boxes was a leaflet offering collectors the opportunity of purchasing the last of the *Circus* models that they needed to complete their sets at $1.00 per model.

There are seven new designs in the *Endangered Animals* set. Three models have been used in previous promotions, but were re-coloured and re-named i.e. "Spotted Owl" (previously the *English Whimsies* Barn Owl) "Bald Eagle" (previously the *Whimsie-land* British Wildlife Golden Eagle), "Polar Bear" (previously the Tom Smith Survival Polar Bear). Please note that the "Polar Bear" has a thicker white glaze applied over the original white glaze.

Backstamp: **A.** Embossed "Wade Eng" on Peregrine Falcon
B. Embossed "Wade England" on other models

No.	Name	Description	Size	U.S. $	Can. $	U.K.
1	Bald Eagle (WL)	Honey brown	35 x 40	3.00	5.00	4.00
2	Florida Panther	Honey brown	35 x 40	3.00	5.00	4.00
3	Green Sea Turtle	Light green	30 x 44	3.00	5.00	4.00
4	Humpback Whale	Grey	20 x 53	3.00	5.00	4.00
5	Manatee	Blue grey	25 x 53	3.00	5.00	4.00
6	Peregrine Falcon	Beige	25 x 45	3.00	5.00	4.00
7	Polar Bear (TS)	White	27 x 45	3.00	5.00	4.00
8	Spotted Owl (EW)	Beige	35 x 20	3.00	5.00	4.00
9	Sturgeon	Blue	27 x 47	3.00	5.00	4.00
10	Timber Wolf	Grey	45 x 28	3.00	5.00	4.00

RICHLEIGH PROMOTIONS
THE CHILDREN OF THE WORLD
1997-1999

The first model in this new series commissioned by Richard and Leigh Leford of Richleigh Promotions, "The Japanese Girl," was produced in two colour ways in winter 1997.

The "Indian Boy" was issued in March 1998 with the "Spanish Girl" and the "Mexican Boy" following in September 1998. All were issued in limited editions of 1,000 with a Certificate of Authenticity, at an original cost of £33.00. Other models planned are "The Dutch Girl," the "English Boy" (dressed as a Guardsman), the "Hawaiian Girl" and the "Greek Boy."

Backstamp: Printed "Children of the World 1000 Ltd Edition Wade" with model name & number and "RP" Logo.

No.	Name	Description	Size	U.S. $	Can. $	U.K. £
1a	Japanese Girl	Black hair; blue kimono; pink fan; light brown base	105	50.00	70.00	35.00
1b	Japanese Girl	Black hair; green kimono; blue fan; light brown base	105	50.00	70.00	35.00
2	The Indian Boy	Blue, white and red feather head-dress; beige-brown clothes; brown wampum belt and moccasins; black tomahawk; grey base	75	55.00	75.00	38.00
3	The Spanish Girl	Black hair and shoes; red dress; brown base	115	50.00	70.00	35.00
4	The Mexican Boy	Dark brown hair; white hat; black suit; red sash; light brown base	105	50.00	70.00	35.00

ROBELL MEDIA PROMOTIONS LTD.
MR. MEN AND LITTLE MISS
1997-1999

"Mr. Happy," a character from the *Mr. Men* childrens story books by Roger Hargreaves, was produced in a limited edition of 2,000 for child members of the Mr. Men and Little Miss Club and was marketed by Robell Media Promotions. The cost of "Mr. Happy"direct from the club was £15.99. In 1998 "Little Miss Giggles" and "Mr. Bump" were added to the set followed by "Mr Snow."

Mr. Happy   Mr. Bump   Little Miss Giggles

Mr. Snow

Backstamp: Black printed "Genuine Wade Porcelain Robell Produced exclusively for the Mr. Men & Little Miss Club Mr. Men and Little Miss TM & © 1997 Mrs. Roger Hargreaves" with "Mr. Happy and Little Miss" logo

No.	Name	Description	Size	U.S. $	Can. $	U.K. £
1	Mr. Happy	Yellow; black eyes/mouth; green base	100	50.00	70.00	35.00
2	Little Miss Giggles	Red hair; yellow bows and nose; blue body; green base	95	40.00	60.00	30.00
3	Mr. Bump	White bandages; blue body; green base	95	40.00	60.00	30.00
4	Mr. Snow	White snowman; black hat/face markings; red and white scarf; pearlised base	120	50.00	70.00	35.00

JAMES ROBERTSON & SONS
ROBERTSON'S JAM GOLLIES AND BANDSTAND

1963-1965

Golliwogs became the trademark of James Robertson & Sons after one of Mr. Robertson's sons visited the United States in the early 1900s. He purchased a golliwog doll for his children, and it was so loved by the family that they decided to use it as their trademark. In 1910 a golliwog first appeared on items from James Robertson Preserve Manufacturers Limited, such as labels and price lists.

Beginning in 1963 a Robertson's promotional campaign offered a series of eight golliwog musicians in exchange for ten paper golliwog labels per model and 6d in postage stamps. George Wade and Son Ltd. produced five models for a trial period only. At some time in 1965, Robertsons changed from using the Wade model to the cheaper Portuguese one.

None of the Golliwogs is marked with a Wade stamp or label, but it is relatively easy to spot a Wade model amongst the hundreds of Golliwogs seen at antique and collector shows. Only the Wade figures are standing on white bases. All the models have a raised "Robertson" mark on the front rim of the base, and all the *Gollies* are black, with blue coats and red trousers.

Wade records confirm that, out of the eight promotional models, it only produced five golliwog musicians: "Accordian Golliwog," "Clarinet Golliwog," "Bass Golliwog," "Saxophone Golliwog" and "Trumpet Golliwog." The three additional models, not confirmed by Wade and most likely produced by another manufacturer, are "Drum Golliwog," "Guitar Golliwog" and "Vocalist Golliwog."

Due to changing race relations laws in Great Britain during the late 1970s and early 1980s, the original name, *Golliwog*, was changed to *Golly Doll* or *Gollies*. The models below are listed by their original names.

Backstamp: A. Embossed "Robertson" (1-5)
B. Red transfer print "Wade England" (6)

No.	Name	Description	Size	U.S. $	Can. $	U.K. £
1	Accordion Golliwog	Blue jacket; red pants; white/yellow accordion	65 x 25	265.00	350.00	150.00
2	Clarinet Golliwog	Blue jacket; red pants; black clarinet	65 x 25	265.00	350.00	150.00
3	Bass Golliwog	Blue jacket; red pants; white/yellow/brown bass	65 x 25	265.00	350.00	150.00
4	Saxophone Golliwog	Blue jacket; red pants; yellow saxophone	65 x 25	265.00	350.00	150.00
5	Trumpet Golliwog	Blue jacket; red pants; yellow trumpet	65 x 25	265.00	350.00	150.00
6	Bandstand	White	50 x 230	200.00	300.00	100.00

S&A COLLECTABLES LTD
JACK THE RIPPER
1999

Commissioned by S&A Collectables in October 1999. The cost direct from S&A was £45.00.

Photograph not available
at press time

Backstamp: Unknown

No.	Description		Size	U.S. $	Can. $	U.K. £
1	Jack the Ripper	Black hat; cloak, bag and knife; white and black shoes; red blood; grey base	Unknown	60.00	90.00	45.00

ST. JOHN AMBULANCE BRIGADE (U.K.)
BERTIE BADGER
1989-1994

"Bertie Badger" was produced in a limited edition of 5,000 as a promotional item for the British St. John Ambulance Brigade in late 1989. It was given as a reward to child members of the brigade after they completed three years of service and training. Those models that are unmarked were produced from 1989 to 1994; those embossed with the Wade mark were made only in 1994.

Backstamp: **A.** Unmarked
B. Embossed "Wade"

No.	Description	Size	U.S. $	Can. $	U.K. £
1	Black/white; white coveralls, shoes	100 x 50	290.00	375.00	140.00

SALADA TEA CANADA
WHIMSEY-ON-WHY

1984

Six models from the *Whimsey-on-Why* sets 1, 2 and 3 were introduced as a short promotional offer by Salada Tea Canada between September and December 1984.

Backstamp: Embossed "Wade England"

No.	Name	Description	Size	U.S. $	Can. $	U.K. £
1	Pump Cottage	Brown thatch; white walls; yellow doors	28 x 39	20.00	25.00	5.00
2	Tobacconist's Shop	Brown roof; red doors	33 x 39	20.00	25.00	5.00
3	The Greengrocer's Shop	Grey roof; green windows, doors	35 x 35	20.00	30.00	8.00
4	The Antique Shop	Purple-brown roof; blue/yellow windows	35 x 37	20.00	30.00	8.00
5	The Post Office	Beige roof; yellow/blue windows	40 x 38	20.00	25.00	10.00
6	Whimsey Station	Red-brown; brown roof	35 x 39	25.00	35.00	15.00

SHARPS CHOCOLATE
HONEY BROWN SMILING RABBIT
1970

The *Honey Brown Smiling Rabbit* was produced in 1970 as a premium with Sharps Chocolate Easter eggs. The box was shaped like a hollow log, and the rabbit was fixed beside an egg containing milk chocolate buttons. The original price was 7/9d.

Backstamp: Unmarked

No.	Description	Size	U.S. $	Can. $	U.K. £
1a	Honey brown; large dark brown eyes	65 x 43	40.00	50.00	25.00
1b	Honey brown; small brown eyes	65 x 43	40.00	50.00	18.00

BO-PEEP
1971

The following year Wade produced the *Honey Brown Bo-Peep*, also as a premium with Sharps Chocolate Easter eggs. The model was fixed beside an egg containing milk chocolate buttons, and was packaged in a box decorated with a design of sheep and trees. The original price was 8/-.

Backstamp: Embossed "Wade England"

No.	Description	Size	U.S. $	Can. $	U.K. £
1a	Honey brown	70 x 28	40.00	50.00	18.00
1b	Honey brown; dark blue hair, apron and flowers	70 x 28	40.00	50.00	25.00

SIMONS ASSOCIATES, INC.

CIRCA 1975

Some time in the mid 1970s, Wade exported a set of 24 *English Whimsies* to Simons Associates, Inc., of Los Angeles, California. The models were packaged in a plastic bubble on a blue card. The front of the card has a colourful design of a tree, smiling sun, baby birds in a nest, butterfly, snail and toadstools. Also printed there is "Whimsies Miniatures Collection Solid English Porcelain," and each package is numbered in the top left corner. On the back is printed: "Collect all these Whimsies miniatures / little creatures from the farm, forest and jungle of solid porcelain," and on the top right hand corner, "Whimsies Wade of England Est. 1810," along with the Union Jack and the American flag.

The values are given for models intact on their cards as they are indistinguishable from Red Rose Tea or English Whimsies models outside the packet. Note that these models were not given the same issue numbers as *English Whimsies*, although they are identical to the originals.

Backstamp: **A.** Embossed "Wade England" (1-3, 5-8)
B. Embossed "Wade England" in a recessed base (4)

No.	Name	Description	Size	U.S. $	Can. $	U.K. £
1	Rabbit	Beige	30 x 30	9.00	7.00	3.00
2	Fawn	Brown; blue ears	30 x 30	8.00	6.00	3.00
3	Mongrel	Dark brown back; light brown front	35 x 35	8.00	6.00	3.00
4	Squirrel	Grey; brown head, legs; yellow acorn	35 x 30	13.00	10.00	6.00
5	Elephant	Grey; some may have black eyes	55 x 50	21.00	16.00	7.00
6	Setter	Brown; black nose	35 x 50	8.00	6.00	3.00
7	Cat	Beige	40 x 17	21.00	26.00	8.00
8	Collie	Golden brown	35 x 35	11.00	9.00	5.00

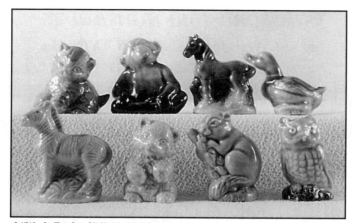

Backstamp: A. Embossed "Wade England" (9-11, 14-16)
  B. Embossed "Wade England" in a recessed base (12, 13)

No.	Name	Description	Size	U.S. $	Can. $	U.K. £
9	Zebra	Light brown; green base	40 x 35	10.00	12.00	5.00
10	Bear Cub	Grey; beige face	30 x 40	8.00	6.00	3.00
11	Fieldmouse	Yellow brown	35 x 25	13.00	12.00	4.00
12	Owl	Dark brown; light brown chest, face	35 x 20	21.00	12.00	7.00
13	Kitten	Dark/light brown; pink or red wool	30 x 30	11.00	9.00	5.00
14	Chimpanzee	Dark brown; light brown face, patches	35 x 35	8.00	6.00	3.00
15	Horse	Grey; green base	35 x 35	16.00	13.00	5.00
16	Duck	Blue/brown; yellow beak	30 x 40	10.00	8.00	3.00

Backstamp: A. Embossed "Wade England" (17-23)
  B. Embossed "Wade England" in a recessed base (24)

No.	Name	Description	Size	U.S. $	Can. $	U.K. £
17	Spaniel	Honey brown; black nose	35 x 35	9.00	6.00	3.00
18	Giraffe	Beige	35 x 35	8.00	6.00	3.00
19	Lion	Light brown; dark brown head, mane	35 x 45	9.00	7.00	3.00
20	German Shepherd	Grey; tan face (formerly Alsatian)	30 x 40	10.00	8.00	3.00
21	Lamb	Fawn; green base	30 x 25	9.00	11.00	5.00
22	Pine Marten	Honey brown	30 x 30	7.00	6.00	3.00
23	Corgi	Honey brown	30 x 35	10.00	8.00	3.00
24	Hedgehog	Dark brown; light brown face	23 x 40	10.00	8.00	3.00

STAFFORDSHIRE HOUSE GIFTS
FIRST WHIMSIES ENGLISH ANIMALS
SET TWO: CIRCA 1954-1958

These models were produced for "Staffordshire House" and were sold in a gift shop in Niagara Falls, Ontario, Canada. Each model is marked with a black, hand written "Made in England" on the base and has "Niagara Falls Canada" on the body of the model. The box for this set is different from the normal Whimsies boxed sets issued, the box has "Whimsies Porcelain Miniatures" on the front with a picture of "Dora the Donkey Soprano" from the *Drum Box* set. The inside of the box is a plain buff brown with silver lettering "Whimsies Porcelain Miniatures by Wade of England" there is also a black and gold label, which reads "A Staffordshire House Gift."

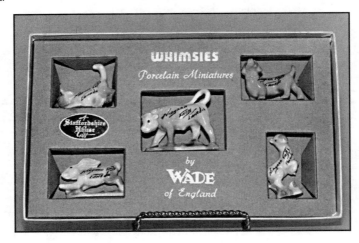

Backstamp: Black ink hand written "Made in England with Niagara Falls Canada"

No.	Name	Description	Size	U.S. $	Can. $	U.K. £
1	Bull	White with brown markings; green base; black lettering	45 x 55	110.00	140.00	70.00
2	Dachshund	Beige; black lettering	35 x 45	120.00	160.00	80.00
3	Hare	White with grey markings; green base; black lettering	30 x 45	50.00	65.00	35.00
4	Kitten	White with grey markings; blue bow; black lettering	30 x 40	125.00	165.00	80.00
5	Lamb	White with brown markings; green base; black lettering	42 x 25	80.00	105.00	50.00
—	Boxed set		—	500.00	670.00	340.00

TOM SMITH AND COMPANY

The world famous Christmas cracker manufacturer, Tom Smith and Company Ltd., collaborated with George Wade and Son Ltd. over a number of years to produce a series of miniature animals exclusively for the Christmas and party cracker market. Each series of animals was used exclusively by Tom Smith for two years, after which time the design rights reverted back to Wade, then they could be reused for other premiums or included in the *English Whimsies* series. In August 1998 Tom Smith Crackers was sold to Napier Industries of Rickmansworth, Herts, UK and the factory was closed.

The first models issued for Tom Smith and Company were eight figures previously used in the 1967-1973 Red Rose Tea Canada series. Next came a set of ten *Safari Park* models. All but two of the models —the "Lion" and the "Musk Ox"— were from either Red Rose Tea Canada or the *English Whimsies* series. The Polar Bear and Koala Bear differ in colour from the *English Whimsies* models. Each is marked with "Wade England" embossed on the rim of the base.

Only the five models in the *Safari Park series* Nos 2,3,4,5, and 7 can be distinguished from those in the *English Whimsies* series; therefore, they have a higher collectors value. All models are listed in alphabetical order for ease of reference.

ANIMATE CRACKERS

1973-1975

Backstamp: Embossed "Wade England" on the rim or in a recessed base

No.	Name	Description	Size	U.S. $	Can. $	U.K. £
1	Alsatian	Dark grey/honey	30 x 40	9.00	7.00	2.00
2	Bluebird (recessed)	Light brown; blue wings	15 x 35	10.00	8.00	4.00
3	Bullfrog (recessed)	Light green	15 x 30	25.00	32.00	10.00
4	Butterfly (recessed)	Honey; blue grey wing tips	10 x 45	10.00	8.00	5.00
5	Fantail Goldfish	Light green/yellow; blue base	30 x 35	10.00	8.00	5.00
6	Pine Marten	Honey	30 x 30	6.00	5.00	2.00
7	Terrapin (recessed)	Dark greenish grey	10 x 40	8.00	6.00	4.00
8	Wild Boar	Beige; green base	30 x 40	15.00	12.00	4.00

ELEPHANT AND PIG

Circa 1975

Wade produced for Tom Smith a very small number of biscuit-glazed miniature elephants and gloss-glazed pigs. The elephant has a hole in the end of the trunk and the pig has a hole in the rump and was intended as indoor firework holders for sparklers.

Elephant

Pig

Backstamp: Unmarked

No.	Name	Description	Size	U.S. $	Can. $	U.K. £
1	Elephant	Charcoal grey	27 x 35	50.00	75.00	25.00
2	Pig	White	25 x 50	50.00	75.00	25.00

SAFARI PARK

1976-1977

Backstamp: Embossed "Wade England"

No.	Name	Description	Size	U.S. $	Can. $	U.K. £
1	Kangaroo	Dark brown; light brown base	45 x 25	18.00	24.00	5.00
2	Koala Bear	Black; brown stump	35 x 25	15.00	25.00	6.00
3	Langur	Light brown; dark brown stump	35 x 30	5.00	7.00	4.00
4a	Lion	Honey brown	30 x 45	15.00	18.00	8.00
4b	Lion	Honey brown; green base	30 x 45	15.00	18.00	8.00
5	Musk Ox	Grey; brown horns	27 x 30	20.00	30.00	12.00
6	Orang-Outan	Ginger	30 x 30	5.00	7.00	5.00
7	Polar Bear	Brown; black nose; grey/blue base	30 x 30	30.00	40.00	20.00
8	Raccoon	Brown; grey-green base	25 x 35	15.00	12.00	4.00
9	Tiger	Golden yellow	35 x 25	15.00	20.00	5.00
10	Walrus	Brown; grey base	30 x 30	12.00	15.00	3.00

CIRCUS

1978-1979

These ten models were set on drum bases, which are marked on their rims. These figures were reissued for Red Rose Tea U.S.A., with only a very slight variation in colour.

Backstamp: Embossed "Wade England"

No.	Name	Description	Size	U.S. $	Can. $	U.K. £
1	Brown Bear	Dark brown	35 x 30	5.00	12.00	4.00
2	Chimpanzee Boy	Beige; blue teapot	40 x 20	10.00	12.00	4.00
3	Chimpanzee Girl	Beige; blue skirt	40 x 20	10.00	12.00	4.00
4	Elephant, Sitting	Blue	30 x 30	8.00	12.00	4.00
5	Elephant, Standing	Blue	30 x 25	8.00	12.00	4.00
6	Lion	Honey brown	40 x 22	5.00	12.00	4.00
7	Pony	Beige	45 x 22	5.00	12.00	4.00
8	Poodle	White; blue skirt	35 x 30	8.00	12.00	4.00
9	Sea Lion	Dark grey	40 x 30	8.00	12.00	4.00
10	Tiger	Honey brown	43 x 20	5.00	12.00	4.00

BRITISH WILDLIFE

1980-1981

Backstamp: Embossed "Wade England"

No.	Name	Description	Size	U.S. $	Can. $	U.K. £
1	Badger	Dark grey	25 x 40	10.00	15.00	5.00
2	Dormouse	Honey; green base	30 x 35	10.00	15.00	5.00
3	Fox	Brown	35 x 40	10.00	15.00	4.00
4	Hare	Honey	50 x 30	10.00	15.00	4.00
5	Mole	Dark grey	25 x 40	10.00	15.00	4.00
6	Partridge	Beige; green base	30 x 20	10.00	15.00	5.00
7	Squirrel	Red-brown	40 x 40	10.00	15.00	4.00
8	Weasel	Beige; green base	35 x 40	10.00	15.00	5.00

FARMYARD ANIMALS

1982-1983

The "Goose" was previously used in the 1971-1979 Red Rose *Miniature Nurseries* series (the earlier model has a pink beak.)

Backstamp: Embossed "Wade England"

No.	Name	Description	Size	U.S. $	Can. $	U.K. £
1	Bull	Dark brown	30 x 50	12.00	18.00	4.00
2	Collie	Honey brown; brown base	25 x 50	12.00	18.00	4.00
3	Cow	Orange-brown	30 x 40	12.00	18.00	4.00
4	Duck Swimming	White; blue base	25 x 30	18.00	24.00	6.00
5	Goat	White; green base	40 x 40	12.00	18.00	6.00
6	Goose	Honey/brown; brown beak	35 x 40	8.00	6.00	4.00
7	Horse	Brown; green base	40 x 30	12.00	18.00	4.00
8	Pig	Pale pink	25 x 40	12.00	18.00	4.00

SURVIVAL ANIMALS

1984-1985

From 1984 onwards, all Tom Smith crackers models were produced in a one-colour glaze. The "Sea Lion" was previously used as the "Seal" in the 1967-1973 Red Rose *Miniature Animals* series; the earlier model is brown on a blue base. The "Bison" had been number 51 of the *English Whimsies* series, where it is honey brown and dark brown.

Backstamp: Embossed "Wade England"

No.	Name	Description	Size	U.S. $	Can. $	U.K. £
1	Armadillo	Dark grey	25 x 45	15.00	20.00	5.00
2	Bison	Dark brown	28 x 40	6.00	8.00	4.00
3	Eagle	Honey	35 x 23	9.00	12.00	4.00
4	Gorilla	Brown	40 x 40	9.00	12.00	4.00
5	Polar Bear	White	27 x 45	9.00	12.00	5.00
6	Sea Lion	Blue	38 x 30	10.00	15.00	6.00
7	Sea Turtle	Green-grey	25 x 45	10.00	15.00	6.00
8	Whale (Baleen)	Blue	25 x 50	9.00	12.00	4.00

NURSERY RHYME CRACKERS

Circa Mid-1980s

At some time in the mid-1980s, Tom Smith issued a box of "Nursery Rhyme" crackers. The box contained a set of six miniature nursery rhymes, the same models used in the Red Rose Tea Canada promotion of 1972-1979.

Backstamp: Embossed "Wade England" on rim

No.	Name	Description	Size	U.S. $	Can. $	U.K. £
1	Hickory Dickory	Red brown/honey brown	45 x 20	6.00	4.00	6.00
2	Humpty Dumpty	Honey brown; blue bow tie; brown wall	45 x 35	7.00	5.00	5.00
3	Little Bo-Peep	Beige; blue apron; green base	45 x 25	5.00	4.00	6.00
4	Old King Cole Type 1	Gap; brown; blue hat and cloak	40 x 35	7.00	4.00	6.00
5	Old Woman Who Lived in a Shoe	Honey brown; red brown roof	40 x 40	7.00	4.00	5.00
6	Wee Willie Winkie	Yellow hair; beige nightshirt	45 x 25	10.00	7.00	6.00

WILDLIFE

1986-1987

These models are reissued *English Whimsies* in all-over, one-colour glazes. Listed below are all the models that have been found in this series, although a number of British collectors have reported finding different figures in their crackers than were illustrated on the outer box (models 9 through 15). It is believed that surplus models from previous Red Rose Tea and Tom Smith promotions were used to fill the orders in time for Christmas sales.

Backstamp: Embossed "Wade England"

No.	Name	Description	Size	U.S. $	Can. $	U.K. £
1	Penguin (EW)	White	45 x 17	10.00	12.00	5.00
2	Rhino (EW)	Grey/brown	25 x 35	8.00	6.00	4.00
3	Leopard (EW)	Honey	17 x 45	6.00	6.00	4.00
4	Kangaroo (EW)	Beige	45 x 25	10.00	15.00	5.00
5	Koala Bear (EW)	Honey	35 x 25	6.00	6.00	4.00
6	Dolphin (EW)	Dark blue	30 x 40	12.00	15.00	5.00
7	Wild Boar (RR/EW)	Beige	30 x 40	8.00	10.00	4.00
8	Orang-Outan (EW)	Dark brown	30 x 30	5.00	7.00	5.00

No.	Name	Description	Size	U.S. $	Can. $	U.K. £
9	Collie (TSF)	Dark brown	25 x 50	15.00	18.00	4.00
10a	Goat (TSF)	White	40 x 40	12.00	18.00	6.00
11	Duck Swimming (TSF)	Blue	25 x 30	18.00	20.00	6.00
12	Squirrel (TSB)	Dark brown	40 x 40	12.00	15.00	4.00
13	Zebra (EW)	Blue-grey	40 x 35	5.00	8.00	8.00
14	Bison (RR/EW)	Brown	30 x 40	5.00	7.00	3.00
15	Hare (TSB)	Brown	50 x 30	10.00	12.00	6.00

Note: The following initials indicate the origin of the models:
EW: *English Whimsies*; RR: Red Rose Canada
TSB: Tom Smith *British Wildlife* set; TSF: Tom Smith *Farmyard* set

MISCELLANEOUS MODELS

1987-1996

Wade re-coloured surplus models from the English Whimsies, Red Rose Tea Whimsies, Whimsie-lands and former Tom Smith Crackers for the Tom Smith Group who included them with other small gifts in their Bric-a-Brac, Catering, De Luxe, Luxury, Gallerie Noel, Table Decoration and Victorian Crackers. Only one or two models were used in each box of crackers and there is no reference to Wade on the outer box. Tom Smith do not keep records of these odd Wade models, and the only way to find them is to look closely at Tom Smith advertising leaflets and packaging where they can be seen amongst plastic toys and paper hats.

1987 ISSUE

Backstamp: Embossed "Wade England"

No.	Name	Description	Size	U.S. $	Can. $	U.K. £
1	Little Bo-Peep	Brown	45 x 25	5.00	6.00	3.00
2	Hickory Dickory Dock	Beige	45 x 20	8.00	10.00	3.00
3	Humpty Dumpty	Brown	45 x 35	8.00	10.00	3.00
4	Old King Cole	Blue	40 x 35	15.00	20.00	10.00
5	Old Woman in a Shoe	Blue	40 x 40	15.00	20.00	10.00
6	Wee Willie Winkie	Blue	45 x 25	15.00	20.00	10.00
7a	Hare (TSB)	Beige	50 x 30	10.00	12.00	4.00
7b	Hare (TSB)	Pale beige	50 x 30	10.00	12.00	4.00
8	Gorilla (TSS)	Dark brown	40 x 40	4.00	6.00	3.00

Note: The following initials indicate the origin of the figures:
EW: *English Whimsies*
RR: Red Rose
TSB: Tom Smith *British Wildlife* set
TSD: Tom Smith *Dogs* set
TSS: Tom Smith *Survival* set

1989 ISSUE

Backstamp: Embossed "Wade England"

No.	Name	Description	Size	U.S. $	Can. $	U.K. £
1	Little Bo-Peep (RR)	Brown; blue apron	45 x 25	5.00	4.00	6.00
2	Hickory Dickory Dock (RR)	Honey/dark brown	45 x 20	6.00	4.00	6.00
3	Wee Willie Winkie (RR)	Beige; yellow hair	45 x 25	10.00	7.00	6.00
4	Kangaroo (EW)	Honey brown	45 x 25	10.00	15.00	5.00
5	Koala Bear (EW)	Beige	35 x 25	6.00	8.00	4.00

1990 ISSUE

Backstamp: Embossed "Wade England"

No.	Name	Description	Size	U.S. $	Can. $	U.K. £
1	Old King Cole (RR)	Brown; blue hat	40 x 35	7.00	4.00	6.00
2	Hare (TSB)	Dark brown	50 x 30	10.00	12.00	6.00
3	Squirrel (TSB)	Blue	40 x 40	6.00	12.00	12.00

1991 ISSUE

Backstamp: Embossed "Wade England"

No.	Name	Description	Size	U.S. $	Can. $	U.K. £
1	Koala Bear (EW)	Honey brown	35 x 25	6.00	8.00	4.00
2	Poodle (RR/TSD)	Dark orange	40 x 45	12.00	15.00	3.00

1992 ISSUE

Backstamp: Embossed "Wade England"

No.	Name	Description	Size	U.S. $	Can. $	U.K. £
1	Bluebird (RR/EW)	Blue	15 x 35	40.00	50.00	12.00
2	Bulldog (TSD)	Beige	35 x 35	10.00	15.00	5.00
3	Mongrel (RR/EW)	Blue	35 x 35	10.00	15.00	3.00

1996 ISSUE

Three *English Whimsies* models were used in assorted Tom Smith crackers. The "Duck" can be found in Tom Smith Catering, De Luxe and Luxury crackers, the "Camel" was used in the Gallerie Noel crackers, and the "Fieldmouse" was in Catering, De Luxe, Luxury and Table Decoration crackers.

Photograph not available
at press time

Backstamp: Unknown

No.	Name	Description	Size	U.S. $	Can. $	U.K. £
1	Camel (EW)	Light brown	35 x 35	9.00	11.00	4.00
2	Duck (EW)	Green	30 x 40	15.00	20.00	6.00
3	Duck Swimming (TS)	Beige	25 x 30	18.00	20.00	6.00
4	Fieldmouse (EW)	Honey	35 x 25	12.00	11.00	3.00
5	Horse	Beige	40 x 30	18.00	20.00	6.00

VILLAGE OF BROADLANDS

1988

Due to high production costs, only five of these models were produced for Tom Smith and Company. A further set of five figures was planned, but never issued.

They come from the same moulds as the following *Whimsey-on-Why* models, but are in different colours:

Whimsey-on-Why	**Village of Broadlands**
Whimsy School	The Chapel
Whimsey Station	The Coach House Garage
Pump Cottage	The Thatched Cottage
The Sweet Shop	The Pink House
The Greengrocers Shop	The Village Store

Backstamp: Embossed "Wade England"

No.	Name	Description	Size	U.S. $	Can. $	U.K. £
1	The Chapel	Grey; green roof; brown door	38 x 51	40.00	55.00	25.00
2	The Coach House Garage	White; grey roof; black beams	35 x 39	40.00	55.00	25.00
3	The Pink House	Pink; grey roof	40 x 40	40.00	55.00	25.00
4	The Thatched Cottage	White; brown roof	28 x 39	40.00	55.00	25.00
5	The Village Store	Brown; brown roof	35 x 35	40.00	55.00	25.00

FAMILY PETS

1988-1989

Backstamp: Embossed "Wade England"

No.	Name	Description	Size	U.S. $	Can. $	U.K. £
1	Cockatoo	Green	35 x 30	8.00	10.00	3.00
2	Guinea Pig	Honey brown	20 x 30	10.00	15.00	6.00
3	Mouse	White	15 x 25	12.00	15.00	4.00
4	Persian Kitten	Blue	25 x 33	8.00	10.00	4.00
5	Rabbit	Brown	30 x 25	8.00	10.00	4.00
6	Shetland Pony	Beige	25 x 30	8.00	12.00	5.00
7	Spaniel Puppy	Honey brown	25 x 30	10.00	12.00	4.00
8	Tropical Fish	Green	20 x 30	10.00	15.00	4.00

WORLD OF DOGS

1990-1991

Only two of these figures were new issues. The others were reissued *English Whimsies* and the first issue of Red Rose Tea Canada models in a new all-over, one-colour glaze.

Backstamp: Embossed "Wade England"

No.	Name	Description	Size	U.S. $	Can. $	U.K. £
1	Alsatian (RR/EW)	Dark brown	30 x 40	10.00	15.00	3.00
2	Bulldog (new)	Beige	35 x 35	10.00	15.00	3.00
3	Corgi (RR/EW)	Honey brown; no eyes, nose	30 x 35	10.00	15.00	3.00
4	Husky (EW)	White	35 x 30	12.00	15.00	3.00
5	Mongrel (RR/EW)	Blue-grey	35 x 35	10.00	15.00	3.00
6	Poodle (RR)	Apricot	40 x 45	12.00	15.00	3.00
7	Spaniel (RR/EW)	Black	35 x 35	15.00	20.00	8.00
8	West Highland Terrier (new)	White	30 x 30	10.00	15.00	3.00

BIRDLIFE SERIES

1992-1993

All the models in the *Birdlife* series, except for the "Wren," had been previously issued, either as *English Whimsies,* as other Tom Smith cracker models or as *Whimsie-land* figures. The "Eagle" and the "Goose" were former Tom Smith models, but this time were produced in different coloured glazes than the originals.

Backstamp: Embossed "Wade England"

No.	Name	Description	Size	U.S. $	Can. $	U.K. £
1	Wren	Beige	33 x 24	15.00	20.00	5.00
2	Duck (WL)	White	45 x 35	12.00	15.00	5.00
3	Cockerel (WL)	Green	50 x 35	12.00	15.00	6.00
4	Partridge (WL)	Beige	35 x 35	12.00	15.00	5.00
5	Barn Owl (EW)	Grey-blue	35 x 25	12.00	15.00	5.00
6	Eagle (TS *Survival*)	Beige	35 x 23	12.00	15.00	5.00
7	Pelican (EW)	Brown	45 x 40	20.00	20.00	5.00
8	Goose (RRT/TS)	Honey	35 x 40	12.00	15.00	5.00

Note: The following initials indicate the origin of the models:
EW: *English Whimsies*
RRT: Red Rose Tea Canada *Miniature Nurseries*
TS: Tom Smith
WL: *Whimsie-land*

SNOWLIFE ANIMALS

1992-1996

All the models in this set, except the "Reindeer," had been previously issued as *English Whimsies*, Tom Smith cracker figures or in the *Whimsie-land* series. The models are produced in a different all-over, one-colour glaze from the originals.

Backstamp: **A.** Embossed "Wade Eng" (1a, 1b)
             B. Embossed "Wade England" (2-10)

No.	Name	Description	Size	U.S. $	Can. $	U.K. £
1	Fox (WL)	Ginger	35 x 35	8.00	10.00	10.00
2	Penguin (EW)	Grey-blue	45 x 17	10.00	12.00	4.00
3	Polar Bear (EW)	White	27 x 45	10.00	12.00	4.00
4a	Reindeer	Gap between legs; beige	30 x 35	12.00	15.00	5.00
4b	Reindeer	No gap; beige	30 x 35	10.00	12.00	4.00
5	Seal Pup (EW)	Grey	17 x 30	15.00	20.00	3.00
6	Snow Goose (RR)	White	33 x 37	12.00	15.00	5.00
7	Snowshoe Hare (TS "Hare")	White	50 x 30	15.00	20.00	3.00
8	Snowy Owl (WL "Owl")	White	35 x 25	15.00	20.00	3.00
9	Walrus (EW)	Beige	30 x 30	12.00	15.00	3.00
10	Whale (Baleen TS)	Grey	22 x 52	8.00	10.00	4.00

Note: The following initials indicate the origin of the models:
        EW: *English Whimsies*
        TS: Tom Smith
        WL: *Whimsie-land*

TALES FROM THE NURSERY

1994-1996

Some of the models from the Red Rose Tea *Miniature Nurseries* were reissued for this set. Two new figures were added in 1994, "Ride a Cock Horse" and a newly modeled "Little Boy Blue." All the models are in an all-over, one-colour glaze. Although there are ten models in this set, the box contains only eight crackers, making some models more difficult to find than others.

Backstamp: Embossed "Wade England"

No.	Name	Description	Size	U.S.$	Can.$	U.K.£
1	Cat and the Fiddle	Light grey	45 x 25	8.00	10.00	3.00
2	Dr. Foster	Dark brown	45 x 25	8.00	10.00	3.00
3	Hickory Dickory Dock	Light brown	45 x 20	8.00	10.00	3.00
4	Humpty Dumpty	Pale blue	45 x 35	8.00	10.00	3.00
5	Little Bo-Peep	Wine	45 x 25	8.00	10.00	3.00
6	Little Boy Blue	Pale blue	45 x 25	10.00	12.00	4.00
7	Little Jack Horner	Honey	40 x 20	6.00	8.00	4.00
8	Queen of Hearts	Apricot	45 x 25	8.00	10.00	4.00
9	Ride a Cock Horse	Green	45 x 35	10.00	12.00	4.00
10	Tom Tom the Piper's Son	Honey	65 x 55	8.00	10.00	3.00

CAT COLLECTION

1996-1997

Eight of these cats are reissued from *English Whimsies*, the *Whimsie-land Series* and from Red Rose Teas *Miniature Nurseries*. Some are in new colours, but others are similar to the Red Rose Tea U.S.A. issues. Two new cat models — one stalking and the other standing — were produced for this series. Although there are only eight crackers in a box, there are ten models in the set.

Backstamp: Embossed "Wade England"

No.	Name	Description	Size	U.S.$	Can.$	U.K.£
1	Cat (EW)	Light brown	40 x 17	8.00	10.00	4.00
2	Cat and the Fiddle (RR)	Dark brown	45 x 25	8.00	10.00	4.00
3	Cat Stalking (new)	Apricot	23 x 43	12.00	15.00	5.00
4	Cat Standing (new)	Light brown	35 x 34	12.00	15.00	5.00
5a	Kitten, lying (WL)	Dark blue	20 x 42	8.00	10.00	4.00
5b	Kitten, lying (WL)	Pale blue	20 x 42	8.00	10.00	4.00
6	Kitten, sitting (EW)	Apricot	30 x 30	8.00	10.00	4.00
7	Leopard (EW)	Honey	17 x 45	4.00	6.00	3.00
8	Lion (EW)	Honey	35 x 45	4.00	6.00	3.00
9	Puss in Boots (RR)	Light grey	45 x 20	8.00	10.00	5.00
10	Tiger (EW)	Honey	35 x 25	15.00	20.00	6.00

Note: The initials after the model indicates its origin.
EW: *English Whimsies*
RR: Red Rose *Miniature Nurseries*
WL: *Whimsie-land Series*

CHRISTMAS TIME CRACKERS

1996-1997

Tom Smith used the *Bear Ambitions* set, which was originally produced as a Wade giftware line, in its Christmas crackers. Four of the models are glazed in different colours from the originals, which were all honey brown.

Backstamp: A. Embossed "Wade England" (3)
B. Embossed "Wade Eng" (1, 2, 4, 5, 6)

No.	Name	Description	Size	U.S. $	Can. $	U.K. £
1	Admiral Sam	Dark brown	50	10.00	12.00	4.00
2	Alex the Aviator	Light brown	45	10.00	12.00	4.00
3	Artistic Edward	Light brown	40	10.00	12.00	4.00
4	Beatrice Ballerina	Honey	50	6.00	8.00	3.00
5	Locomotive Joe	Dark brown	50	10.00	12.00	4.00
6	Musical Marco	Honey	45	6.00	8.00	3.00

HEDGEROW AND SEALIFE PARTY TIME CRACKERS

1998

There were two new Tom Smith Party Cracker Animal series produced for 1998-1999, Hedgerow and Sealife. Each set contained eight models, but the Tom Smith boxes contained only six crackers, which meant collectors would have to buy more than one box of crackers to complete a full set.

All the models had been used in Previous Promotions (some as many as four times). The models were produced in new all over one-colour glazes except for the Mole and the Badger, which are lighter colours than the originals. Models are listed in Alphabetical order for ease of reference. Tom Smith closed down in 1999.

Backstamp: Embossed "Wade England"

HEDGEROW - 1998

Although all the hedgerow animals are all previously issued models, they are all in new colours.

No.	Name	Description	Size	U.S. $	Can. $	U.K. £
1	Badger (TS)	Pale Grey	25 x 40	6.00	8.00	4.00
2	Butterfly (RRC)	Blue	10 x 45	7.00	10.00	4.00
3	Hare (TS)	Light brown	50 x 30	6.00	8.00	4.00
4	Mole (TS)	Pale Grey	25 x 40	6.00	8.00	4.00
5	Mouse (EW)	Apricot	40 x 25	7.00	10.00	4.00
6	Otter (RRC)	Dark Brown	30 x 35	7.00	10.00	4.00
7	Rabbit (RRC)	Honey	30 x 30	7.00	10.00	4.00
8	Squirrel (RRC)	Apricot	35 x 30	7.00	10.00	4.00

Note: The following initials denote the series the model originated from.
EW: *English Whimsies*
KA: King Aquariums Ltd
RRC: Red Rose Tea Canada
TS: Tom Smith UK

SEALIFE - 1998

The "Whale" is a brighter blue than the original 1984 "Survival Whale."

No.	Name	Description	Size	U.S. $	Can. $	U.K. £
1	Angel Fish (EW)	Light green	35 x 40	7.00	10.00	4.00
2	Dolphin (EW)	Light grey	30 X 40	7.00	10.00	4.00
3	Seahorse (EW)	Apricot	50 x 17	7.00	10.00	4.00
4	Seal on Rock (RRC)	Dark brown	35 x 35	7.00	10.00	4.00
5	Turtle (EW)	Light green	15 x 50	7.00	10.00	4.00
6	Walrus (EW)	Honey	30 X 30	7.00	10.00	4.00
7	Whale (Baleen TS)	Bright blue	22 x 52	7.00	10.00	4.00
8	Whelk (Sea Snail KA)	Bright blue	30 X 35	7.00	10.00	4.00

SPILLERS DOG FOODS LTD.
RETRIEVER
1991

Commissioned by Spillers Dog Foods, this model could be obtained by sending in a certain number of tokens from packets of the dog food.

Backstamp: Embossed "Wade England"

No.	Description	Size	U.S. $	Can. $	U.K. £
1	Honey brown; green base	26 x 53	30.00	40.00	18.00

MARGARET STRICKLAND
POLACANTHUS MONEY BOX, THE ISLE OF WIGHT DINOSAUR
1994

Margaret Strickland, a resident of the Isle of Wight, England, commissioned the *Polacanthus Money Box*. This model is an artists impression taken from the skeleton of a Polacanthus dinosaur, whose remains have only been found on the Isle of Wight. It was produced in May 1994, in a limited numbered edition of 2,000.

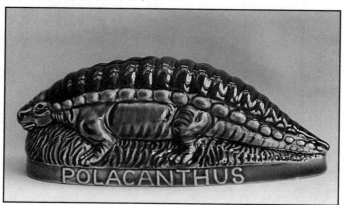

Backstamp: Black transfer "Wade" in Isle of Wight outline, numbered

No.	Description	Size	U.S. $	Can. $	U.K. £
1	Honey/dark brown; green base; coin slot in top	79 x 205	85.00	110.00	50.00

TRAUFLER

A slip-cast Sheep in two colours and sizes and the Cockerel Salt Pot and the Hen Pepper Pot were produced by Wade for Traufler, a tableware manufacturer, to compliment its imported tablewares, which featured sheep, shepherds and farmyard scenes. These models were also produced by another manufacturer and are also unmarked. Those figures not made by Wade have darker faces, more eyelashes and ears that are closer to their faces.

SHEEP

1992

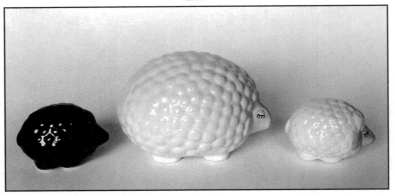

Backstamp: Unmarked

No.	Name	Description	Size	U.S. $	Can. $	U.K. £
1a	Sheep, Large	Cream; pink face	85 x 145	32.00	45.00	24.00
1b	Sheep, Large	Black	85 x 145	32.00	45.00	24.00
2a	Sheep, Small	Cream; pink face	65 x 45	30.00	40.00	20.00
2b	Sheep, Small	Black	65 x 45	30.00	40.00	20.00

COCKEREL SALT POT AND HEN PEPPER POT

1992

Backstamp: Unmarked

No.	Name	Description	Size	U.S.$	Can.$	U.K.£
1a	Cockerel Salt Pot	White; red/black markings	110 x 55	30.00	40.00	20.00
1b	Cockerel Salt Pot	Yellow; pink comb; black markings	115 x 80	30.00	40.00	20.00
2a	Hen Pepper Pot	White; red/black markings	90 x 55	30.00	40.00	20.00
2b	Hen Pepper Pot	Yellow; pink comb; black markings	90 x 70	30.00	40.00	20.00

DAVID TROWER ENTERPRISES
POPEYE COLLECTION
1997-1998

"Popeye," a much loved cartoon character who made his cartoon debut in 1933, was the first model issued in an intended series of four to be modeled by Ken Holmes and produced by Wade Ceramics for David Trower Enterprises. The three other models are "Brutus," "Olive Oyl and Swee'pea," and "Wimpy." The models were sold in colourful presentation boxes with certificates of authenticity. "Popeye's" original price was £35.00 and was issued in a limited edition of 2,000. "Brutus," was issued in a limited edition of 1,500 and "Olive Oyl,"and "Wimpy" were issued in limited editions of 2,000, at a cost of £36.00.

Backstamp: **A.** Printed "Wade Popeye ™ & © 1997 King Features Synd Inc. Limited Edition of 2000 © David Trower Enterprises"
B. Printed "Wade Brutus ™ & © 1997 King Features Synd Inc. Limited Edition of 1500 © David Trower Enterprises"
C. Printed "Wade Olive Oyl and SweePea ™ & © 1998 King Features Synd Inc. Limited Edition of 2000 © David Trower Enterprises"
D. Printed "Wimpy TM & © 1998 King Features Synd Inc Wade"

No.	Name	Description	Size	U.S.$	Can.$	U.K.£
1	Popeye	White hat with black band; brown pipe; red collar with black band; black shirt with yellow buttons, navy blue cuffs; yellow belt with white buckle; navy blue trousers; black shoes; brown circular base	120	55.00	70.00	50.00
2	Brutus	Blue hat/trousers; black hair/eyes/beard/ T-shirt; orange shirt; brown belt; white buckle	129	55.00	75.00	45.00
3	Olive Oyl and Swee'pea	Olive: black hair, skirt and shoes; red blouse; blue belt; Sweepea: white hat; red suit	Unknown	75.00	90.00	45.00
4	Wimpy	Brown hat/shoes; dark blue jacket; white shirt; red tie; orange trousers; blue belt	130	65.00	90.00	45.00

THE NURSERY RHYMES COLLECTION

1998-1999

The first model in the new Nursery Rhymes collection was "Humpty Dumpty," followed by "Goosey Gander" in April 1999 and "Little Bo-Peep" in September 1999. Each model was produced in a limited edition of 1,000 and issued with a Certificate of Authenticity. The cost was £32.00 each.

Humpty Dumpty, Goosey Gander

Backstamp: Printed "Wade from the Nursery Rhyme Collection World Wide Limited Edition of 1,000 © 1998 Wade Ceramics Ltd © 1998 D.T.Ents" with name of model

No.	Name	Description	Size	U.S.$	Can.$	U.K.£
1	Humpty Dumpty	Red hat; white shirt/base; blue bow tie; dark green and blue trousers/shoes; pale blue wall	115	50.00	70.00	35.00
2	Goosey Gander	White goose; black hat, jacket, shoes; red waistcoat; grey base	127	50.00	70.00	35.00
3	Little Bo-Peep	Grey bonnet; yellow hair; dark blue bows; white dress; pale blue bustle/hem; brown staff; black shoe; green base	127	50.00	70.00	35.00

21ST CENTURY KEEPSAKES
MEMORIES COLLECTION
1998-1999

"Andy Pandy" issued in November 1998 was the first model in the *Memories Collection* which is a series of characters from 1950s British BBC Television. "Looby Loo and Ted" from the Andy Pandy program followed in February 1999. Other models in the Memories series are "Bill and Ben The Flowerpot Men" from a TV program of the same name

The characters were all string puppets used in the above mentioned children's television programs first seen in the early 1950s. The models were produced in limited editions of 1,500 and issued with a certificate of authenticity at a cost of £39.00 each. A special limited edition of 500 of the "Bill and Ben" and "Little Weed" models had gold edged petals; these models were mailed to the first 500 purchasers.

Backstamp: **A.** Printed "Limited Edition 1500 Wade England" with name of model and 21ST Century logo (1, 2)
B. Printed "Bill & Ben Little Weed Limited Edition Of 500 With Gold Edged Petals Wade England" with 21ST Century logo (3)

No.	Name	Description	Size	U.S.$	Can.$	U.K.£
1	Andy Pandy	Blue hat; blue and white striped suit; white pom poms; collar/shoes; brown stool	123	65.00	90.00	45.00
2	Looby Loo and Ted	Brown teddy with red bow; Looby Loo: yellow hair; red bows; white blouse; blue skirt/shoes	100	65.00	90.00	45.00
3a	Bill and Ben and Little Weed	Yellow weed flower; gold edged petals; brown hats; reddish brown bodies; black hands, boots; dark brown base	115	Unknown		
3b	Bill and Ben and Little Weed	Yellow weed flower; brown hats; reddish brown bodies; black hands, boots; dark brown base	115	60.00	80.00	40.00

UK INTERNATIONAL CERAMICS LTD.
THE FLINTSTONES COLLECTION
1996-1998

"Fred and Wilma Flintstone," from a popular television series of the 1970s, were the first two models offered as a pair, in a limited edition of 1,500. "Betty and Barney Rubble" followed a few months later. The original issue price for the first four models was £68.00 for the pair.

"Pebbles" and "Bamm-Bamm" complete the *Flintstones* collection. Original cost from UKI was £85.00. Please note that "Bamm Bamm" and "Pebbles" were issued in a limited edition of 1,000 which means that five hundred collectors who purchased the earlier four models (1,500 of each) would not be able to complete the set.

Backstamp: **A.** Printed "™, The Flintstones™ Limited Edition of 1500 © 1996 H-B Prod. Inc © UKI Ceramics Ltd Licensed by CPL" With name of model

No.	Name	Description	Size	U.S.$	Can.$	U.K.£
1	Fred	Black hair/eyes/spots on coat; blue neck scarf; orange coat; stone base	120	80.00	110.00	55.00
2	Wilma	Brown hair; black eyes; red mouth; white necklace/dress; stone base	125	80.00	110.00	55.00
3	Barney	Yellow hair; black eyes; brown coat; stone base	105	80.00	110.00	55.00
4	Betty	Black hair/eyes/dress strap; red mouth; white button; pale blue dress; stone base	115	80.00	110.00	55.00
5	Bamm Bamm	Orange hat; white hair; olive green club; orange/black spotted shorts; grey base	100	90.00	120.00	60.00
6	Pebbles	Orange hair; green dress; blue pants; grey base	100	90.00	120.00	60.00

FELIX THE CAT

1997

This *Felix the Cat* model was modelled by Andy Moss, and was produced in a limited edition of 1,500. Each figure came with a numbered certificate and was in a special presentation box. The original cost was £38.00.

Backstamp: Black printed "WADE TM™ 1997 FTC PROD. INC. Limited edition of 1500 ™ UKI CERAMICS LTD Licensed by El Euro lizenzen, Munchen"

No.	Description	Size	U.S. $	Can. $	U.K. £
1	Black cat and lettering; white face and base; red tongue	135	98.00	130.00	65.00

NODDY AND BIG EARS

STYLE TWO

1997

"Noddy" and "Big Ears," created by Enid Blyton in her famous *Noddy* books, are the first two models in an intended set of four. Unlike their 1950s predecessors, these models are slip cast (hollow) and much larger. They were sold as a pair at £68.00.

"Mr. Plod the Policeman" and "Tessie Bear" were added to the *Noddy* set in 1999, and were issued in a limited edition of 1,500 at a cost of £85.00. (For Noddy and Big Ears Style One, see page 62).

Backstamp: **A**. Black printed "Wade © UKI Cer. Ltd 1997 © D.W. 1949/90 Licenced by BBC WL Ltd" with name of model
Limited Edition 1500
B. Printed "Wade Limited Edition 1,500 © 1998 EBL Ltd - A.R.R. © UKI Ceramics Ltd, 1998"
with name of model

No.	Name	Description	Size	U.S. $	Can. $	U.K. £
1	Big Ears	Red hat; dark blue coat; yellow bow tie with red stripes; yellow trousers with green strips; brown shoes; white base	138	95.00	130.00	65.00
2	Noddy	Dark blue hat, bows; red shirt/shoes/light blue shorts; yellow scarf with red spots; white base	110	95.00	130.00	65.00
3	Mr. Plod	Dark blue uniform; yellow star and buttons; white base	140	90.00	120.00	60.00
4	Tessie Bear	Yellow bear; White/pink hat; blue bow; pink blue skirt; white base	110	90.00	120.00	60.00

THE WADE CLASSICAL COLLECTION
DEER, POLAR BEAR AND MONKEY
1997

UK International Ceramics commissioned a set of three Art Deco style models which were originally intended to be a limited edition of 1,000 sets, but because of difficulties with copyright laws, only 260 sets were actually sold. The rest were withdrawn from sale and subsequently destroyed. The sets that were sold had a numbered Certificate of Authenticity. The three models could be purchased by mail order only at a cost of £85.00 during January of 1998.

Deer

Polar Bear

Monkey

Backstamp: A. Printed "Wade Deer First in the Series of Wade Classical Collection Exclusive to UKI Ceramics Produced in a Limited Edition of 1,000 © Wade Ceramics Ltd ©UKI Ceramics Ltd"
   B. Printed "Wade Polar Bear Second in the Series of Wade Classical Collection Exclusive to UKI Ceramics Produced in a Limited Edition of 1,000 © Wade Ceramics Ltd ©UKI Ceramics Ltd"
   C. Printed "Wade Monkies Third in the Series of Wade Classical Collection Exclusive to UKI Ceramics Produced in a Limited Edition of 1,000 © Wade Ceramics Ltd ©UKI Ceramics Ltd"

No.	Name	Description	Size	U.S. $	Can. $	U.K. £
1	Deer	Off-White	133 x 101	200.00	250.00	100.00
2	Polar Bear	Grey	101 x 127	200.00	250.00	100.00
3	Monkey	Beige	114 x 88	200.00	250.00	100.00

TOM AND JERRY

1998

This large size version of *Tom and Jerry* standing on round bases were commissioned by UK International Ceramics in a limited edition of 1,500. The cost direct from UKI was £75.00 for the pair.

Backstamp: **A.** Printed "Wade Tom from Tom & Jerry ☐ ©1997 Turner ENT. Co. A.R.R. Limited Edition of 1500 © UKI Ceramics LTD Licensed by CPL"
B. Printed "Wade Jerry from Tom & Jerry ☐© 1997 Turner ENT. Co. A.R.R. Limited Edition of 1500 © UKI Ceramics LTD Licensed by CPL"

No.	Name	Description	Size	U.S. $	Can. $	U.K. £
1	Tom	Grey and white; pink inside ears; black eyebrows, eyes, nose and whiskers; white base	135	75.00	100.00	50.00
2	Jerry	Brown and beige; black eyebrows, eyes, nose and whiskers; white base	110	75.00	100.00	50.00

TAURUS THE BULL

1999

"Taurus The Bull" is the first model in a new *Animal Collection* commissioned by UKI Ceramics. Produced in a limited edition of 350, the original cost direct from UKI was £38.50.

Backstamp: Printed "Wade Limited Edition of 150 ©Wade Ceramics Ltd. © UKI Ceramics Ltd. Taurus the Bull Produced Exclusively for UKI Ceramics Ltd in an Exclusive Worldwide Edition Tel: 01394386662 Fax: 01394 386742"

No.	Name	Description	Size	U.S. $	Can. $	U.K. £
1	Taurus the Bull	Cream bull and base; dark brown fill under stomach	140 x 180	55.00	80.00	38.50

THE CATKINS COLLECTION

1999

The *Catkins* models first appeared as UK Fair models in 1998-1999. In April 1999, UKI Ceramics introduced their new series of catkin models "Out for a Duck Catkins" and "Clown Catkins." Other models "Sailor," "Town Crier," "Olympic 2000," "Witch," "Scotsman" and "Millennium Celebrations Catkins" are planned for late 1999. Each model was issued in a limited edition of 750 at a cost of £28.00.

Backstamp: Unknown

No.	Name	Description	Size	U.S. $	Can. $	U.K. £
1	Clown Catkins	White hat and trousers with black bobbles; black collar; yellow tunic; multi-coloured base	120	45.00	60.00	30.00
2	Out For a Duck Catkins	Black cap; white cricketing clothes with black stripe on jumper; brown bat and ball; green base	120	45.00	60.00	30.00

ROBERT WILLIAMSON AND PETER ELSON
GINGERBREAD MAN AND GINGERBREAD CHILDREN
1995-1996

A hollow model of a giant gingerbread man was commissioned by Robert Williamson and Peter Elson. It was available for sale at the 2nd U.K. Fairs Wade Show in Birmingham. Following the success of the "Giant Gingerbread Man," a hollow model of the "Gingerbread Children" (a waving girl and boy) was produced in a limited edition of 2,000, (they were sold at the Dunstable Wade show in September 1996). The original cost of both models was £15.00 each.

Backstamp: Embossed "Wade"

No.	Name	Description	Size	U.S. $	Can. $	U.K. £
1	Gingerbread man	Ginger brown	105 x 80	68.00	90.00	35.00
2	Gingerbread children	Brown; dark green base	84 x 84	68.00	90.00	35.00

UNKNOWN COMPANY

Sometimes models are found in North America, the United Kingdom or even as far away as Australia which cannot be categorized in any company promotion, due to the fact that they were not found in original packaging or seen listed in company promotional advertising. Collectors from the U.K. could have transported models to North America, and models found in the U.K. could have been transported from North America.

KODIAK BEAR

Circa 1965

No one seems to be able to identify the series for which the "Kodiak Bear" was produced or why it was made. It may have been a prototype model produced for the first Red Rose Tea premiums, then rejected due to high production costs (its open arms required more fettling). As a result, the "Kodiak Bear" was not put into full production, and any models produced may have been used up in miscellaneous premiums. A second variation of the bear is slightly smaller in size and has a small gap between his legs.

Backstamp: A. Embossed "Wade England"
B. Unmarked

No.	Description	Size	U.S. $	Can. $	U.K. £
1a	Beige brown; green base	40 x 25	60.00	75.00	20.00
1b	Brown; honey brown face, chest, stomach	40 x 25	60.00	75.00	20.00
1c	Light brown; black nose; green base	40 x 25	60.00	75.00	20.00
1d	Red-brown	40 x 25	60.00	75.00	20.00

UNKNOWN COMPANY
3 FOR 49¢ WHIMSIES
CIRCA 1972

A small number of red carded Whimsies have been discovered in Canada and the U.S.A. There has been no further information found as to who for and when these models were produced. It is probable that they were for a chain of North American Dime Stores. A Fieldmouse on one of the red card models has a recessed base, as did some of the early 1967-1973 Canadian Red Rose Tea models. Others are from the 1971-1984 *English Whimsies* series, which would suggest that surplus stock was distributed to this company. A date of early 1970s is estimated for these models. The values given are for models intact on their cards, as they are indistinguishable from Red Rose Tea or *English Whimsie* models outside the packet.

Backstamp: A. Embossed "Wade England" in recessed base (1, 3)
          B. Embossed "Wade England" on rim (2, 4)

No.	Name	Description	Size	U.S. $	Can. $	U.K. £
1	Bear Cub	Honey brown	34 x 20	12.00	15.00	10.00
2	Bison, large	Honey brown	34 x 46	12.00	15.00	10.00
3	Duck	Blue/brown; yellow beak	30 x 40	12.00	15.00	10.00
4	Fieldmouse	Honey brown	35 x 25	12.00	15.00	10.00
5	Setter	Brown; grey green base	35 x 50	7.00	5.00	2.00

UNKNOWN COMPANY
MISCELLANEOUS WHIMSIE MODELS

These models, in all over one colour glazes, are promotional models and most likely Redco Foods (Red Rose Tea U.S.A.) or Tom Smith (Miscellaneous) Cracker Models.

Backstamp: Embossed Wade England on rim

No.	Name	Description	Size	U.S. $	Can. $	U.K. £
1	Collie (TS)	Beige	25 x 50	8.00	10.00	4.00
2	Duck(EW)	Beige	30 x 40	8.00	10.00	4.00
3a	Duck swimming (TS)	Light blue	25 x 30	8.00	10.00	4.00
3b	Duck swimming (TS)	White	25 x 30	8.00	10.00	4.00
4a	Elephant (EW)	Dark grey	55 x 50	12.00	15.00	10.00
4b	Elephant (EW)	Pale grey	55 x 50	8.00	12.00	8.00
5	Langur Type 3 (EW)	Brown	35 x 30	5.00	7.00	4.00
6	Little Jack Horner (RRC/TS)	Blue	40	6.00	4.00	6.00
7a	Persian Kitten (TS)	Apricot	25 x 33	8.00	10.00	4.00
7a	Persian Kitten (TS)	Black	25 x 33	8.00	10.00	4.00
7b	Persian Kitten (TS)	Dark brown	25 x 33	8.00	10.00	4.00
7c	Persian Kitten (TS)	Honey brown	25 x 33	8.00	10.00	4.00
7c	Persian Kitten (TS)	White head; light grey body; pale blue ball of wool	25 x 33	10.00	15.00	7.00
7a	Persian Kitten (TS)	White	25 x 33	8.00	10.00	4.00
8	Rabbit open ears (RR/EW)	Grey body; white face; black eyes; pink nose	30 x 30	25.00	35.00	12.00

Note: The black kitten is suspect, as Wade rarely reglaze models black. In the known black models that were reglazed by Wade, the original design (fur/stripes) on the model can still be seen beneath the black glaze, as in the *English Whimsie* black "Zebra" and black "Poodle" models. Some models have been deliberately painted black by persons unknown to mislead collectors; these suspect models have a heavy coat of paint applied over the original Wade glaze.

The following initials indicate the origin of the model.
EW: *English Whimsies*
RRC: Red Rose Tea Canada
TS: Tom Smith

TOAD OF TOAD HALL
2000

INDEX

A

B

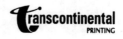

Printed in Canada